M000195830

"You spent more than 1000 hours doing this research for us, that's really great – we just have to pick up the book and it's done..." (**WTVR-TV**, Richmond)

"Very helpful to lots of families when the kids say, I'm bored...and I don't want to go to same places again!" – (**WISH-TV**, Indianapolis)

"Dividing the state into many sections, the book has something for everyone...everywhere." – (**WLVT-TV**, Pennsylvania)

"These authors know first-hand that it's important to find hands-on activities that engage your children..." (**WBNS-TV**, Columbus)

"A family that's a great source for travel ideas..." (**WBRA-TV**, Roanoke)

"What a great idea...this book needed to be done a long time ago!" (**WKYT-TV**, Lexington)

"A fabulous idea...places to travel that your kids will enjoy" (**WOOD-TV**, Grand Rapids)

"The Zavatskys call it a dream come true, running their own business while keeping the family together. Their goal, encourage other parents to create special family travel memories." - (**WLVT-TV,** Pennsylvania)

"It's a wonderful book, and as someone who has been to a lot of these places...you hit it right on the money!" – (**WKRC-TV**, Cincinnati)

Praise for the "Kids Love" Guidebook Travel Series
Customer Comments (actual letters on file)

"I wanted to tell you how helpful all your books have been to my family of 6. I rarely find books that cater to families with kids. I have your Indiana, Ohio, Kentucky, Michigan, and Pennsylvania books. I don't want to miss any of the new books that come out. Keep up the great ideas. The books are fantastic. I have shown them to tons of my friends. They love them, too." – H.M.

"I bought the Ohio and Indiana books yesterday and what a blessing these are for us!!! We love taking our grandsons on Grammie & Papaw trips thru the year and these books are making it soooo much easier to plan. The info is complete and full of ideas. Even the layout of the book is easy to follow...I just wanted to thank you for all your work in developing these books for us..." – G.K

"I have purchased your book. My grandchildren and I have gone to many of the places listed in your book. They mark them off as we visit them. We are looking forward to seeing many more. It is their favorite thing to look at book when they come over and find new places to explore. Thank you for publishing this book!" - B.A.

"At a retail price of under $17.00, any of the books would be well worth buying even for a one-time only vacation trip. Until now, when the opportunity arose for a day or weekend trip with the kids I was often at a loss to pick a destination that I could be sure was convenient, educational, child-friendly, and above all, fun. Now I have a new problem: How in the world will we ever be able to see and do all the great ideas listed in this book? I'd better get started planning our next trip right away. At least I won't have to worry about where we're going or what to do when we get there!" – VA Homeschool Newsletter

"My family and I used this book this summer to explore our state! We lived here nearly our entire life and yet over half the book we never knew existed. These people really know what kids love! Highly recommended for all parents, grandparents, etc.." – Barnes and Noble website reviewer

KIDS ♥ LOVE MISSOURI

Your Family Travel Guide to Exploring "Kid-Friendly" Missouri

500 Fun Stops & Unique Spots

George & Michele Zavatsky

Dedicated to the Families of Missouri

In a Hundred Years...It will not matter, The size of my bank account...The kind of house that I lived in, the kind of car that I drove...But what will matter is...That the world may be different Because I was important in the life of a child.

- author unknown

For the latest major updates corresponding to the pages in this book visit our website:

www.KidsLoveTravel.com

- **REMEMBER:** *Museum exhibits change frequently. Check the site's website before you visit to note any changes. Also, HOURS and ADMISSIONS are subject to change at the owner's discretion. Note: FAMILY ADMISSION RATES generally have restrictions. If you are tight on time or money, check the attraction's website or call before you visit.*

- **INTERNET PRECAUTION:** *All websites mentioned in KIDS LOVE MISSOURI have been checked for appropriate content. However, due to the fast-changing nature of the Internet, we strongly urge parents to preview any recommended sites and to always supervise their children when on-line.*

- **EDUCATORS:** *There are suggestions for finding FREE lessons plans embedded in many listings as helpful notes for educators.*

ISBN-13: 978-0-9822880-4-7

KIDS ♥ MISSOURI ™   Kids Love Publications, LLC

TABLE OF CONTENTS

(Amusements, Animals & Farms, Museums, Outdoors, State History, Tours, etc.)

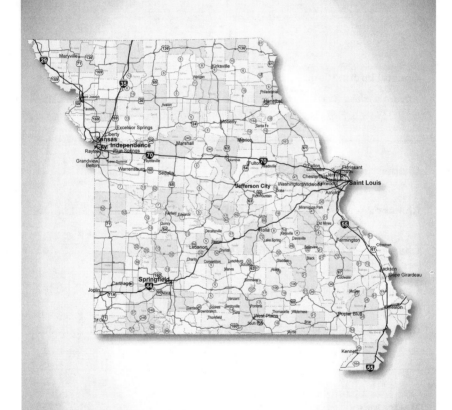

State Detail Map

(With Major Routes and Cities Marked)

Chapter Area Map

(Chapters arranged alphabetically by chapter name)

CITY INDEX *(Listed by City, Area, Page Numbers)*

CITY INDEX *(Listed by City, Area, Page Numbers)*

HOW TO USE THIS BOOK

(a few hints to make your adventures run smoothly:)

BEFORE YOU LEAVE:

- Each chapter represents a two hour radius area of the state or a Day Trip. The listings are by City and then alphabetical by name, numeric by zip code. Each listing has tons of important details (pricing, hours, website, etc.) and a review noting the most engaging aspects of the place. Our popular Activity Index in back is helpful if you want to focus on a particular type of attraction (i.e. History, Tours, Outdoor Exploring, Animals & Farms, etc.).

- Begin by assigning each family member a different colored highlighter (for example: Daniel gets blue, Jenny gets pink, Mommy gets yellow and Daddy gets green). At your leisure, begin to read each review and put a highlighter "check" mark next to the sites that most interest each family member or highlight the features you most want to see. Now, when you go to plan a quick trip - or a long van ride - you can easily choose different stops in one day to please everyone.

- Know directions and parking. Use a GPS system or print off directions from websites.

- Most attractions are closed major holidays unless noted.

- When children are in tow, it is better to make your lodging reservations ahead of time. Every time we've tried to "wing it", we've always ended up at a place that was overpriced, in a unsafe area, or not super clean. We've never been satisfied when we didn't make a reservation ahead of time.

- If you have a large family, or are traveling with extended family or friends, most places offer group discounts. Check out the company's website for details.

- For the latest critical updates corresponding to the pages in this book, visit our website: www.kidslovetravel.com. Click on *Updates*.

ON THE ROAD:

- Consider the child's age before you stop at an exit. Some attractions and restaurants, even hotels, are too formal for young ones or not enough adventure for teens.

- Estimate the duration of the trip and how many stops you can afford to make. From our experience, it is best to stop every two hours to stretch your legs or eat/snack or maybe visit an inexpensive attraction.

- Bring along travel books and games for "quiet time" in the van. (see tested travel products on www.kidslovetravel.com) As an added bonus, these "enriching" games also stimulate conversation - you may get to know your family better and create memorable life lessons.

ON THE ROAD: *(cont.)*

- In between meals, we offer the family snacks like: pretzels, whole grain chips, nuts, water bottles, bite-size (dark) chocolates, grapes and apples. None of these are messy and all are healthy.
- Plan picnics along the way. Many Historical sites and State Parks are scattered along the highway. Allow time for a rest stop or a scenic byway to take advantage of these free picnic facilities.

WHEN YOU GET HOME:

- Make a family "treasure chest". Decorate a big box or use an old popcorn tin. Store memorabilia from a fun outing, journals, pictures, brochures and souvenirs. Once a year, look through the "treasure chest" and reminisce. "Kids Love Travel Memories!" is an excellent travel journal and scrapbook template that your family can create (available on www.kidslovetravel.com).

WAYS TO SAVE MONEY:

- Memberships - many children's museums, science centers, zoos and aquariums are members of associations that provide FREE or Discounted reciprocity to other such museums across the country. AAA Auto Club cards offer discounts to many of the activities and hotels in this book. If grandparents are along for the ride, they can use their AARP card and get discounts. Be sure to carry your member cards with you as proof to receive the discounts.
- Supermarket Customer Cards - national and local supermarkets often offer good discounted tickets to major attractions in the area.
- Internet Hotel Reservations - if you're traveling with kids, don't take the risk of being spontaneous with lodging. Make reservations ahead of time. We don't use non-refundable, deep discount hotel "scouting" websites (ex. Hotwire) unless we're traveling on business - just adults. You can't cancel your reservation, or change them, and you can't be guaranteed the type of room you want (ex. non-smoking, two beds). Instead, stick with a national hotel chain you trust and join their rewards program (ex. Choice Privileges) to accumulate points towards FREE night stays.
- State Travel Centers - as you enter a new state, their welcome centers offer many current promotions.
- Hotel Lobbies - often have a display of discount coupons to area shops and restaurants. When you check in, ask the clerk for discount pizza coupons they may have at the front desk.
- Attraction Online Coupons - check the websites listed with each review for possible printable coupons or discounted online tickets good towards the attraction.

MISSION STATEMENT

At first glance, you may think that this is a book that just lists hundreds of places to travel. While it is true that we've invested thousands of hours of exhaustive research to prepare this travel resource…just listing places to travel is not the mission statement of these projects.

As children, Michele and I were able to travel extensively throughout the United States. We consider these family times some of the greatest memories we cherish today. We, quite frankly, felt that most children had this opportunity to travel with their family as we did. However, as we became adults and started our own family, we found that this wasn't necessarily the case. We continually heard friends express several concerns when deciding how to spend "quality" and "quantity" family time. 1) What to do? 2) Where to do it? 3) How much will it cost? 4) How do I know that my kids will enjoy it?

Interestingly enough, as we compare our experiences with our families when we were kids, many of our fondest memories were not made at an expensive attraction, but rather when it was least expected.

It is our belief and mission statement that if you as a family will study and use the contained information to create family memories, these memories will grow a stronger, tighter family. Our ultimate mission statement is, that your children will develop a love and a passion for quality family experiences that they can pass to another generation of family travelers.

We thank you for purchasing this book, and we hope to see you on the road (*and hear your travel stories!*) God bless your journeys and Happy Exploring!

Happy Exploring,

George, Michele, Jenny and Daniel

General State Agency & Recreational Information

Call *(or visit websites)* for the services of interest. Request to be added to their mailing lists.

- **MISSOURI TOURISM**: www.visitMO.com

- **MISSOURI STATE PARKS & HISTORIC SITES**: www.mostateparks.com. State Park Activity Sheets: http://mostateparks.com/kids.htm. History & Heritage Teachers Guides: http://www.dnr.mo.gov/shpo/educawar.htm.

- **KANSAS CITY TOURISM**: www.visitkc.com

- **MISSOURI AGRICULTURAL SEASONAL FARMS**: www.agrimissouri.com/pdf/agritourismmap.pdf

- **ST. LOUIS TOURISM**: www.explorestlouis.com

Travel Journal & Notes:

AIRPORTS - All children love to visit the airport! Why not take a tour and understand all the jobs it takes to run an airport? Tour the terminal, baggage claim, gates and security / currency exchange. Maybe you'll even get to board a plane.

ANIMAL SHELTERS - Great for the would-be pet owner. Not only will you see many cats and dogs available for adoption, but a guide will show you the clinic and explain the needs of a pet. Be prepared to have the children "fall in love" with one of the animals while they are there!

BANKS - Take a "behind the scenes" look at automated teller machines, bank vaults and drive-thru window chutes. You may want to take this tour and then open a savings account for your child.

CITY HALLS - Halls of Fame, City Council Chambers & Meeting Room, Mayor's Office and famous statues.

ELECTRIC COMPANY / POWER PLANTS - Modern science has created many ways to generate electricity today, but what really goes on with the "flip of a switch". Because coal can be dirty, wear old, comfortable clothes. Coal furnaces heat water, which produces steam, that propels turbines, that drives generators, that make electricity.

FIRE STATIONS - Many Open Houses in October, Fire Prevention Month. Take a look into the life of the firefighters servicing your area and try on their gear. See where they hang out, sleep and eat. Hop aboard a real-life fire engine truck and learn fire safety too.

HOSPITALS - Some Children's Hospitals offer pre-surgery and general tours.

NEWSPAPERS - You'll be amazed at all the new technology. See monster printers and robotics. See samples in the layout department and maybe try to put together your own page. After seeing a newspaper made, most companies give you a free copy (dated that day) as your souvenir. National Newspaper Week is in October.

PETCO - Various stores. Contact each store manager to see if they participate. The Fur, Feathers & Fins™ program allows children to learn about the characteristics and habitats of fish, reptiles, birds, and small animals. At your local Petco, lessons in science, math and geography come to life through this hands-on field trip. As students develop a respect for animals, they will also develop a greater sense of responsibility.

PIZZA HUT & PAPA JOHN'S - Participating locations. Telephone the store manager. Best days are Monday, Tuesday and Wednesday mid-afternoon. Minimum of 10 people. Small charge per person. All children love pizza – especially when they can create their own! As the children tour the kitchen, they learn how to make a pizza, bake it, and then eat it. The admission charge generally includes lots of creatively made pizzas, beverage and coloring book.

KRISPY KREME DONUTS - Participating locations. Get an "inside look" and learn the techniques that make these donuts some of our favorites! Watch the dough being made in "giant" mixers, being formed into donuts and taking a "trip" through the fryer. Seeing them being iced and topped with colorful sprinkles is always a favorite with the kids. Contact your local store manager. They prefer Monday or Tuesday. Free.

SUPERMARKETS - Kids are fascinated to go behind the scenes of the same store where Mom and Dad shop. Usually you will see them grind meat, walk into large freezer rooms, watch cakes and bread bake and receive free samples along the way. Maybe you'll even get to pet a live lobster!

TV / RADIO STATIONS - Studios, newsrooms, Fox kids clubs. Why do weathermen never wear blue/green clothes on TV? What makes a "DJ's" voice sound so deep and smooth?

WATER TREATMENT PLANTS - A giant science experiment! You can watch seven stages of water treatment. The favorite is usually the wall of bright buttons flashing as workers monitor the different processes.

U.S. MAIN POST OFFICES - Did you know Ben Franklin was the first Postmaster General (over 200 years ago)? Most interesting is the high-speed automated mail processing equipment. Learn how to address envelopes so they will be sent quicker (there are secrets). To make your tour more interesting, have your children write a letter to themselves and address it with colorful markers. Mail it earlier that day and they will stay interested trying to locate their letter in all the high-speed machinery.

GEOCACHING AND LETTERBOXING

Geocaching and Letterboxing are the ultimate treasure hunt and can add excitement and fun to your driving, camping and hiking experiences. Geocaching employs the use of a GPS device (global positioning device) to find the cache.

Letterboxing uses clues from one location to the next to find the letterbox; sometimes a compass is needed. Both methods use the Internet advertising the cache, providing basic maps and creating a forum for cache hunters.

GEOCACHING

The object of Geocaching is to find the hidden container filled with a logbook, pencil and sometimes prizes! Where are Caches? Everywhere! But to be safe, be sure you're treading on Public Property. When you find the cache, write your name and the date you found it in the logbook. Larger caches might contain maps, books, toys, even money! When you take something from the cache you are honor-bound to leave something else in its place. Usually cache hunters will report their individual cache experiences on the Internet. (www.geocaching.com)

- ## GPS RECEIVER

    You'll need a GPS receiver that will determine your position on the planet in relation to the cache's "waypoint," its longitude/latitude coordinates. You can buy a decent GPS receiver for around $100. More expensive ones have built-in electronic compasses and topographical maps, but you don't need all the extras to have fun geocaching.

LETTERBOXING

The object is similar to geocaching — find the Letterbox — but instead of just signing and dating the logbook, use a personalized rubber stamp. Most letterboxes include another rubber stamp for your own logbook. The creator of the letterbox provides clues to its location. Finding solutions to clues might require a compass, map and solving puzzles and riddles! This activity is great fun for the entire family! (www.letterboxing.org)

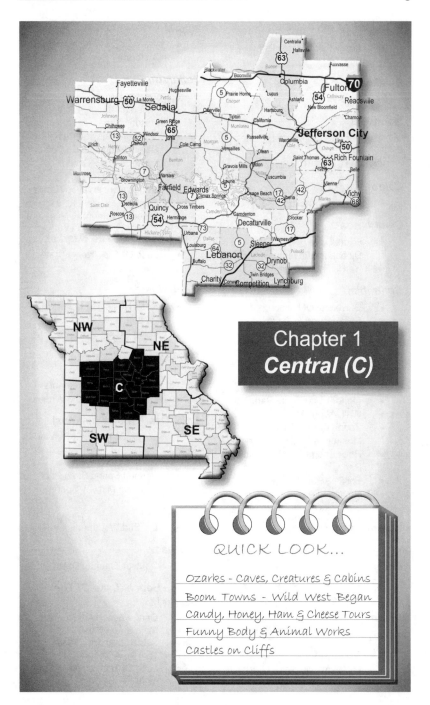

Chapter 1
Central (C)

QUICK LOOK...

Ozarks - Caves, Creatures & Cabins
Boom Towns - Wild West Began
Candy, Honey, Ham & Cheese Tours
Funny Body & Animal Works
Castles on Cliffs

Arrow Rock
- Arrow Rock State Historic Site

Blackwater
- Blackwater

Boonville
- Boone's Lick State Historic Site
- Old Cooper County Jail

California
- Burgers' Smokehouse

Camdenton
- Bridal Cave
- Dinospace Adventure
- Ha Ha Tonka State Park

Columbia
- University Of Missouri
- Shakespeare's Pizza
- State Historical Society Of Missouri
- The Candy Factory
- Youzeum
- 63 Diner
- Finger Lakes State Park
- Walk-About Acres
- Boone County Historical Museum & Visitors Center
- Rock Bridge Memorial State Park
- For The People Pow Wow
- Heritage Festival
- Shryocks Annual Corn Maze

Columbia (Hartsburg)
- Hartsburg Pumpkin Festival

Competition
- Stoney Acres Sheep Dairy And Cheese Plant

Dixon
- Meyer Tree & Berry Farm

Fort Leonard Wood
- Museum Complex At Fort Leonard Wood

Fulton
- Winston Churchill Memorial & Library

Jefferson City
- Central Dairy
- Jefferson Landing State Historic Site
- Missouri Highway Patrol Safety Education Center
- Missouri State Capitol Complex
- Runge Conservation Nature Center
- Missouri Veterinary Museum

Kaiser (Lake Of The Ozarks)
- Lake Of The Ozarks State Park

Knob Noster
- Knob Noster State Park
- Whiteman Air Force Base Open House

Lake Ozark
- Bagnell Dam
- Lake Ozark Amusements
- Tom Sawyer Paddle-Wheeler

Lake Ozark (Four Seasons)
- Lodge Of The Four Seasons

Lebanon
- Bennett Spring State Park
- Lebanon Midway Speedway

Linn Creek
- Big Surf Waterpark

Marthasville
- Deutsch Country Days

Osage Beach (Lake Of The Ozarks)
- Osage Beach Amusements
- Main Street Music Hall
- Sea Rocket Thrill Rides
- Tan-Tar-A Resort
- Lake Of The Ozarks Holiday Light Park

Osage City
- Clark's Hill-Norton State Historic Site

Pittsburg
- Pomme De Terre State Park

Sedalia
- Bothwell Lodge State Historic Site
- Katy Depot And Railroad Heritage Museum
- Missouri State Fair

Versailles
- Jacob's Cave

Warsaw
- Harry S Truman Dam & Reservoir Visitor Center
- Harry S Truman State Park
- Lost Valley Hatchery And Visitor Center

Waynesville
- Old Stagecoach Stop

Williamsburg
- Crane's Museum And Country Store

Travel Journal & Notes:

Sites and attractions are listed in order by City, Zip Code, and Name. Symbols indicated represent:

Festivals   Restaurants   Lodging

ARROW ROCK STATE HISTORIC SITE

Van Buren Street & Van Buren (Hwy 41) **Arrow Rock** 65320

- ☐ Phone: (660) 837-3330 **www.mostateparks.com/arrowrock.htm**
- ☐ Hours: Daily 10:00am-4:00pm (March-November). Winters only open Friday thru Sunday and winter holiday Mondays.
- ☐ Admission: The Missouri state park system does not charge entrance fees. However, there are fees associated with camping, lodging, tours, museums and certain special events.
- ☐ Tours: Guided tram tours of the village of Arrow Rock are provided for a nominal fee by the Friends of Arrow Rock.

The spirit of Missouri's frontier years lingers in this quiet, historic village town. You can tour an old jail, courthouse and the home of artist George Caleb Bingham. Dine at the Old Tavern. Sample a delicious, family-style meal in a charming log cabin restaurant. Meals include choice of smoked pork chop, buffalo brisket, country ham, fried or grilled honey-glazed chicken breast accompanied by spinach salad and fruit salad, scalloped potatoes, green beans, homemade breads, fabulous desserts, and coffee/tea/lemonade. This restaurant is guaranteed to be highlight of any tour.

A visitor center, hiking and camping are available. The site's visitor center museum features exhibits that tell about Arrow Rock and the historic "Boone's Lick Country." Visitors can watch a 20-minute video "Arrow Rock: Frontier Town of the Boone's Lick." The kids will like looking at the dioramas of famous people who lived in town. The Bingham Home, built by Missouri's preeminent artist of the 1800s, George Caleb Bingham, has been restored and furnished as it might have been when he lived there. The Huston Tavern, dating back to 1834, stands ready to serve you its traditional hearty fare. The old courthouse, a town doctor's home, a stone jail and other historic buildings are part of a walking tour offered at the site. The Pierre a Flèche (Rock of Arrows) hiking trail is a nearly one and one-half mile loop in the southern half of the site (see site map). The trailhead is in the visitor center parking lot. The River Landing Trail runs along the old warehouse road from town to the river landing - a spot that connected Lewis and Clark's trails and goods traveling the Missouri. So much history moved through this town, it's like walking through a mini-US History lesson in person. Basically, this whole town IS the historic site.

BLACKWATER
125 Main Street (3 miles north of I-70 at exit 89) **Blackwater** 65322

☐ **www.blackwater-mo.com**
☐ Admission: FREE.

As pioneers moved west, little "boom" towns were created. One such town was Blackwater, a common strop for coal and water used by the Missouri Pacific Railroad. After much restoration, you drive into this town and get a feeling you're on the set of a Western movie. Blackwater offers a jail replica, an exact replica of the Missouri-Pacific Depot, country school building, telephone museum, veterans memorial, water gardens and a 10-room, renovated 1887 hotel. Today you can stand near the windmill over the original town well and close your eyes and step back in time to the days of the Wild West. You can almost hear the steam whistle and smell the pungent coal smoke of the Missouri Pacific. You can almost hear the cattle bellowing. You can almost hear the music and voices from the Arcade saloon. Many buildings have been turned into gift shops so there is much browsing for old-fashioned treats involved in your visit.

The Telephone Museum showcases a lifetime collection of telephone memorabilia, including some items dating to the days before direct-dial systems. (Open April-Thanksgiving 9:00am-5:00pm).

BOONE'S LICK STATE HISTORIC SITE
Route 187 (Northwest of Boonville) **Boonville** 65233

☐ Phone: (660) 837-3330 (Arrow Rock)
  www.mostateparks.com/booneslick.htm
☐ Hours: The historic site grounds are open from sunrise to sunset year-round.
☐ Admission: The Missouri state park system does not charge entrance fees. However, there are fees associated with camping, lodging, tours, museums and certain special events.

BOONE'S LICK STATE HISTORIC SITE (cont.)

This is the site of the salt manufacturing business once owned and operated by Daniel Boone's sons, Daniel and Nathan started in 1805. Brine water was poured into iron kettles and heated to boiling on a stone furnace. As the water evaporated, salt crystallized in the bottom of the kettle. The salt was shipped by keelboat on the Missouri River to St. Louis. Salt, which was indispensable at the time for preserving meat and tanning hides, was produced at the site until approximately 1833.

It was Boone who created Boon's Lick Trail through the Saint Charles countryside, out of which grew the Santa Fe Trail and later the Oregon Trail – critical paths for early pioneers seeking a better life in the western United States. A self-guided gravel trail leads down a hillside to the salt springs and an outdoor exhibit explains the history of the site. Picnic sites available. Tour Boone's family home and pioneer village in neighboring Defiance, Missouri.

OLD COOPER COUNTY JAIL

614 East Morgan Street (just a couple miles north of I-70) **Boonville** 65233

- ☐ Phone: (660) 882-7977 **www.friendsofhistoricboonville.org/oldjail.html**
- ☐ Hours: Open for tours Monday-Friday, 9:00am-5:00pm. During summer also open Saturday and Sunday afternoons, 2:00-4:00pm.
- ☐ Miscellaneous: Another historic property in town is the HAIN HOUSE (Fourth & Chestnut). For a small fee, you can tour this typical 19th century, single-family dwelling built and owned by one extended Swiss family for 170 years.

A small museum, maintained by the Friends of Historic Boonville, can be found in the old Cooper County Jail on Morgan Street. The jail was used from 1847 to 1978, longer than any other lockup in Missouri. It housed outlaw Frank James and was the site of many public hangings. Slaves quarried the 2.5 foot thick limestone blocks which they used for construction of the two story building. Ironically, this was the site of slave sales and the round rings bolted to the outer walls of the dungeon rooms held prisoners and slaves shackled by their feet. Jail cells were installed upstairs. Every cell has its own history, its own stories to tell. The graffiti-carved limestone rock walls stand as silent witnesses to a way of life beyond our comprehension. While this site may be a little too deep in late 1800s history for young ones, those who have begun to study US Civil War era history will learn much emotionally.

DID YOU KNOW ? Boonville was the site of the first actual clash of arms between Union and pro-Confederate Missouri State Guard troops. Several markers in the town commemorate the First Battle of Boonville on June 17, 1861, and the Second Battle of Boonville in September 1863, as well as Gen. Sterling Price's raid through the town in October 1864.

BURGERS' SMOKEHOUSE

32819 Hwy. 87 (along Moreau River, 3 miles south of town, off Hwy 87)
California 65018

- ☐ Phone: (800) 345-5185 **www.smokehouse.com**
- ☐ Hours: Weekdays 8:00am-4:00pm. Store open one hour later Saturdays by chance.
- ☐ Admission: FREE.

Take a tour of this "scented" and artsy smokehouse operated by the Burger family for more than 50 years. The visitors center features dioramas that depict the seasons of the year. Other exhibits display ingredients, pictures, and artifacts that explain the art of meat curing. As you enter the Visitor's Center over a covered bridge, windows on the left open to a Spring diorama scene while the other windows on the right overlook a Winter scene. Water runs under the bridge and through the dioramas continuously. After exiting the bridge, you enter a Fall setting depicting a farmyard that features a handmade waterwheel. Slim (a little hillbilly boy) sits in the hayloft to welcome you to the Country Ham Smokehouse. You proceed around the next corner and there is Missouri in the Summertime. Wild turkey, deer, squirrel, and an assortment of wildlife as it appears in the Missouri Ozarks, are a part of this large diorama. From the bottom of the pool, up the cliffs to the sky is 2 1/2 stories high, making it one of the largest dioramas in the United States. As you proceed down the hall, you'll end up in the retail store. Tell the receptionist you would like to see the video tour of the smokehouse in the theatre. Now that you know the process, try some samples. If you're still hungry, purchase a sandwich in their shop.

BRIDAL CAVE

526 Bridal Cave Rd (2 miles north of Camdenton on Highway 5)
Camdenton 65020

- Phone: (573) 346-2676 www.bridalcave.com
- Hours: Daily 9:00am-5:00pm. Closes at 4:00 winter, open until 6:00pm summer.
- Admission: $15.00 adult (13+), $7.00 child (5-12).

Legend holds that an American-Indian couple wed at the cave site in the early 1800s. Since then, more than 2,100 couples from around the world have exchanged vows in the stalactite adorned Bridal Chapel. Hour-long tours offer views of giant columns, delicate soda straw configurations and the crystal-clear waters of Mystery Lake. Kind of a spooky place to get married-don't you think?

DID YOU KNOW ? Camdenton is home to several Marinas (near Rte 5, near bridges or at resorts) that have boat rentals - even houseboats. Often a motel or cottages are near the marina.

DINOSPACE ADVENTURE

1163 South Hwy 5 (a mile south of the Hwy 5 and Hwy 54 intersection)
Camdenton 65020

- Phone: (573) 346-5516 **www.dinospaceadventure.com**
- Hours: Tuesday-Saturday 9:00am-5:00pm (Memorial Day-Labor Day). Friday & Saturday 9:00am-5:00pm (Labor Day-November & March-Memorial Day). Closed December-February.
- Admission: General $6.00 (ages 2+).
- Educators: wonderful space-related curriculum unit studies (w/activities) are found here: www.dinospaceadventure.com/starlab.html

Orion Center's DinoSpace Adventure is a unique combination of science center and theme park with serious exhibits for adults and fun activities for kids. From dinosaurs to outer space and everything in between, it's all here. Just south of Camdenton on Hwy. 5, the center is a fun favorite with school groups and travelers. The 5,500-square-foot museum features exhibits on geology, archaeology, natural history and more. One exhibit space is called the Bone Room which features a life-size cast of the head of Stan the T-Rex. Outside, the DinoSpace Adventure Park has up to a dozen hands-on activities. Take what you learned in the science museum outside to the fun park launching balls from trebuchets, riding zip lines and pretending that you can overcome dinosaurs.

HA HA TONKA STATE PARK

1491 State Road D **Camdenton** 65020

- ☐ Phone: (573) 346-2986 **www.mostateparks.com/hahatonka.htm**
- ☐ Hours: Daily from 8:00am-sunset.
- ☐ Admission: The Missouri state park system does not charge entrance fees. However, there are fees associated with camping, lodging, tours, museums and certain special events.

Your family may not have any dragons to slay, but you'll find many wild creatures in a natural setting as you amble toward Ha Ha Tonka Castle located in Ha Ha Tonka State Park, near Camdenton on the Niangua arm of the Lake of the Ozarks. The Castle was built after European-style castles and, after a series of fatal events, what remains are the stark, devastated outside walls that majestically stand on the edge of the cliff. Ha Ha Tonka is a geological wonderland: sinkholes, caves, a huge natural bridge, soaring bluffs, and Missouri's twelfth largest spring. Scenic trails lead thru deep ravines and bowls caused by collapsed caves, past a 100 foot natural bridge and a theater like pit called the Colosseum (used for Native American tribal meetings?). Fifteen miles of trail traverse the park, leading visitors to spectacular scenery, natural wonders and the famous castle ruins. Accessible, paved walkways and rugged, rocky trails provide every hiking experience, from a casual boardwalk stroll to an overnight backpack trip.

DID YOU KNOW ? Ha Ha Tonka State Park is host to several geocache and letterbox sites.

UNIVERSITY OF MISSOURI

Columbia

- ☐ **www.missouri.edu/visitors/**

Visit the oldest land-grant university west of the Mississippi and the Historic Francis Quadrangle on the MU Campus, site of the historic MU Columns, and (believe it or not) Thomas Jefferson's original tombstone. Here's some other highlights of a campus visit:

UNIVERSITY OF MISSOURI (cont.)

- **MIZZOU TIGERS** - Faurot Field, football home games.
- **MUSEUM OF ART & ARCHEOLOGY** - Pickard Hall. http://maa. missouri.edu/. The Museum of Art and Archaeology features major works of art, plus ancient art and artifacts such as death masks. The unique costumes, masks and other special exhibits will surprise and delight most visitors.
- **MUSEUM OF ANTHROPOLOGY** - Swallow Hall. http:// anthromuseum.missouri.edu/. The Anthropology Museum focuses on the native peoples of the country and those in Missouri, as well as the early settlements of Missouri. The permanent exhibition gallery focuses on American Indian cultures from across North America and on Missouri prehistory, from B.C. to the present. Both museums have special features that kids like - from mummified animals - to American Indian artifacts, and a replica of a settlers cabin.
- **ENTOMOLOGY MUSEUM** - Agricultural Building.
- **BUCK'S ICE CREAM PARLOR ON THE MU CAMPUS**, (573) 882-4100. One of Columbia's best kept secrets, Buck's is located on the southeast corner of College & Rollins in Eckles Hall. Here, the MU Food Science Department makes and serves some of the best ice cream and yogurt to be found - Tiger Stripe ice cream, a rich vanilla swirled with chocolate fudge is a Columbia favorite!

DID YOU KNOW? Missouri Mules are proud symbols of the "Show-Me State" and mascots of the MU School of Veterinary Medicine.

SHAKESPEARE'S PIZZA

Columbia - *225 South Ninth Street 65201. Phone: (573) 449-2454 (The District) www.Shakespeares.com. Miscellaneous: Another location is at 3304 Broadway Business Park Court, (573) 447-1202. If you want pizza this is the place to go. They sell by the slice during lunch. They also offer subs, salads and garlic bread. Prices range from about $3-5 for lunch and $4-10 for dinner. Go early evening to avoid the crowds. The best part, by reservation, you and up to five friends or relatives can make and bake your own Shakespeare's pizza at the downtown shop, then enjoy watching the pizza bake. Which of their fresh pizza toppings did you choose? Their meats are* *made just for them and their veggies are cut fresh upon ordering, not frozen. I guess the best part is really the tasting!*

STATE HISTORICAL SOCIETY OF MISSOURI

1020 Lowry Street (University of Missouri campus) **Columbia** 65201

- Phone: (573) 882-7083 or (800) 747-6366
  http://shs.umsystem.edu/about/visit.shtml
- Hours: Monday-Friday 8:00am-4:45pm, Saturday 8:00am-3:30pm.
- Admission: FREE.
- Miscellaneous: Downtown Columbia has lots of little shops and restaurants to do a walk-around. Educators: the best thing about this historical site is their online Education page, especially if you're preparing to write an essay about Famous Missourians.

In Columbia, the most famous painting of the Civil War era hangs at the State Historical Society of Missouri. George Caleb Bingham's "Order No. 11" depicts the Union order to clear the civilian population from Missouri's western counties near the Kansas border. The purpose was to check guerrilla activity in the region, but the harsh measure only served to increase the bloodshed as William Quantrill, "Bloody Bill" Anderson and others raised terror in the hearts of anyone connected with the Union war effort. Outside of this painting, there's not much for kids. Better to visit their online resources or stop in with older youth to physically research state history.

THE CANDY FACTORY

701 E. Cherry Street, downtown **Columbia** 65201

- Phone: (573) 443-8222 **www.CandyFactory.biz**

Chocolate, candies, milk shakes, all scrumptious treats, what could be better? How about a cookie dipped in chocolate? The Candy Factory takes your favorite snacks and treats, like Oreos, Nutter Butters, potato chips and dips them in chocolate for a sweet treat. The potato chip chocolates are surprisingly good - the perfect blend of sweet and salty. Your choices include original, salty kettle cooked and jalapeno kettle cooked. Watch them roll cherry filling or dip caramel apples. Walk down candy cane lane past viewing windows watching a chocolate enrober do its thing or view the goings on in the candy cooking kitchens and chocolate molding room. The in store favorite to share at home is their Ultimate Chocolate Pizza. They are open daily for shopping and viewing. Call ahead for daily hours and best viewing hours.

YOUZEUM

608 Cherry Street (corner of 6th and Cherry Streets) **Columbia** 65201

- Phone: (573) 886-2006 **www.youzeum.org**
- Hours: (Youzeum - all ages) Friday 10:00am-5:00pm, Saturday 10:00am-6:00pm. (Explore & More - ages 7 years and younger) Tuesday, Thursday & Wednesday 9:00am-12:00pm, Friday 9:00am-5:00pm, Saturday 10:00am-6:00pm.
- Admission: $8.00 adult (14+), $5.00 child (4-13).

Visit Mid-Missouri's only interactive science center that's all about YOU! Kids learn how the body works and have fun doing it at the YouZeum with an interactive zip through the human body in a 3-D film and a virtual jog on the Katy Trail. For instance, you'll be able to walk through the brain and see how it works, fight 'germ-wars' on an interactive video screen and ride a bicycle on a virtual trail. Some things are gross (but kinda funny), some practical science. All lead students to the conclusion that knowledge about their bodies (even the gross stuff) can keep them healthy longer.

63 DINER

Columbia - *5801 N Highway 763 (3 miles north of town) 65202. Phone: (573) 443-2331 www.63diner.com. Hours: Tuesday-Saturday 11:00am-9:00pm. Turn back the clock and join us in the original location for old-fashioned quality and service. Enjoy a 50s ambience with all of your 63 favorites including the B-52 Steak Sandwich and their signature banana split. Open Tuesday - Saturday for lunch & dinner. You won't have trouble finding the place...just look for the red Cadillac jutting from the front of the building.*

FINGER LAKES STATE PARK

1505 E. Peabody Road **Columbia** 65202

- Phone: (573) 443-5315 **www.mostateparks.com/fingerlakes.htm**
- Admission: The Missouri state park system does not charge entrance fees. However, there are fees associated with camping, lodging, tours, museums and certain special events.

This old strip mining area is now used for swimming, fishing, and canoeing. Holes left from the strip mining have resulted in excellent swimming lakes and one even has a sandy beach. Note that the swimming holes are extremely deep, and there are no shallow areas. There is also a campground, picnic sites and mountain bike paths.

YOUTH RIDING AREA - This area is located north of the Motocross Track. This small riding area has be set aside for children under the age of 12 years and who are riding ORVs 80cc or under. Adult supervisor is required at all times. On race days, the youth track is closed along with the main track.

WALK-ABOUT ACRES

6800 North Kircher Road (I-70 and Hwy 63 intersection take Route PP northeast 7.5 miles) **Columbia** 65202

☐ Phone: (573) 474-8837 **www.walk-aboutacres.net**
☐ Hours: Tuesday-Saturday 9:00am-5:00pm, Sunday 1:00-5:00pm.
☐ Tours: Guided field trips are $4.00 per person, which includes rolling a beeswax candle and planting a plant. Small unguided tours with no activities are free of charge, however we do accept donations towards our animal feed bills to help cover costs. For an additional $1.00 you could include one of our delicious honey ice creams. You really need to make a reservation to visit the farm if you want a tour. April-November.

Walk-About Acres is a working farm featuring locally produced honey and honey products. Walk About Acres introduces visitors to showy peacocks, cuddly rabbits, a friendly turkey, kissing llamas, Nubian milk goats and bees. Visit the bee yard to see how bees live and work in their hive. Moms like shopping for their various potted plants.

BOONE COUNTY HISTORICAL MUSEUM & VISITORS CENTER

3801 Ponderosa Street **Columbia** 65203

☐ Phone: (573) 443-8936 **http://boonehistory.org/Museum.htm**
☐ Hours: Wednesday, Friday, Saturday & Sunday 12:30-4:30pm. Longer summer hours. Call or see website for details.

Tour the Boone County Historical Museum which features a sampler exhibit of the lives and events that shaped the settlement of Boone County

- from Daniel Boone and his Boone's Lick Trail to the establishment of the University of Missouri. Each display highlights the Western Expansion along the Booneslick Trace and on native Americans. Kids find out what broadax is, check out a weaving loom and a collection of antique toys, such as an airplane pedal car. Then go next door to the Maplewood, a 19th Century rural farmstead which features a gracious 2 story home and original outbuildings.

ROCK BRIDGE MEMORIAL STATE PARK

5901 South Hwy. 163 **Columbia** 65203

☐ Phone: (573) 449-7402 **www.mostateparks.com/rockbridge.htm**
☐ Admission: The Missouri state park system does not charge entrance fees. However, there are fees associated with camping, lodging, tours, museums and certain special events.

Geologic formations are the main features of this day-use park, which sits atop Devil's Icebox Cave. Cave tours are only recommended for healthy, strong teens and adults. Trails lead visitors to the natural rock bridge, sinkholes and springs. Nature programs are offered and picnic areas are available. Bats love this area in the summer but only come out to feed at dusk. The Cave trails are also supported by wood boardwalks. From the caves, the boardwalk meanders through the woods and keeps visitors' feet dry inches above the stream that flows through the Rock Bridge. Displays tell visitors more about the cave system and the area's history. Additional information can be gained from using the Devil's Icebox Self-Guiding Trail booklet, which is available for a small fee at the park office.

FOR THE PEOPLE POW WOW

Columbia - *Boone County Fairgrounds. American Indian traditional dance. Honored guest, Larry Sellers; played Cloud Dancing on the Dr. Quinn, Medicine Woman TV program. American Indian art vendors; Indian fry bread and foods; raffles. Held in the open air, covered pavilion at the Boone County Fairgrounds, rain or shine. All drums are welcome. Limited seating available; bring your own chairs. Free camping and RVs. Small Admission. http://msptv.org/powwow.htm (Memorial Day weekend)*

HERITAGE FESTIVAL

Columbia - *Historic Maplewood Farm in Nifong Park. www.gocolumbiamo.com. The festival celebrates the history of mid-Missouri with demos and displays of cowboys and a chuckwagon, a Lewis and Clark encampment, Native American teepees, trades people exhibiting their wares, hayrides, storytelling, entertainment stages and lots of kettle corn. (third weekend in September)*

SHRYOCKS ANNUAL CORN MAZE

Columbia - *2927 County Road 253 (12 miles east of Columbia on I-70 betw. Exit 137 & 144). Phone: (573) 592-0191. Fall fun with corn maze featuring 12 acres of corn and over four miles of trails!, plus a three story gumball machine and petting zoo. Allow at least one hour and 15 minutes to get through the maze. Groups will take longer. A portion of all ticket sales benefit the Boy Scouts and Girl Scouts of Mid-Missouri. Hours: Thursday, Friday, and Sunday: 2:00pm-dark Saturday: 10:00am - 10:00pm (flashlight nights). Admission. (starts mid-summer but best in fall)*

HARTSBURG PUMPKIN FESTIVAL

Columbia (Hartsburg) - *Downtown. This quaint river town brings in over 100 craft vendors and offers a petting zoo, pony rides, food booths and tons of pumpkins and pumpkin-related games and food. Hartsburg is filled with musical entertainment, every holiday and other decorations, and tens of thousands of pumpkins. The festival features pumpkin carving, pumpkin pie eating competitions, hayrides in the pumpkin patch, pumpkin painting, apple butter making, and a straw maze. (mid-October weekend)*

STONEY ACRES SHEEP DAIRY AND CHEESE PLANT

11399 Claxton Road **Competition** 65470

☐   Phone: (417) 668-5560 **www.stoneyacres.biz**
☐   Hours: Please call ahead for appointment or stop in by chance.
☐   Admission: FREE.

Missouri's only licensed sheep dairy also is home to a small cheese plant. Visitors may milk the sheep and bottle feed the lambs when the time and season are right. Their shop has cheese, soaps and other items for sale…all made from sheep's milk which gives their cheese products a slightly different flavor and creamy white color. All their consumer products are made in small batches to maintain quality.

MEYER TREE & BERRY FARM
13018 Highway D **Dixon** 65459

- ☐ Phone: (573) 759-7998 **http://meyertreeandberryfarm.com/**
- ☐ Hours: (Blueberries) Tuesday & Thursday 8:00am-Noon and 5:00pm-8:00pm. Saturday 8:00am-6:00pm, Sunday Noon-5:00pm. (late-June - late-September). (Pumpkins) Weekdays Noon-6:00pm, Saturday 8:00am-6:00pm, Sunday Noon-5:00pm (late-September - October).
- ☐ Tours: the farm offers group tours by appointment.

Three acres of blueberries, ripe and ready for picking in June, and a pumpkin patch the whole family will love in the fall. During the pumpkin season, late September through October, this popular you-pick farm has hay wagon rides and bonfires.

MUSEUM COMPLEX AT FORT LEONARD WOOD
495 South Dakota Avenue **Fort Leonard Wood** 65473

- ☐ Phone: (573) 596-0780 **www.wood.army.mil/ccmuseum/index.htm**
- ☐ Hours: Monday-Friday 8:00am-4:00pm, Saturday 10:00am-4:00pm. Closed during inclement weather.
- ☐ Admission: Free

The history and contributions of the military police, Army engineers and chemical warfare units during conflicts dating to the Revolutionary War are on display in a three-museum complex. Land-mine warfare, tactical bridging, demolition and explosives, arms, chemical warfare. Military Police vehicles are on display in the vehicle park located across the street from the museum. Kids think seeing the Army barracks (everything in place) is pretty cool.

WINSTON CHURCHILL MEMORIAL & LIBRARY

501 Westminster Avenue (Westminster College campus) **Fulton** 65251

- Phone: (573) 642-3361 **www.churchillmemorial.org**
- Hours: Daily 10:00am-4:30pm.
- Admission: $6.00 adult, $5.00 senior, $4.00 youth (12-18), $3.00 child (6-11).
- Educators: trying to get a hold of the character and accomplishments of a great man in the history books may love this curricula online: www.churchillmemorial.org/schoolprograms/curricula/Pages/default.aspx.

In 1946, Sir Winston Churchill made his famous Iron Curtain speech at Westminster College, which is listed on the National Register of Historic Places. How did the church and memorial land in Fulton? The Living Memorial 13-minute film explains. Interactive exhibits, artifacts and a film focus on one of the 20th century's most well-known statesmen, Winston Churchill. See the podium Churchill used to make that speech and watch a film of him delivering it. Look for his famous top hat (autographed). On the outside and above the museum is the church that was so damaged during the London Blitz in 1940 that it was scheduled to be demolished until Fulton asked that it be shipped to Westminster College so it could be reconstructed as a tribute to Winston Churchill. Visitors can also experience a London air raid through a light and sound show. You won't want to miss the Berlin Wall sculpture "Breakthrough."

Sculpted by Churchill's grand-daughter, "Breakthrough" is carved from eight sections of the Berlin Wall. The museum center was designed to provide a place for students to come and learn about themselves and their lives through Churchill, making history relevant to their present and future. Doesn't this sound like a fun way to explore the life and character of such a famous historical statesman?

CENTRAL DAIRY

Jefferson City - *610 Madison St. 65101. Phone: (573) 635-6148 www.centraldairy.biz. Ice cream has never been so good. Be prepared for a tough decision as you view the flavors behind the long glass window. There are over 40 flavors of ice cream to try and this is the home of the $1.00 triple, hand-dipped cones and unbelievable banana splits. A trip to our hometown dairy for an enormous scoop of ice cream has been a tradition in Jefferson City since the 1930s.*

JEFFERSON LANDING STATE HISTORIC SITE

Jefferson Street and Capitol Avenue **Jefferson City** 65101

- ☐ Phone: (573) 751-2854 **www.mostateparks.com/jeffersonland.htm**
- ☐ Admission: The Missouri state park system does not charge entrance fees. However, there are fees associated with camping, lodging, tours, museums and certain special events.

Jefferson Landing State Historic Site is significant as a rare surviving Missouri River landing. The Lohman Building, built in 1839, is a sturdy stone structure that served as a tavern and hotel, and in its heyday also housed one of the city's largest warehouse and mercantile businesses. Today, the main floor contains a visitor center with exhibits on transportation. The ground floor of the building still serves as the city's Amtrak train station. Don't you love walking on those brick "cobblestone street" hallways?

MISSOURI HIGHWAY PATROL SAFETY EDUCATION CENTER

1510 East Elm Street **Jefferson City** 65101

- ☐ Phone: (573) 751-3313 **www.mshp.dps.mo.gov**
- ☐ Hours: 8:00am-5:00pm
- ☐ Admission: FREE. Groups of 10 or more people should call for a reservation (573) 526-6149.

Nowhere in the state of Missouri is there such a comprehensive display of information concerning traffic safety law enforcement, drug abuse and other items relating to the history of the Missouri Highway Patrol. Exhibits focus on the services and responsibilities of the Highway Patrol, both on and off the highways. Test your emergency reaction time and see wreckage of a car crash where passenger's lives were saved wearing seat belts. It seems funny to think patrolmen cased the streets in a 1931 Model A Ford Roadster at one time. See one up close.

MISSOURI STATE CAPITOL COMPLEX

201 West Capitol Avenue **Jefferson City** 65102

- ☐ Phone: (573) 751-2854 **www.mostateparks.com/statecapcomplex/**
- ☐ Admission: The Missouri state park system does not charge entrance fees. However, there are fees associated with camping, lodging, tours, museums and certain special events.

For updates & travel games visit: **www.KidsLoveTravel.com**

☐   Audio Tours: are downloadable from the Audio Tours link online BEFORE you get there. In a hurry? Self-guided tour maps are available at the Capitol Tour Reservation desk located on the first floor. Capitol tours are given Monday through Saturday every hour on the hour (excluding the noon hour) for walk-in guests. Reservations are required for groups of 10 or more. On Sundays, tours are given at 10:00am, 11:00am, 2:00pm and 3:00pm.

☐   Educators: an audio online site of interviews and facts about former Missouri slaves is at this extension: www.mostateparks.com/statecapcomplex/ statemuseum/slaverysechoes.htm.

STATE CAPITOL - As your family approaches the complex, many notice the Missouri Capitol Building looks a lot like the D.C. Capitol building. Very ominous outside and very stately inside. All four floors of Missouri's Capitol are open to the public. A 30-minute guided tour is the best way to experience the historic and decorative features of the building. Two things you must try to see while on tour (if available, obey signs on doors): Legislature in session (January thru mid-May) and the Mural in the House Lounge. Both are "active" spaces. The mural is colorful and busy but kids love trying to make out the different facial expressions and count how many people are in the mural. Oh, and wouldn't the Governor's office be a handsome room to work in? A walk around the Capitol grounds highlights more of Missouri's history, including Karl Bitter's bronze relief of the signing of the Louisiana Purchase Treaty, which sits on the terrace overlooking the Missouri River.

MISSOURI STATE MUSEUM - Part of the original Capitol plans called for a ground-floor museum that showcased Missouri's cultural and natural history. Now operated by the Missouri Department of Natural Resources, the Missouri State Museum features exhibits, dioramas and changing displays.

•   HISTORY HALL - Be a history detective as you explore the hands-on exhibits and try to answer questions asked along the way. Try on 19th century clothing, design a flag and learn about the equipment soldiers carried during the war. "Slavery's Echoes" is where quotes from interviews with former slaves give first-hand accounts of working conditions, family life, housing and treatment they endured. Also in the display, you'll find "hands-on" artifacts like shackles and clothing, along with an audio stories. Scavenger Hunt: http://www.mostateparks. com/statecapcomplex/statemuseum/se_scavengerhunt.pdf.

MISSOURI STATE MUSEUM (cont.)

- NATURAL RESOURCES HALL - Displays the products of the state's forests, fields and mines. This gallery displays Missouri's natural resources on the south wall, human resources on the north wall and the story of how the two have interacted in the center.

RUNGE CONSERVATION NATURE CENTER
(Mo. Hwy. 179 - 1/2 mile north of Highways 50/63) **Jefferson City** 65102

- ☐ Phone: (573) 526-5544 **http://mdc.mo.gov/areas/cnc/runge/**
- ☐ Hours: (Area) 6:00am-9:00pm. (Buildings) Tuesday, Wednesday, Friday, Saturday: 8:00am-5:00pm, Thursday 8:00am-8:00pm.
- ☐ Admission: FREE.

Enjoy the wonders of Missouri's habitats and the fish, forest and wildlife resources found in the Show-Me State. There are hiking trails and wildlife habitats outdoors, while the nature center features indoor exhibits. Kids love "Bubba", an enormous model of a bullfrog, the 2500 gallon aquarium full of native state fish and the walk-thru cave. Age a fish using an enormous fish scale and learn how and why we tag fish. Follow a river otter with a tracking device and see a rare swamp rabbit that can swim. This is a great little Missouri natural history stop and it's free.

MISSOURI VETERINARY MUSEUM
2500 Country Club Drive (50 west to Rte 179 exit) **Jefferson City** 65109

- ☐ Phone: (573) 636-8737 **www.mvma.us**
- ☐ Hours: Monday-Friday, 9:00am-4:00pm & Saturday by appointment.

The only museum in the United States that is devoted solely to veterinary medicine is located in Jefferson City. On display are veterinary artifacts and instruments, many over 100 years old. The museum houses over 3,500 artifacts dating from the 1st century to present. The interactive museum is appropriate for both children and adults. Hands-on learning center for kids: Visitors touch and explore materials, such as bones, animals skins and hairballs. Other discovery materials are specimens showing stages of a calf embryo and various animal diseases. Be prepared for the unusual such as a hog catcher, huge horse pills and giant syringes. What strange objects does a veterinarian find in a cow's stomach? What did a veterinarian use in 1929 to give Fido his medicine? Discover the answers to these questions at the Veterinary Museum.

LAKE OF THE OZARKS STATE PARK

403 Highway 134 (off Hwy. 54 on Route A)
Kaiser (Lake of the Ozarks) 65047

- Phone: (573) 348-2694 **www.mostateparks.com/lakeozark/cave.htm**
- Admission: The Missouri state park system does not charge entrance fees. However, there are fees associated with camping, lodging, tours, museums and certain special events. Tours run $4.00-$6.00 (Mid-April thru mid-October).

The wooded hills and miles of shoreline provide a getaway from nearby attractions. The park offers camping, camper cabins, a yurt, marinas, beaches, trail rides and hiking trails. The park's visitor center is located at Ozark Caverns, the site of the cave tours. The center features a variety of educational exhibits, particularly displays on the cave environment and animal life within the cave system. (Visitor Center open 9:00am-5:00pm daily except closed in winter).

OZARK CAVERNS - Cave is located in the park and can be explored using handheld lanterns. Guided one hour tours give you a view under the Ozark hills of bats, salamanders and interesting cave formations like the Angel Showers. The spectacular Angel's Shower is among the highlighted sights. The perpetual flow of water seems to spring directly from the rocks above into two massive basins below. Visitors center exhibits about the natural features of the cave.

KNOB NOSTER STATE PARK

873 SE 10 Knob Noster 65336

- Phone: (660) 563-2463 **www.mostateparks.com/knobnoster.htm**
- Admission: The Missouri state park system does not charge entrance fees. However, there are fees associated with camping, lodging, tours, museums and certain special events.

Dominated by second growth hardwood forest, this park contains restored remnants of open woodlands and grasslands. It has a nature center, small lakes, a campground, hiking trails, an equestrian trail and campground. Several small lakes in the park cater to the fisherman, and non-motorized boats may be used. The nature center is open daily during business hours.

WHITEMAN AIR FORCE BASE OPEN HOUSE

Knob Noster - *Highway 23 off Highway 50. Once a year you can visit the home base of the Stealth bomber. Usually held a summertime weekend, the open house is set up so you can climb into older planes, view displays about aircraft and the air force, and see guard dogs, a mobile command station, and other military items. Includes an air show and aerial demonstrations throughout the day. (mid-September weekend)*

BAGNELL DAM

1 Willmore Lane **Lake Ozark** 65049

☐   Phone: (900) 451-4117 **www.lakeareachamber.com**

WILLMORE LODGE VISITORS CENTER & MUSEUM - Lodge serves as offices of the Lake Ozark area Chamber of Commerce and houses a museum with a great big view of the Dam. The visitors center is your first stop when arriving in the area to orient yourself and pick up the latest coupon booklets. The museum exhibits tell about the area before Bagnell Dam was built and the construction of the dam. Occasionally, a guide will offer a short free tour of the dam showing how electricity is generated and how the dam was built. What are the dozens of rooms in this building named after?

BAGNELL DAM - OMA & NOMA DAYS FESTIVAL

Lake Ozark - *Experience yesteryear as we celebrate the first crossing of the Bagnell Dam by Oma and Noma Degraffenreid in 1931. Dress in era style clothing and enjoy an old fashioned festival with events such as, outhouse racing, frog jumping, watermelon seed spitting, pie eating contests, to name a few. Held at the south end of Bagnell Dam. www.omanomadays.org. (mid-May weekend)*

DID YOU KNOW? The Lake of the Ozarks area has a number of oddities, but one that remains a mystery is on the west side of Highway 5 to State Road 135-3. It's a shoe fence with dozens of shoes of all shapes, styles, and colors on the fence post. Each year it grows and changes as new shoes are added. In the same vicinity is the Cup Tree. Some believe that there was once a natural spring here and people left their cups and mugs for other travelers. While not necessarily sanitary, its intent was quite hospitable and quite colorful with cups and mugs of all colors and sizes dancing in the breeze.

LAKE OZARK AMUSEMENTS
Lake Ozark 65049

- **CASTLE ROCK** - 2620 Bagnell Dam Blvd. CastleRock has a figure eight track that takes on the Ozark's hills and has some sharp turns. It's a small enough track that you can pass someone twice while being thrilled by the speeds available. They also have a kiddie track and a slick track. Also has 18-hole mini golf, climbing wall and ejection bungee seat.

- **SUGAR CREEK MINI GOLF** - 3001 Bagnell Dam Blvd. Sugar Creek Mini Golf gives you a special flavor of the Ozarks. Nestled in shaded trees and Ozark terrain, Sugar Creek offers 36 holes woven through scenes from the 1880's: church, saloon, main street and a water wheel. When the temps swelter you will find this attraction a favorite for many, young and old.

TOM SAWYER PADDLE-WHEELER
1006 Bagnell Dam Boulevard (docks near Bagnell Dam) **Lake Ozark** 65049

☐   Phone: (573) 365-3300 or (888) 366-7759 **www.tom-huck.com**

Take a narrated, 90-minute cruise on a circa 1800s paddlewheeler. The cruise includes the main channel of Lake of the Ozarks, and some interesting coves. They offer sightseeing and dinner cruises. Rates and times are posted online in May each year. Before or after the ride, try Huckleberry's Restaurant - Cajun style bar and grill located on the dock.

LODGE OF THE FOUR SEASONS
Lake Ozark (Four Seasons) - *315 Lodge of Four Seasons Drive 65049. Phone: (573) 365-3000, (800) THE-LAKE or (888) 265-5500 (reservations) www.4seasonsresort. com. This is a true lodge setting with rock or stone walls, fireplace in the lobby and cozy furnishings. While the main lodge is older, the condos are new and furniture and carpeting in the lodge rooms has been updated recently. This resort area also offers a*

full-service marina offering boat, water ski and personal watercraft rentals, parasailing, fishing guides, lake cruises, gasoline and a store. They also have a full-service spa on the property. Good for a few days of retreat and recreation in the Ozarks.

BENNETT SPRING STATE PARK
26250 Hwy 64A **Lebanon** 65536

- ☐ Phone: (417) 532-4338 (Park Office) or (417) 532-4307 (Lodging)
  www.mostateparks.com/bennett.htm or www.bennettspringstatepark.com
- ☐ Admission: The Missouri state park system does not charge entrance fees. However, there are fees associated with camping, lodging, tours, museums and certain special events.
- ☐ Miscellaneous: Lebanon is a hub for handfuls of canoe rental and guided tours and dozens of family campgrounds.

Bennett Spring, the fourth largest state park in Missouri, has a daily output of over 100 million gallons of water, rising out of a narrow cave. Native Americans were the first to enjoy its beauty and benefits, and referred to it as "Eye of the Sacred One." Bennett Spring was one of Missouri's first state parks. Today it is still one of the most beautiful and most popular in the state's system. Many things draw people here, but the reason that tops the list is the fishing - trout fishing. The hatchery in the park adds fish to the stream daily. Stop in at the hatchery for a quick tour.

In addition to fishing, park visitors can enjoy 12 miles of hiking trails, with an abundance of wildlife and wildflowers to be found along the paths. Area outfitters can provide float trips on the Niangua River. The Nature Interpretive Center is a great place to get an overview of the park's wildlife, as well as learn the history of the spring. There's an outdoor swimming pool, tent camping and RV sites, motel rooms, single cabins, duplexes and four-plexes available. Feed you cravings at the rustic C.C.C. Dining Lodge. Built in 1930, the Dining Lodge offers a varied cuisine of just bring in your catch and they will cook it for you!

LEBANON MIDWAY SPEEDWAY
22304 Route B **Lebanon** 65536

☐ Phone: (417) 588-4430 **www.lebanonmidwayspeedway.com**

Spring through fall, race fans can watch the action on this dirt-track speedway in Lebanon. April-September. $8.00-$25.00; ages 10 and younger are FREE.

BIG SURF WATERPARK
954 State Road Y (off Hwy. 54 at State Rt. Y) **Linn Creek** 65052

☐ Phone: (573) 346-6111 **www.bigsurfwaterpark.com**
☐ Hours: Daily, (Memorial Day-Labor Day)
☐ Admission: $25.00 adult (11-59), $20.00 junior (4-10), $14.00 senior (60+). Discounts after 3:00pm.

Big Surf Waterpark – Features 27 acres of water fun including a wave pool, three-story Zambezi Falls water experience, whirlpool spa, rapid rides, body flumes, lazy river and Tropical Splash Island for young children.

DEUTSCH COUNTRY DAYS

Marthasville - *Luxenhaus Farm, Highway O. A living history event that takes place on a farm that is home to 19 restored historic buildings. This is the only time the farm is open to the public. Usually 60+ crafts and skills demonstrators share their skills: rugs, crosscut sawing, sheep shearing, natural dyeing, paper marbling, primitive folk-art gourds and kloppelei (bobbin lace). Admission. (third weekend in October)*

OSAGE BEACH AMUSEMENTS
Osage Beach (Lake of the Ozarks)

- **MINER MIKE'S ADVENTURE TOWN** - 4515 Hwy 54. Admission: www.minermikes.com. Ride packages $8.00-$14.00. Over 100 token operated games are available and must be purchased separately. You may purchase the rides individually, and each ride requires 4 tokens per child. One adult may ride free with a paying child. Open year-round except winter.

- **PIRATES COVE ADVENTURE GOLF** - 5850 US 54. Admission: $7.95 adult, $6.95 child. www.piratescove.net/location/14. Your choice of 2 courses, the Captains Course, or the more challenging Blackbeard's Challenge.

- **PUTT N STUFF FAMILY FUN CENTER** - 5440 Highway 54. March - October. Phone: (573) 348-2127. One-stop fun for the family. Two 18-hole mini-golf courses with waterfalls, caves and fans to keep you cool; bumper cars; skee ball; video games; a children's merry-go-round; figure-eight go-cart track with a kiddies' track.

- **GRAN RALLY KARTS** - 5730 US 54. Phone: (573) 348-2012.

MAIN STREET MUSIC HALL

1048 Main Street (note GPS address is 5845 Highway 54) Osage Beach (Lake of the Ozarks) 65065

☐ Phone: (573) 348-9500 or (800) 348-9501 **www.lakemusichall.com**
☐ Hours: (Showtime) is at 8:00pm. Christmas shows in late November and December are at 7:00pm. Call or see website for latest schedule.
☐ Admission: $17.00 adult, $15.00 senior, $8.00 child (5-12).

The Main Street Music Hall is a live music show that is now in it's 15th season at the Lake of the Ozarks in Osage Beach, Missouri. Located in the Landing On Main Street Shopping Village, the show offers a wide variety of musical enjoyment as well as comedy that is sure to bring a laugh and a smile to people of all ages. The show consists of two hours of current and classic country, gospel, and patriotic songs, as well as a trip through time with their medley of songs from the 1960's through today.

SEA ROCKET THRILL RIDES

1192 Lake Shore Drive (leaves from various ports around town) Osage Beach (Lake of the Ozarks) 65065

☐ Phone: (573) 286-4306 **www.searocketrides.com**
☐ Hours: 9:00am-sundown (Sunday - Friday), 9:00am-Noon only on Saturdays. May-September.
☐ Admission: $20.00-$30.00 per person, depending on length of ride. Must be 6 or older to ride. Discount Coupon online.

Take a 30-minute ride aboard the Sea Rocket. It's fast, and up to 12 passengers at a time can cruise the Lake of the Ozarks in this offshore-type speedboat.

TAN-TAR-A RESORT

494 Tantara Drive (Route KK) **Osage Beach (Lake of the Ozarks)** 65065

☐   Phone: (573) 348-3131 or (800) 826-8272 **www.tan-tar-a.com**

Parents who long for the nostalgia of old-fashioned lakeside resorts will appreciate this established resort property. Although the resort has been around a while, their rooms are clean and roomy and the resort is right on the lake. There are two pools at Tan-Tar-A. The larger complex has a large pool that has a maximum depth around 4 ft. There is also a hot tub and a fairly decent water slide for the kids. The spa also has an indoor pool. Other amenities: bowling, horseback riding, boat rentals, tubing, miniature golf, an arcade and hiking trails. There are restaurants on the property but, for convenience, they may be pricey for a family budget. Tan-Tar-A covers quite a few acres with hills, so make sure to use the shuttle service if you don't want to drive around or try to walk to everything. (And speaking of driving around, make sure to grab a map when you check in! If you don't you might get lost). Average basic room rate: $150/night. Recent guests suggest requesting the main building. Every activity (except the pools) requires an additional fee.

- **TROPIC ISLAND CRUISES** - Offers a 90 minute narrated cruise that covers about 2.5 miles of the lake and a good bit of local flavor storytelling. Daily Scenic Cruises: Tuesday-Sunday 3:00-4:30pm. Juices, soft drinks and cocktails available. Public Scenic Cruise Rates: Adults: $16, Ages 4 - 12: $10, 3 & under: Free. www.tropicislandcruises.com.

- **TIMBER FALLS INDOOR WATERPARK** - This indoor waterpark offers four water slides, a lazy river for floating, an activity pool where water basketball and other games are played, and a three-story tree house that dumps water every so often. Hours vary. www.tan-tar-a.com/1/timber_falls.htm. Separate admission: $17.00-$22.00.

LAKE OF THE OZARKS HOLIDAY LIGHT PARK

Osage Beach (Lake of the Ozarks) - *Osage Beach City Park. More than 80 giant, animated displays at the Osage Beach City Park. Admission: $10.00 a car. (starts daily weekend before Thanksgiving thru New Years Day)*

CLARK'S HILL-NORTON STATE HISTORIC SITE

(I-70 exit 128) Osage City 65101

- ☐ Phone: (573) 449-7402 www.mostateparks.com/clarkshill.htm
- ☐ Admission: The Missouri state park system does not charge entrance fees. However, there are fees associated with camping, lodging, tours, museums and certain special events.

The Lewis and Clark Expedition camped near this site and Clark climbed the hill to see the confluence of the Missouri and Osage rivers. He made observations and took measurements of the rivers from a rock on the hilltop, noting that he passed two Indian Mounds to get to the top. On June 1-3, 1804, they camped at the base of what is now known as Clark's Hill. Today, a half-mile interpretive trail passes American Indian mounds to an overlook of the rivers. The rock where Clark stood and the location of the crew's campsite below can also be seen from the overlook. Interpretive signs along the trail discuss the history of the area. This site is open daylight hours. There is no admission to hike the trail.

POMME DE TERRE STATE PARK

Route 64B Pittsburg 65724

- ☐ Phone: (417) 852-4291 www.mostateparks.com/pommedeterre.htm
- ☐ Admission: The Missouri state park system does not charge entrance fees. However, there are fees associated with camping, lodging, tours, museums and certain special events.

Pomme de terre, French for "potato," can be translated "apple of the earth," which is a fitting interpretation when referring to Pomme de Terre State Park. Visitors can launch a boat and find a quiet cove to fish for bass, walleye, catfish, crappie or even muskie. A fishing pier and marina or one of the park's two public swimming beaches provide a great place to cool off or lounge in the sun. The park offers two hiking trails that wind through several scenic areas and picnic sites in the forest or near the lake. Overnight accommodations include more than 250 campsites, many located near the lake shore, on both sides of the lake.

BOTHWELL LODGE STATE HISTORIC SITE
19349 Bothwell State Park Road **Sedalia** 65301

☐ Phone: (660) 827-0510 **www.mostateparks.com/bothwell.htm**

☐ Admission: The Missouri state park system does not charge entrance fees. However, there are fees associated with camping, lodging, tours, museums and certain special events.

☐ Tours: (Castle) $4.00 adult (13+), $2.50 child (6-12), $15.00 family. Monday & Thursday-Saturday 10:00am-4:00pm & Sunday 11:00am-4:00pm (April - mid-September). Weekends & Holiday Mondays 10:00am-4:00pm & Sunday 11:00am-4:00pm (mid-September - March). The last tour begins at 3:00pm.

☐ Educators - Teacher's guides are available to assist school groups planning a visit.

Between 1897 and 1928, this castle was built for a well-known Sedalia lawyer named John Homer Bothwell. The 12,000-square-foot lodge is constructed atop three caves and was built in four different sections...on the side of a cliff. Not only is the house handsomely appointed, Bothwell Lodge State Historic Site offers nature lovers hiking trails, bike paths, a picnic area and playground equipment for the kids. Guided tours take you through the 3-story house, pointing out the unusual design elements of the owner.

KATY DEPOT AND RAILROAD HERITAGE MUSEUM
600 East Third Street **Sedalia** 65301

☐ Phone: (660) 826-2222 **www.sedaliakatydepot.com**

☐ Hours: Monday-Friday 9:00am-5:00pm. Saturday 10:00am-3:00pm. (April-December). Monday-Friday 9:00am-5:00pm (January-March).

☐ Miscellaneous: Folks can rent bikes at the Trailside Café or take a short walk on the Katy Trail to the only tunnel on the trail.

The great railroad town of Sedalia is home to the Sedalia Katy Depot, constructed in 1896 on the Missouri-Kansas-Texas (M-K-T or "Katy") line. One of the largest depots between Kansas City and St. Louis, this depot features Henry the telegrapher and Jeanie, a young girl who describes her family's recent trip to the 1904 St. Louis World's Fair. Children can be an engineer for a day and drive a train while learning more about the train station operations at the turn of the last century. The youth activity area also has a place where kids can pretend to sell train tickets. One of the exhibits is a working telegraph. This is also the hub of the visitors bureau where you can find assistance in exploring the rest of the town.

MISSOURI STATE FAIR

Sedalia - State Fairgrounds, Hwy 65 (2503 W. 16th Street). The 11-day fair showcases the best of Missouri agriculture; competitions; professional entertainment; rural lifestyle experiences; hands-on science, technology and innovation; family-friendly amenities for infants to mature adults; and action-packed activities. The Missouri State Fair is the perfect blend of activities for a memorable family outing. The midway carnival includes games and rides for children and thrill seekers of all ages. The nightlife on the fairgrounds kicks up each evening with free music on the Budweiser Stage and music stars performing on the stage of the Pepsi Grandstand. Admission. www.mostatefair.com. (eleven days in August).

JACOB'S CAVE

23114 Highway TT (1 mile off State Highway 5) **Versailles** 65084

☐   Phone: (573) 378-4374 **www.jacobscave.com**
☐   Hours: 9:00am-5:00pm (Memorial Day - Labor Day), Closes at 4:00pm rest of year.
☐   Admission: $12.00 adult, $6.00 child (4-12).

Known for its reflecting pools, ceiling sponge-work, prehistoric bones and one of the world's largest geodes. Find evidence of ice ages and three earthquakes.

HARRY S TRUMAN DAM & RESERVOIR VISITOR CENTER

15968 Truman Road **Warsaw** 65355

☐   Phone: (660) 438-7317 or (660) 438-2216 (Visitor Center) **www.nwk.usace.army.mil/ht/**
☐   Hours: 9:00am-5:00 (summer). Closes at 4:00pm spring & fall. (March-October). Closed winters.

Atop Kaysinger Bluff, the center offers spectacular views of the lake, dam and the city of Warsaw. Exhibits using touch screens conveying history and culture of Osage Valley and the process of turning the moving energy from water to electricity are available. The theater offers a must-see short movie on

Osage Valley history and construction of the dam. Wildlife and water safety videos are also available for viewing. The staff will be available to answer questions and to provide Annual Day Use Passes, water safety materials, lake area brochures and maps.

HARRY S TRUMAN STATE PARK

28761 State Park Road Warsaw 65355

☐ Phone: (660) 438-7711 or (800) 334-6946
  www.mostateparks.com/trumanpark.htm
☐ Admission: The Missouri state park system does not charge entrance fees. However, there are fees associated with camping, lodging, tours, museums and certain special events.

Surrounded by water on three sides, this park encompasses the tip of a peninsula that juts into Truman Lake. Water activities such as swimming, boating and fishing are featured, as are a marina, boat ramps, hiking trails and campgrounds. Hiking trails wind through the woods and out to rocky overlooks, offering breathtaking views of the lake and an occasional glimpse of the abundant wildlife. Fox, coyote, deer, wild turkey and beaver make their homes in the forest and grasslands of Truman State Park. Anglers of all skill levels will be challenged to hook a variety of fish in the lake's cool, clear waters.

LOST VALLEY HATCHERY AND VISITOR CENTER

28232 Hatchery Avenue (located east of Highway 65 at the Truman Dam access road on County Road 620 just NE of Warsaw) **Warsaw** 65355

☐ Phone: (660) 438-4465 **http://mdc.mo.gov/areas/hatchery/lostvalley/**
☐ Hours: (Visitor Center) Tuesday-Saturday 9:00am-4:00pm (year-round).

The Lost Valley Fish Hatchery is the largest state-owned, warm water hatchery in Missouri and one of the largest in the nation. The hatchery houses a large visitors center, where guests can learn about the fish. A variety of exhibits focusing on fishing and aquatic themes include an over-sized native Missouri mussel model, a model of hatchery water flow, how to legally measure fish, computer games, fishing line knot- tying, and many other demonstrations and displays. The visitor may view the hatchery production room from two large windows inside the visitor center. A scenic pullout on the access road overlooks most of the rearing ponds and a portion of Truman Lake. Fishing for youth 15 years of age and younger is allowed in a pond on site during Visitor Center hours. Tackle and bait are available at the Visitors Center. There is no charge for fishing or the use of the equipment or bait.

OLD STAGECOACH STOP

(Downtown - On the east side of the square, in the middle of the block on Linn Street, sits the white two-story Old Stagecoach Stop)
Waynesville 65583

- ☐ Phone: (573) 762-9683 or (573) 435-6766 **www.oldstagecoachstop.org**
- ☐ Admission: FREE.
- ☐ Tours: Saturday 10:00am-4:00pm (April-September). A tour with a guide in-period costume takes about 45 minutes.
- ☐ Miscellaneous: FROG ROCK is at 300 Historic Route 66. This huge rock is painted as a frog (named W.H. Croaker) and overlooks the city of Waynesville. Frog Fest is held in the frog's honor the first full weekend in May. Laughlin Park is not far away and has a spring for trout fishing, swimming or visitors can utilize the park's walking trail.

Built in 1854, the Old Stagecoach Stop is a 10-room-house museum where every room is NOT set up in the same time period. Each of the rooms has been restored to a different use or era in the building's history. It was used as a Civil War hospital, hotel, boarding house and dentist's office. The building is a two story structure. There are ten rooms, nine restored to various periods in the building's history (1854-now). A tour with a guide in period costume takes about 45 minutes.

OLD SETTLERS DAY

Waynesville - *Old Stagecoach Stop. Old Settlers Day is celebrated the last Saturday in July which has a full weekend. The Old Stagecoach Stop sponsors this Old Settlers Day. It is the oldest city festival. Events are scheduled in the City Park, one block west, along with food and craft vendors. (last Saturday in July).*

CRANE'S MUSEUM AND COUNTRY STORE

10665 Old Hwy 40 **Williamsburg** 63388

☐   Phone: (573) 254-3311 **www.cranes-country-store.com** or
www.cranesmuseum.org

The country store has lots of old-time and classic clothing and assorted gifts. Serves one-meat-one-cheese $1.00 dollar sandwiches.

The 1800s regional history museum displays rare toys, American Indian artifacts, primitive hardware and tools, a recreated 1929 White Eagle gas station and Victorian items. Marlene's Restaurant is an extension of Crane's Museum. Marlene's offers a full-service cafe environment serving sandwich plates for around $5.00 as well as an Old-Fashioned Ice Cream Parlor. Museum charges small admission to folks 10 and older. Open daily.

Travel Journal & Notes:

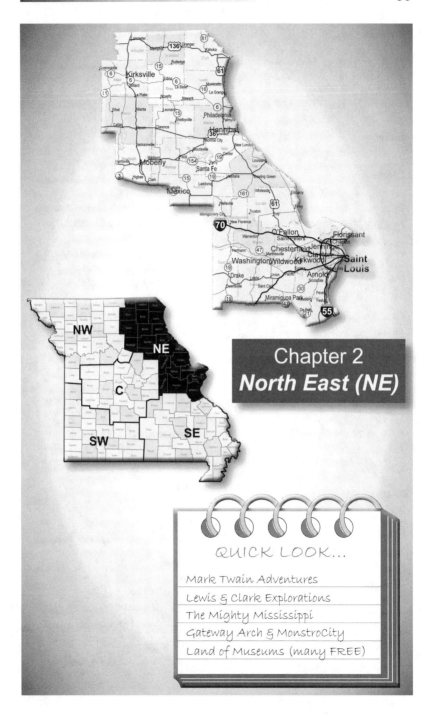

Chapter 2
North East (NE)

QUICK LOOK...

Mark Twain Adventures

Lewis & Clark Explorations

The Mighty Mississippi

Gateway Arch & MonstroCity

Land of Museums (many FREE)

Alton, IL
- National Great Rivers Museum

Athens (Revere)
- Battle Of Athens State Historic Site

Ballwin
- Castlewood State Park

Clarksville
- Clarksville Visitor Center, River Heritage Center

Defiance
- Daniel Boone Home And Boonesfield Village

DeSoto
- Washington State Park

East St. Louis, IL
- Gateway Geyser
- Gateway Grizzlies

Eureka
- Route 66 State Park
- Six Flags St. Louis
- Wild Canid Survival & Research Center (Wolf Sanctuary)
- Yogi Bear's Jellystone Park Camp Resort

Festus
- The Pumpkin Patch

Florida
- Mark Twain Birthplace State Historic Site & Park

Glencoe
- Wabash Frisco And Pacific Steam Railway

Grafton, Il
- Pere Marquette State Park & Visitors Center
- Raging Rivers Waterpark

Gray Summit
- Purina Farms
- Shaw Nature Reserve

Hannibal
- Adventures Of Tom Sawyer Diorama Museum
- Big River Train Town
- Cameron Cave
- Hannibal Tours
- Mark Twain Boyhood Home Complex
- Mark Twain Cave Complex
- Mark Twain Dinette
- Mark Twain Himself
- Mark Twain Riverboat
- Molly Brown Birthplace & Museum
- Ole Planters Restaurant
- Sawyer's Creek Fun Park
- Paddlewheel Popcorn & Candy Company
- Tom Sawyer Days

Hartford, IL
- Camp River Dubois, Lewis & Clark State Historic Site

Hermann
- Deutschheim State Historic Site & Museum

Imperial
- Mastodon State Historic Site

Kahoka
- Clark County Mule Festival

Kirksville
- Still National Osteopathic Museum
- Thousand Hills State Park
- Shrine Pro Rodeo

La Grange
- Wakonda State Park

La Plata
- Jackson Country Connections

Louisiana
- Asl Pewter Foundry

Macon
- Long Branch State Park

Mexico
- Audrain Historical Society Museum Complex
- Binders Hilltop Apple And Berry Farm

Monroe City
- Mark Twain Landing

Montgomery City
- Graham Cave State Park

New London
- Starlight Alpaca Ranch

Robertsville
- Robertsville State Park

St. Charles
- Fast Lane Classic Cars
- First Missouri State Capitol State Historic Site
- Katy Trail State Park
- Lewis And Clark Boat House And Nature Center
- Rt Weiler's Restaurant
- Fete De Glace Ice Carving Competition
- Lewis And Clark Heritage Days
- Festival Of The Little Hills

St. Louis
- Double Key Treasure Hunts
- Flamingo Bowl
- St. Louis Rams Football
- Dental Health Theater
- Eat-Rite Diner

St. Louis (cont.)
- Eugene Field House & St. Louis Toy Museum
- Gateway Arch
- Gateway Arch Riverboat Cruises
- St. Louis Cardinal's Busch Stadium Tours
- The Old Courthouse
- City Museum
- Scott Joplin House State Historic Site
- St Louis Blues Hockey
- Union Station
- Soulard Market
- Crown Candy Kitchen
- Bob Kramer's Marionnette Theater
- Earthways Center
- The Sheldon
- Ted Drewes Frozen Custard
- Forest Park
- Missouri Botanical Garden
- St. Louis Art Museum
- St. Louis Science Center
- St. Louis Zoo
- Missouri History Museum
- Miniature Museum Of Greater St. Louis
- Museum Of Transportation
- Grant's Farm
- America's Incredible Pizza Company
- Suson Park
- Old Chain Of Rocks Bridge
- The Hill
- St. Louis Storytelling Festival
- Celebrate St. Louis - Fair St. Louis
- St. Louis Holiday Magic

St. Louis (Chesterfield)
- Faust Park

St. Louis (Fenton)
- Swing-A-Round Fun Town

St. Louis (Ferguson)
- Challenger Learning Center - St. Louis

St. Louis (Hazelwood)
- Big Foot 4 X 4 Inc.
- St. Louis Mills Mall, Sportstreet

St. Louis (Kirkwood)
- Magic House: St. Louis Children's Museum
- Powder Valley Conservation Nature Center
- Laumeier Sculpture Park

St. Louis (Lemay)
- Jefferson Barracks Historic Park

St. Louis (Maplewood)
- Piwacket Children's Theater

St. Louis (Maryland Heights)
- Aquaport
- Thies Farm & Greenhouses

St. Louis (University City)
- Fitz's American Grill & Bottling Co.

St. Louis (White Haven)
- Ulysses S. Grant National Historic Site

Troy
- Cuivre River State Park

Valley Park
- World Bird Sanctuary

Wayland
- Iliniwek Village State Historic Site

West Alton
- Jones - Confluence State Park

Wildwood
- Babler Memorial State Park
- Hidden Valley Ski Resort

Sites and attractions are listed in order by City, Zip Code, and Name. Symbols indicated represent:

 Festivals   Restaurants   Lodging

RIVER FERRIES OVER THE MISSISSIPPI RIVER INTO ILLINOIS

☐ **www.greatriverroad.com/SecondaryPages/ferries.htm**
☐ Note: If you are planning a visit to any of the ferries in the Middle Mississippi Valley and believe the ferries might not be operating due to flood conditions or ice please call the numbers below for current information.

Early American ferries consisted of rafts, rowboats and horse boats that could cross rivers where demand for transportation existed but where there weren't any easy crossings. The advent of railroads and bridges put most ferries out of business and motorized vessels replaced the earlier forms of transportation of those that survived. For modern travelers, the remaining ferries in operation can save time as well as providing scenic river views.

GOLDEN EAGLE FERRY - (618) 396-2535. This ferry takes vehicles across the Mississippi River between the small town of Golden Eagle in Calhoun County in Illinois and St. Charles County in Missouri. To reach the Golden Eagle Ferry from Pere Marquette State Park or Grafton, cross the Brussels Ferry and continue on County Road 1 until you see the signs directing you to the ferry. From the Missouri side of the Mississippi River take MO-94 to County Road B north of St. Charles. Take CR-B west to Golden Eagle Ferry Road. Take Golden Eagle Ferry Road to the ferry. Daily from 8:00am-9:00pm. Toll fees: Car or pickup truck $6.00 one-way or $11.00 round trip. Motorcycles $4.00, bicycles or pedestrians $3.00.

GRAFTON FERRY - (636) 899-0600. The Grafton Ferry is located on the Illinois side at the foot of Illinois Route 3, just upriver of the Grafton public boat ramp. On the Missouri side, it terminates just off of Grafton Ferry Road alongside the St. Charles County Airport. From there it is a short ride to highway 94 and about 10 miles to the St. Charles city line. Toll Fees: $8.00 one way, $5.00 for motorcycles, $4.00 for bicycles, & $3.00 for pedestrians with reduced rates for round trips. Daily except major winter holidays.

NATIONAL GREAT RIVERS MUSEUM

#1 Lock and Dam Way, Melvin Price Lock & Dam Illinois Route 3 intersects I-270 approx. two miles east of the Mississippi River. Take IL Route 3 North to Hwy 143 west 2 miles) **Alton, IL 62024**

- ☐ Phone: (877) 462-6979 **www.mvs.usace.army.mil/Rivers/ngrm.html**
- ☐ Hours: Daily 9:00am-5:00pm except major winter holidays.
- ☐ Admission: FREE.
- ☐ Tours: Free tours of the Melvin Price Locks and Dam are conducted daily at 10:00am, 1:00pm and 3:00pm. Also explained are what causes floods, with emphasis on the Great Flood of 1993 and how the Corps of Engineers fights these destructive acts of nature, and what future strategies are being developed to limit their impact.
- ☐ Educators: They have a in-house link (http://education.wes.army.mil/ navigation/navigate.html) to an amazing array of simple and in-depth lessons, games and projects related to navigation and water science of great rivers-all presented on a very teachable level.

The Museum features state of the art interactive displays and exhibits that help visitors understand the many aspects of the Mississippi River and how humans interact with it. A large model of the bluffs of the region is in the center of the museum and provides info on the various wildlife from prairie plants and trees to birds and other animals. An aquarium displays the various species of fish that inhabit the Mississippi River. Stir river sediment banks; make a stairway of water; or make your own map. One display explains how the Mississippi has been used as a highway, not only by humans but by migrating waterfowl, and chronicles the different types of vessels used from canoes to steamboats to modern day barges. The Pilot House simulator allows visitors to see what it's like to guide a 1,000 foot tow of barges under a bridge or through a lock. We took on the challenge (harder than it seems) of steering a barge as a parent/child team and finally successfully made it through. This activity, and the dam tour, are the kids' favorites. It sure is eventful when a big barge comes through during the 45-minute lock tour!

BATTLE OF ATHENS STATE HISTORIC SITE

Hwy. CC **Athens (Revere)** 63465

☐ Phone: (660) 877-3871 **www.mostateparks.com/athens.htm**

☐ Admission: The Missouri state park system does not charge entrance fees. However, there are fees associated with camping, lodging, tours, museums and certain special events.

☐ Tours: Tours of the Thome-Benning House are offered free of charge. From April through October, they are available daily 10:00am-4:00pm.

The Battle of Athens State Historic Site interprets the battle, town history, and contains buildings that were part of the once-thriving town. Today, the historic site encompasses much of the former town of Athens. Several buildings have been preserved and are undergoing restoration. Foremost is the Thome-Benning house, locally known as "the Cannonball House," which still exhibits two holes made through the kitchen walls by a cannonball during the battle. Visitors can tour the house, visit the Thome mill ruins, participate in guided tours of the historic town site or take advantage of numerous recreation opportunities. There are hiking trails, a lake for fishing, picnic areas, a playground, a campground and 1.5 miles of Des Moines River frontage.

CASTLEWOOD STATE PARK

1401 Kiefer Creek Road **Ballwin** 63021

☐ Phone: (636) 227-4433 **www.mostateparks.com/castlewood.htm**

☐ Admission: The Missouri state park system does not charge entrance fees. However, there are fees associated with camping, lodging, tours, museums and certain special events.

The Meramed River, with limestone bluffs towering above it, flows through this park, making it popular for canoeing and fishing. The park is great for day-use activities like picnicking, hiking, mountain biking and horseback riding. River Scene Trail: this three-mile loop is the most spectacular trail in the park and highlights the park's most memorable features. The trail climbs to and then traverses a series of bluffs overlooking the Meramec River. It then goes down a long wood staircase that takes you from the top of the bluffs to the valley below. From there, the trail takes you through an up-close and personal look at the river and the bottomland surrounding it. Along the way, you will pass panoramic vistas, remnants of the historic resort era and floodplain forest. This trail is designated for hiking and bicycling (hiking only on the bluff portion).

CLARKSVILLE VISITOR CENTER, RIVER HERITAGE CENTER

204 North 2nd Street Clarksville 63336

☐ Phone: (573) 242-3132 **www.clarksvillemo.us/riverheritagemuseum.html**

☐ Miscellaneous: While kids may not be interested in shopping in historic downtowns, they may like Clarksville. Several varied artists have set up shop here such as: Clarksville Glassworks, Bee Naturals, The Bent Tree Gallery, Dawn of Creation Art Studio and the Great River Pottery and Wood Shop. You'll find these working artist shops on First and Second Streets. Often, the artist is in residence to demo their work.

500 foot bluffs overlook the Mississippi River. This Center contains large displays and hundreds of items and artifacts relative to the various cultural societies that lived along the Mississippi, Illinois and Missouri rivers. Displays span the last 100 years, but the emphasis is on tools and equipment used during 1870-1970 period by the families living along the rivers. Displays include, commercial and sport fisheries, the mussel-shell pearl button industry, water fowling, furbearer harvesting, family fish markets, vintage boats and outboard motors, and a typical river man's workshop.

The center has a viewing platform with a spotting scope. It looks out onto the Mississippi River, and the U.S. Lock and Dam #24, providing a close vantage point to view all river boat and barge traffic and a 'front row seat' in the midst of one of the largest winter migrating areas for the bald eagles. Why are eagles attracted to this stretch?

EAGLE DAYS

Clarksville - *Visitors Center. Special exhibits, guided eagle-viewing tours and live eagle exhibits. Every winter bald eagles come to this town to fish along the river bluffs and around the locks. FREE. (late January weekend)*

DANIEL BOONE HOME AND BOONESFIELD VILLAGE

1868 Highway F (I-70 or Hwy 40-61 to Hwy. 94 south then 5 miles west on Hwy F) **Defiance** 63341

☐ Phone: (636) 798-2005 **www.lindenwood.edu/boone**

☐ Hours: Daily 9:00am-5:00pm. During Daylight Savings Time open until 6:00pm.

☐ Admission: (1-hour tour) $7.00 adult, $6.00 senior (55+), $4.00 child (4-11). (2-hour tour) $12.00 adult, $10.00 senior (55+), $6.00 child (4-11).

☐ Tours: Your choice of a 1-hour home or village tour or both for additional fee. Tours start on the hour. A fifteen minute video on the life of Daniel Boone is played in the theater before each tour.

This site offers visitors a look at life as a frontiersman. The Boone Home is nearly 200 years old and it's where Daniel Boone lived later in life and died. Costumed guides give one hour tour of the home and the 19th century village buildings focusing on Boone family history and life on the frontier. (Buildings available in the village are the schoolhouse, dressmaker's shop, carpenter's shop, Old Peace Chapel, general store, grist mill, and home of Squire Boone.) Volunteers in the village may be splitting rails, dipping candles, woodworking, playing the fiddle or frontier games like hoop and stick or stilts. Try it. In the school house, students can quickly pretend they are a pioneer student. Before each tour there is a 15 minute video of Daniel Boone's Life shown in the theater.

WASHINGTON STATE PARK

13041 State Hwy 104 **DeSoto** 63020

☐ Phone: (636) 586-0322 **www.mostateparks.com/washington.htm**

☐ Admission: The Missouri state park system does not charge entrance fees. However, there are fees associated with camping, lodging, tours, museums and certain special events.

This park was once a ceremonial ground for prehistoric Indians. Today, petroglyphs - American Indian rock carvings - are a special attraction. These carvings, or petroglyphs, are believed to have been made around A.D. 1,000 and give clues to the lives of the prehistoric Indians who once inhabited this part of Missouri. In addition to a lodge, there are quaint stone hiking shelters, a picnic pavilion, and the beautifully laid stone slabs that make up the 1,000

Steps Trail. The three hiking trails at Washington State Park provide every experience, from an easy stroll with bluff-top views of the river to a vigorous excursion through 10 miles of rugged Ozark terrain. The park offers a pool, float trips, cabins, hiking and backpacking trails, a store and camping.

GATEWAY GEYSER

185 W. Trendley Avenue (Front Street and Trendley Avenue)
East St. Louis, IL 62201

☐ Phone: (618) 346-4905 **www.hydrodramatics.com/gateway_geyser.htm** or **www.meprd.org/MMMP.htm**

☐ Hours: The Geyser Fountain runs from April thru October. It usually runs twice a day at Noon, 3:00pm, 6:00pm, 9:00pm daily, but only for 15 minutes. Schedule subject to change. The FAA has placed time restrictions on the Geyser.

☐ Admission: FREE.

Currently the tallest fountain in the world, the Gateway Geyser rises as a testimonial to the engineering expertise and 16-year effort of Hydro Dramatics. Soaring to nearly 630-feet, the geyser's height mirrors that of St. Louis' famed Gateway Arch, located directly across the Mississippi River. The center fountain is complemented by four auxiliary fountains, which represent the four rivers that converge in the St. Louis area. The "park" setting around the geyser is FREE of charge to wander through.

GATEWAY GRIZZLIES

GCS Stadium (I-70 exit IL 3 south. The stadium faces riverfront St. Louis)
East St. Louis, IL 62206

☐ Phone: (618) 337-3000 **www.gatewaygrizzlies.com**

The Gateway Grizzlies minor league baseball team plays in the outdoor GCS Stadium. The 6,000 seat stadium includes reserved box seats, picnic table seats (for families/groups), general and lawn seats. This stadium is the area's own "field of dreams," It's minor league baseball at its finest in a small venue and for a small price. Game tickets run $5.00-$9.00. There's a kids zone area where children can climb and play ball on their "turf." They get the kids involved on the field and every week there are theme nights (ex. Hat night, bobbleheads).

ROUTE 66 STATE PARK

97 North Outer Road **Eureka** 63025

☐ Phone: (636) 938-7198 **www.mostateparks.com/route66.htm**
☐ Hours: Visitor Center: 9:00am-4:30pm daily (April thru October). Weekends only (November to mid-December). Closed winters.
☐ Admission: The Missouri state park system does not charge entrance fees. However, there are fees associated with camping, lodging, tours, museums and certain special events.

In Eureka, the 419-acre Route 66 State Park includes picnic areas, walking trails and a remodeled visitor center offering a peek into the past with artifacts and displays from the route's 82-year history. Route 66 State Park showcases the history and mystique of a highway that has been called "The Main Street of America." The historic Route 66 has come to represent American mobility, independence and spirit of adventure, and the park has captured the essence of the highway in its displays and array of recreation options. Bridgehead Inn, a 1935 roadhouse, serves as Route 66 State Park's visitor center. It houses Route 66 memorabilia and interprets the environmental success story of the former resort community of Times Beach, which once thrived on the location of the park. A gift shop, specializing in hundreds of Route 66 items, is also located in the visitor center building. Although the kids may only recognize the black-n-white Route 66 road signs on display, they'll have fun looking at the corny neon signs and pictures of the small roadside stops.

SIX FLAGS ST. LOUIS

4900 Six Flags Road (I-44 exit 261) **Eureka** 63025

☐ Phone: (636) 938-4800 **www.sixflags.com**
☐ Hours: Vary by season. Open daily in summer 10:30am-9:00pm. Hurricane Harbor closes at 8:00pm. Call or visit website for Spring/Fall hours.
☐ Admission: $39.99 General, $31.00 (child under 48"). Ages 2 and under are FREE. Multi-visit discounts and online discounts are available. Parking $15.00. Additional fees for some concerts and special events.

Six Flags St. Louis continues its tradition of bringing new thrills to the popular theme park. Admission to the park also includes the Hurricane Harbor water park for the same price. The water park has expanded with the exciting Wahoo Racer attraction. Six Flags has also added a spectacular nighttime parade, appropriately named "Glow in the Park" and several live stage shows. The littlest visitors will enjoy pint-sized rides and friendly characters in Looney Tunes Town while bigger brothers and sisters can experience more than 100 rides and attractions throughout the park. Special events including Fright Fest in October and the Country Fair in the fall extend the season of fun well beyond summer. Hurricane Harbor Water Park is free with Six Flags admission.

WILD CANID SURVIVAL & RESEARCH CENTER (WOLF SANCTUARY)

6750 Tyson Valley Road (Washington University property, 20 miles southwest of ST. Louis) **Eureka** 63025

☐ Phone: (636) 938-5900 **www.wildcanidcenter.org**

☐ Admission: (Public 1-hour Tour) $8.00/person. Extra $2.00 for 2-hour Program/Tour.

☐ Tours: The Tour is a one hour guided walking tour of the wolf enclosures. The walk is outdoors approximately a 1/2 mile round trip. Public tours are offered Fridays, Saturdays and Sundays. On a public tour you are grouped with other visitors. Public tours generally range in size from 1-40 people and have a set start time of 1:00pm. Optional 2-hour Program/Tours are available at additional cost and start at 10:00am. Advance Reservations are required for all Programs.

☐ FREEBIES: a free download of the WolfQuest: Survival of the Pack computer game is available here: http://wildcanid.wolfquest.org/

The place was founded in the 1970's to help promote the survival of the wolf, which has become endangered all over the world. The original founder was Wild Kingdom host Marlin Perkins. All fees you are charged go directly to this effort. You can either schedule a group tour or go for an individual tour. The tour begins indoors with a movie as well as other hands-on activities while learning about the evolution of the wolf through fossils, paw prints and old pelts Outside, endangered wolves are born and reared on the property for reintroduction to the wild. Your guide will lead you on the trail to view the wolves and African wild dogs and swift foxes that live in their own packs in natural areas. (FYI wear comfortable shoes, flip flops are not the appropriate footwear for this trek.) Evening campfire programs share how wolves communicate - with live "sound bites."

YOGI BEAR'S JELLYSTONE PARK CAMP RESORT

5300 Fox Creek Road **Eureka** 63025

☐   Phone: (800) 861-3020 **www.eurekajellystone.com**

Conveniently located just ¼ mile from the gate of Six Flags and nestled among 35 wooded acres; this family resort offers all the fun and adventure of a back-to-nature vacation combined with first class resort amenities including FREE WIFI, pool, mini-golf, video arcade, train rides, arts & crafts, a variety of outdoor games, and daily character visits from Yogi Bear. A full time Rec Director is on hand to make sure there's never a dull moment. Exciting theme events and planned activities change weekly.

The large campground has sites for all sizes of RVs. Visitors who consider themselves to be traditional hotel guests will love the resort's cozy cottages. Each cottage sleeps six and features two bedrooms, kitchen, bath, and sitting area. A covered dining porch and outdoor grill make family picnics a breeze. Plus, each cottage has a fire pit so your family can end the perfect day roasting S'mores and telling tales around the campfire. Hookups are around $30 and cabins range from $80-$120 per night.

SANTA'S MAGICAL KINGDOM

Eureka - *Yogi Bear's Jellystone Park is transformed into a magical paradise that includes a thirty-five-acre display of animated scenes, spectacular special effects, and millions of lights celebrating the holiday season.*

THE PUMPKIN PATCH

Festus - *14560 Dry Fork Road. www.albesm.com/pumpkinpatch/pumpkinpatch.html Phone: (636) 931-3901 . In the fall, there's a corn maze, children's train rides, apple butter making and weekend wagon rides down to the pumpkin patch. (pumpkin patch begins late September thru October)*

MARK TWAIN BIRTHPLACE STATE HISTORIC SITE & PARK

37352 Shrine Road **Florida** 65283

☐ Phone: (573) 565-3449 **www.mostateparks.com/twainsite.htm**
☐ Admission: The Missouri state park system does not charge entrance fees. However, there are fees associated with camping, lodging, tours, museums and certain special events.
☐ Tours: From November through March, the museum is open Friday through Sunday from 10:00am-4:30pm with the exception of Thanksgiving, Christmas and New Year's days. Tours are offered during these times. The museum is closed Monday through Thursday. Summertime, the museum is open daily. A fee of $2.50-$4.00 is charged for the tours.
☐ Miscellaneous: near town (24000 Route 107, in the Mark Twain Lake area) is GRANDMAS COUNTRY MUSIC SHOW featuring live country music on the first, third and fifth Saturdays of each month. Kiddies FREE. Admission for those over 10.

The two-room cabin where Samuel Langhorne Clemens was born is on-site, surrounded by a modern museum with memorabilia of Mark Twain, the name Clemens adopted as a writer. Exhibits and audio visual programs dot the perimeter of the cabin (indoors). They have a handwritten manuscript of the Adventures of Tom Sawyer on display. The Visitors Center has a bird watching station for waterfowl. The park overlooks Mark Twain Lake and offers fishing, boating, hiking trails, campsites and swimming beaches.

WABASH FRISCO AND PACIFIC STEAM RAILWAY

109 Grand Avenue (Old State Road & Washington Street) **Glencoe** 63038

☐ Phone: (636) 587-3538 **www.wfprr.org**
☐ Hours: The Railroad is open every Sunday, May through October rain or shine. Trains start their scheduled departures from the station at 11:00am with trains departing about every 20 minutes. The final train leaves at 4:15pm. The ride is a two-mile round trip lasting about 30 minutes and travels along the scenic Meramec River.
☐ Admission: A $4.00 donation is asked per ticket. Children 3 years old and younger ride free.

Just outside of St. Louis is this 12-inch-gauge miniature steam railroad that takes passengers on a two-mile round trip ride along the scenic Meramec River every Sunday, May through October. The ride takes only about 30 minutes. Afterwards, picnic at the tables near the station. Perfect place to bring that young model train fan.

PERE MARQUETTE STATE PARK & VISITORS CENTER

Illinois Route 100 (take the ferry over from St. Charles to Grafton)
Grafton, IL 62037

☐   Phone: (618) 786-3323 or (618) 786-2331 (Lodge)
    http://dnr.state.il.us/lands/landmgt/PARKS/R4/PEREMARQ.HTM
☐   Admission: Admission to Illinois State Parks is FREE. Camping and lodge
    fees apply for overnights.
☐   Tours: The Sam Vadalabene Bike Trail runs from this State Park to the City
    of Alton, approx. 20 miles. The entire trail is paved and a map is available
    showing the location of historic sites, restaurants, and local attractions.
☐   Miscellaneous: The Lodge consists of both new facilities as well as those
    constructed by the CCC. Native stone and rustic timbers of the original Lodge
    blend with the new to provide first class accommodations in an historical
    setting. The mammoth stone fireplace in the lobby soars to a roof height of
    50 feet. There are 50 spacious guest rooms and 22 stone guest cabin rooms.
    Among the facilities available are a restaurant, gift shop, indoor swimming
    pool, whirlpool, game room and tennis court.

Pere Marquette State Park comprises over 8,000 acres making it Illinois' largest state park. Named for Jacques Marquette, a French missionary who was a member of a European expedition led by Louis Joliet. They were the first Europeans to reach the confluence of the Mississippi and Illinois rivers. A large stone cross located east of the main park entrance along Route 100 commemorates their historic landing. The park is famous for the beauty of its fall colors and as a home for bald eagles in the winter. In addition to the spectacular views of the Illinois and Mississippi rivers from several scenic overlooks (can you find the Piasa Bird?), visitors can take advantage of a variety of year-round recreational activities, including hiking, biking, horseback riding, camping, fishing, boating, and taking part in interpretative programs. The Visitor Center welcomes you with a three-dimensional map of the park, a 300-gallon aquarium, and a wealth of other displays and exhibits concerning the Illinois River, wildlife habitats, local history and geology. Pere Marquette Lodge provides elegant dining, with a Sunday brunch that draws people from Missouri as well as Illinois. The dining room seats 150 people and offers a choice of family style dining or selections from the menu. Many comment that this is a nice haven to escape to quiet nature.

RAGING RIVERS WATERPARK

100 Palisades Parkway (along Great River Road, take Grafton ferry or bridge to Alton) **Grafton, IL** 62037

- ☐ Phone: (618) 786-2345 **www.ragingrivers.com**
- ☐ Hours: Daily 10:30am to 6:00pm or later (Memorial Day Weekend-Labor Day).
- ☐ Admission: $16.95-$19.95 per person (age 3+). Save $5.00 after 3:00pm. Parking $5.00.
- ☐ Miscellaneous: Locker rooms, showers, concessions. No coolers.

Raging Rivers WaterPark is cool when it's hot! Form the zoomin' Cascade Body Flumes, to the tube (or tubeless) wave pool, to a lazy Endless River, there's something for everyone. SwirlPool is a two-bowl attraction that's really 3 rides in one. Slide quickly down the tunnel flume, spin swiftly in the giant vortex, then drop into a deep pool of water. (for the more daring, try this ride at night) The milder Runaway Rafts Ride takes you on a 600 foot long journey down the hillside and then thru swift water and wild rapids. Or, ride the tubed Shark Slide that floats down a flume into a catch pool. Itty Bitty Surf City and TreeHouse Harbor are for the younger set.

PURINA FARMS

200 Checkerboard Drive (I-44 west past Six Flags over Mid-America to the Gray Summit exit. Turn right onto Hwy 100) **Gray Summit** 63039

- ☐ Phone: (314) 982-3232 **www.purina.com/events/**
- ☐ Hours: Open seasonally mid-March through mid-November, closed all major Holidays. Reservations Required. Summer open Tuesday-Sunday starting at 9:30am and running through 4:00pm closing. Spring and Fall open Wednesday-Friday only starting at 9:30am and running through 3:00pm closing.
- ☐ Admission: Free admission and parking, however, a nominal fee may be charged for special events.
- ☐ Miscellaneous: While at the Visitor's Center, visitors can browse through the Purina Farms Store to pick up Purina mementos or breed-specific sculptures, ornaments and shirts. Food services also are provided at the Visitor's Center.

At Purina Farms, learn how people and animals relate in everyday life. Visit a mini-Victorian house filled with cuddly kittens, watch a sheep herding demonstration, explore a barn or hold piglets and bunnies. Purina Farms combines a tourist center and two canine competition areas. Show and field events as well as hands-on activities and exhibits reinforce the bond between pets and their people. Located on the grounds of the oldest and largest animal nutrition center in the world, the Ralston Purina Pet Food Company and Purina Mills have interesting educational displays, videos and hands-on activities focused on animal care. The Visitors Center hosts regularly scheduled obedience shows and grooming demonstrations. Plus, the center has interactive stations like Scent Boxes (lets you smell how a dog smells things) and Vision displays show the differences between your vision and that of dogs and cats.

Instead of just displaying Purina products and benefits, the complex features more of a petting zoo. Kids can pet Purina's own dogs and cats, milk a cow, and play in the hayloft at the Farm Animal Barn. The Pet Center building's key attraction is a 20-foot-tall, multilevel cat house, complete with windows, stairways, rocking chairs and other furnishings, creating a feline paradise. A staircase surrounding the structure provides visitors with an eye-level view of the cat house's inhabitants. Kind of a huge dollhouse (cat house) that you can walk around!

The Canine Competition Center is designed specifically for field and test competition with a spacious arena for herding trials and tests, lure coursing and whippet races.

SHAW NATURE RESERVE
Hwy. 100 & I-44 **Gray Summit** 63039

- Phone: (636) 451-3512 **www.shawnature.org**
- Hours: (Nature Reserve) Daily, 7:00am until sunset. (Visitor Center) Monday-Friday 8:00am-4:30pm, Saturday & Sunday 9:00am-5:00pm. (Bascom House) Monday-Sunday 10:00am-4:00pm.
- Admission: $3.00 adult (13+), $2.00 senior (65+), Child 12 & under are FREE.
- Tours: The Wilderness Wagon Departs from the Visitor Center Saturday and Sunday afternoons from May – June and September - October (weather permitting) on the hour: 1:00, 2:00 and 3:00. This is a great relaxing way to view what SNR has to offer.

The Nature Reserve is dedicated to returning the land to its condition before European-style agriculture. Plant scientists are actively reintroducing "heritage" plants to this reserve to grow alongside almost 1,000 species of native plants. Glades are the "crown jewels" of habitat preservation at the nature reserve. Glades are sunny areas where rock is at the surface, so the land can't be used for crops. The starting point of the woodland trail system, trails departing here lead visitors through glades, prairie, woodlands, and bottomland forests, and provide access to the Meramec River. Restrooms, drinking water, and a sheltered picnic area are available.

If you want a "Little House on the Prairie" feel, take the weekend Wilderness Wagon tours. The narrated wagon ride travels the 3 mile Trail House Loop Road, with stops at the Trail House and wetland bus stop. $1.00 per person. It's a great way to shorten the hike to the river or to the wetlands if you have small children or non-hikers in your group. Get off at either stop and get picked up later. You'll feel like a pioneer heading west as you hear about comparisons to early pioneer life and what living conditions were like. Would you rather live in a teepee or a sod house? Near the end of the trail, you'll see a real sod house built into the side of an earthen mound.

ADVENTURES OF TOM SAWYER DIORAMA MUSEUM

323 N. Main Street (next to historic Grant's Drug Store, down the hill
and around the corner from the Mark Twain Home and Museum.)
Hannibal 63401

- ☐   Phone: (314) 221-3525
- ☐   Hours: Monday-Friday 8:00am-6:00pm, Saturday & Sunday 9:00am-5:00pm.

An excellent overview of Mark Twain's The Adventures Of Tom Sawyer can be seen in these sixteen hand carved scenes. Art Sieving spent five years creating these dioramas, his painstaking artistry evident in every detail. Look for the scene of tom whitewashing the fence, tom and Becky on Jackson's Island and then in a cave. A candy shop is in the front portion of the building.

BIG RIVER TRAIN TOWN

320 N 3rd Street **Hannibal** 63401

- ☐   Phone: (573) 221-1966.
- ☐   Small admission.

All Aboard! To Train Town. Where toy trains come alive. New and Vintage toy trains. Take a journey to a time where the Golden Age of railroading and toy trains were a part of most everyone's life. So stroll back and enjoy our operating and interactive layouts, along with toy train memorabilia and a depot store. Bring your camera and smiles. Open Daily.

CAMERON CAVE

300 Cave Hollow Road (1 mile South of Hannibal on Highway 79)
Hannibal 63401

☐ Phone: (573) 221-1656 **www.marktwaincave.com**
☐ Hours: Daily 9:00am-6:00pm (most days). Open until 8:00pm most summer days. 10:00am-4:00pm (November-March).
☐ Admission: $15.95 adult, $9.95 child (8-12), $2.10 child (7 and under). Additional fees for other activities and tour upgrades.
☐ Tours begin at Mark Twain Cave Visitors Center.

Visit the Northern Hemisphere's most complex cave, Cameron Cave, Missouri's newest show cave. You'll see the cave nearly as it was when first discovered. This lantern guided tour takes you through this complex maze cave. The tour last 1 ½ hours and several visitors on the tour will carry lanterns. This is a natural cave with no artificial or artistic lighting. Guests lanterns casting shadow (and light) on formations makes this cave feel like you're in a mystery novel. Don't a lot of the formations look like honeycombs? There are only 3 maze type caves in North America and two of them are right here!

HANNIBAL TOURS

Hannibal 63401

Along the Mississippi River you come across a little town that Mark Twain made famous. Twain grew up here on the banks of the river and featured this town in some of his best-loved stories. Admission Charged. Call for current rates.

• **HANNIBAL TROLLEY** - 220 N Main. (573) 221-1161. Just as the trolleys that once "clanged" their bells along Hannibal's streets, the Hannibal Trolley Company also serves as transportation to and from some of Hannibal's attractions. 60 minute tour hits all the important stops in town. You may depart and re-board our trolley at the Mark Twain Cave, Sawyer's Creek, Rockcliffe Mansion, and the depot. Trolleys run open air in summer months and are enclosed in early spring and late fall.

HANNIBAL TOURS (cont.)

- **TWAINLAND EXPRESS** - 400 N Third. (573) 221-5593. Let the sights and sounds of a trip on Twainland's "Choo-Choo" (Hannibal's only passenger train) take you away for the best of Historic Hannibal. Comfortable and slow-paced tours for all ages. "Choo-Choo" by Mark Twain's Home, Lighthouse on Cardiff Hill, Millionaire's Row, Sawyer's Creek, Welshman's Home, Old Jail Museum, Garth Library, Orpheum Theater, Mark Twain Cave, the Mighty Mississippi River, plus so much more! Trains run open air during summer, enclosed early spring and fall. This shuttle is made to look like a train and offers one-hour sightseeing tours blending historical facts with humorous stories. $5.00-$8.25 per person.

- **MARK TWAIN CLOPPER** - A short 20-minute tour of downtown and the river is carried out in a horse-drawn wagon. Memorial Day thru Labor Day: $5.00 adult, $2.50 child.

MARK TWAIN BOYHOOD HOME COMPLEX

120 North Main Street Hannibal 63401

- ☐ Phone: (573) 221-9010 **www.marktwainmuseum.org**
- ☐ Hours: Daily, 9:00am-5:00pm. Open until 6:00pm (June-August). In addition to daily schedule, the complex opens at Noon on Sunday (November-March).
- ☐ Admission: $9.00 adult, $7.50 senior (60+), $5.00 child (6-12).
- ☐ Tours: There are a total of 8 properties to see. We suggest at least 90 minutes to view all of the buildings.
- ☐ Educators: Wonderful creative writing and reading comprehension for various ages is found under the Education icon>For Teachers>Lesson Plans. Miscellaneous: Annually on Memorial Day weekend in September, Main Street Hannibal honors Mark Twain and his literary works with a Twain literature-inspired theme festival. Festival goers are encouraged to dress in theme attire (ex. Roughing It would have a Wild West theme).

A tour of the museum properties includes the actual buildings that inspired many famous scenes in Samuel Clemens' (pen name Mark Twain), most well-known novels, including The Adventures of Tom Sawyer and Adventures of Huckleberry Finn. The museum includes 8 properties where young Sam Clemens lived, played and had the adventures he would later use as inspiration for his stories. The Interpretive Center, located directly behind the Mark Twain Boyhood Home, begins the visitor experience.

Visitors may then visit the Huck Finn House, a reproduction of the home of Tom Blankenship, the young boy Twain knew in his youth and later labeled as the model for Huckleberry Finn.

Visitors are then directed to the Boyhood Home, the house that inspired Twain's imagination. Life size white figures of an adult Twain residing in each room, give visitors the feeling of returning with Twain to the boyhood home of his memories. Visitors can almost imagine a young Sam Clemens sneaking out the window, like Tom in The Adventures of Tom Sawyer. Be sure to notice the stairwell going to the second floor at the inside of the house, and then remember Tom Sawyer sneaking in to overhear Aunt Polly and the others planning the boys' funeral. On summer afternoons, Mark Twain re-enactors begin conversations with guests, in character.

Across the street stands the Becky Thatcher House (currently undergoing restoration), the childhood home of Laura Hawkins, immortalized in The Adventures of Tom Sawyer as Becky Thatcher. There is a Children's Play Discovery Area as well, where children can dress up as Becky or Tom would have in the mid-1800s or play some games that were also popular in that time period, such as checkers. As a different touch, the site also serves as a bookstore with a large selection of Twain's books and many children's classics and souvenirs.

Next door is the Justice of the Peace Office. This is J.M. Clemens Law Office where Samuel Clemen's father presided as Justice of the Peace. The courtroom here provided the inspiration for the trial scene in Tom Sawyer. Samuel's dad died when he was 11 and he was taken from school and placed in the office of the Hannibal Courier as a printer's apprentice.

The next museum building is Grant's Drug Store. It is set up like an old drug store in Sam Clemens' day with bottles of herbs and treatments arranged on shelves.

The Museum Gallery, located on Main Street just two blocks south of the Boyhood Home holds a wealth of Twain artifacts, exhibits featuring scenes from five of Twain's most popular books as well as a replica steamboat pilot house. The first floor features five of Twain's books. You can walk through a simulated cave as Tom Sawyer or sit on a raft similar to the one that took

MARK TWAIN BOYHOOD HOME COMPLEX (cont.)

Huck Finn down the river. Actual artifacts include Mark Twain's writing desk, white linen coat, top hat and well-worn pipe. Upstairs is more of an art gallery with many drawings done by Norman Rockwell as illustrations of editions of Tom Sawyer and Huckleberry Finn books. Although he left Hannibal in 1853, Clemens didn't begin writing "The Adventures of Tom Sawyer" until 20 years later.

After your day in Hannibal, we promise your kids will feel like they were dropped into the middle of Twain's books. Don't be surprised if your kids act out scenes from Twains tales as they wander the old-fashioned town streets. DID YOU KNOW ? For a $10.00 contribution to the endowment fund they will let you sign the whitewashed fence outside.

MARK TWAIN CAVE COMPLEX

300 Cave Hollow Road Hannibal 63401

- ☐ Phone: (573) 221-1656 **www.marktwaincave.com**
- ☐ Hours: Daily 9:00am-6:00pm most spring & fall days. Open until 8:00pm (summer). Daily 10:00am-4:00pm (November-March).
- ☐ Admission: $15.95 adult, $9.95 child (8-12), $2.10 (7 and under). Upgraded tours available at additional fees.
- ☐ Tours: Allow 60-90 minutes for tour.
- ☐ Note: Walkways are level and smooth and there are no steps. Persons of any age can easily make the tour. Bring a light wrap as the cave is 52 degrees year around. Wear sensible walking shoes and be sure to bring your camera. Just a few steps away across the creek from the Visitor Center is Sticks and Stones and a sluice where kids of all ages can pan for semi-precious gemstones (extra fee). MARK TWAIN CAVE CAMPGROUNDS are on location for RV or tent camping w/ hookups, showers, playground. www.marktwaincave.com/campground.html.

Samuel Clemens explored the cave as a child, and later, under the pen name of Mark Twain, wrote about his adventures. Mark Twain wrote, "By and by somebody shouted, "Who's ready for the cave? Everybody was. Bundles of candles were procured and straight away there was a general scamper up the hill." The historic tour begins with a video presentation which explains the geology of caves and how this particular cave was discovered. An experienced guide will escort you on a one-hour tour featuring points of interest mentioned in five of Mark Twain's writings. Visit the Mark Twain Cave where Tom and Becky got lost while running from Injun Joe. Other formations to look for are Aladdin's Palace and the Cathedral. The cave was also a hideout for the notorious outlaw Jesse James and provided refuge for slaves seeking freedom via the Underground Railroad. What is really a dull cave suddenly is full of intrigue as stories are woven and images conjured up in kids minds.

MARK TWAIN DINETTE

Hannibal - 400 N. 3rd Street (Historic District next to Mark Twain Home) 63401. Phone: (573) 221-5511. Lunch and dinner buffet daily plus a large menu to choose from. Saturday & Sunday Breakfast Buffet, full menu upon request. Outdoor seating available. Breakfast w/ super buffets on weekends, burgers, tenderloin, catfish specialty for dinner. Try the homemade root beer. Open daily 6:00am-9:00pm.

MARK TWAIN HIMSELF

Planter's Barn Theater, 319 North Main Street **Hannibal** 63401

- ☐ Phone: (573) 231-0021 or (866) 492-0021
  www.marktwainhimself.com or **www.heritagestage.com**
- ☐ Hours: Call or visit website for current schedule.
- ☐ Admission: $16.00 adult, $14.00 senior & child.

Just a few steps from the Mark Twain Boyhood Home and Museum is a live, one man show that captures Twain's humor and satire. Performing on the 1849 stage in a barn on Dead Man's Alley (same stage as Clemens played), the actor Twain returns to the bank of the Mississippi River. Laugh along with Tom Sawyer and catch a glimpse of America through the eyes of Huckleberry Finn. Seasonally they put on a show titled A Shepherd's Tale (during Christmas season) and the Gospel of Mark (near Easter), all presented by veteran stage actor Richard Garey. Served with lots of laughter and a Victorian Tea of cake, cookies, coffee, and tea, this is great theater.

MARK TWAIN RIVERBOAT

100 Center Street (foot of Center Street at the Mississippi River - Center Street Landing) **Hannibal** 63401

☐   Phone: (573) 221-3222 **www.marktwainriverboat.com**
☐   Hours: (Sightseeing) Daily @ 1:30pm (May), Daily @ 11:00am, 1:30pm & 4:00pm (Memorial Day-Labor Day), Daily @ 1:30pm & 4:00pm (September & October). Boarding begins 30 minutes before departure.
☐   Admission: (Sightseeing) $14.00 adult (13+), $11.00 child (5-12).
☐   Tours: Various cruises available but the Sightseeing tour features commentary on river history, legends, and sights. This cruise features an open snack bar with sandwiches and beverages. No reservations are required for the sightseeing cruises.

To Mark Twain, the most exciting aspect of growing up in Hannibal was living just two blocks from the Mississippi River, and there was nothing he was prouder of in later years than his career as a riverboat pilot. Today a nostalgic riverboat named after Twain plies the mighty river giving visitors the opportunity to experience a taste of "Life on the Mississippi." During the day, the Mark Twain Riverboat offers One Hour Sightseeing Cruises.

MOLLY BROWN BIRTHPLACE & MUSEUM

505 North Third Street **Hannibal** 63401

☐   Phone: (573) 221-2100 or (573) 221-2477 **www.visitmollybrown.com**
☐   Hours: Monday 10:00am-3:00pm, Thursday-Saturday 10:00am-4:00pm. Sunday 11:00am-4:00pm. Closed Tuesday & Wednesday.
☐   Admission: $4.00 adult, $3.00 child.

Did you know Molly Brown was on her way to Hannibal when the Titanic went down? Come learn more about this "Unsinkable" heroine of the Titanic…a woman of means who still had a Midwestern mentality to work hard to survive (she coordinated rowing activities to keep the lifeboat moving and keep the frightened women warm). The story circulated that when first interviewed by reporters in New York, they asked to what she attributed her survival. "Typical Brown luck," she supposedly said, "We're unsinkable." The label stuck, and she became a national celebrity. Visit the place where America's most fascinating rags to riches story began on July 18, 1867. Just a few short blocks from downtown, Margaret (Molly) Tobin Brown's original Irish immigrant's cottage is restored to its 1860's condition. One of six children of John and Johanna Tobin, Molly lived and worked in Hannibal until age 18. She rose to fame after moving to Colorado and marrying J.J. Brown who, seven years later, struck the largest vein of gold known at that time! View her home as it might have been when she was a girl and explore a little Titanic memorabilia as well.

OLE PLANTERS RESTAURANT

Hannibal - 316 N Main Street 63401. Phone: (573) 221-4410. A Main Street staple for more than 30 years, Ole Planters has a full-service lunch and dinner menu, specializing in hickory smoked pork and beef, homemade tenderloins and unforgettable homemade pies. Ask about the famous guests who have stopped by to grab a bite. Lunch/Dinner most days. Closed Tuesday and Sunday nights. Closed January-February.

SAWYER'S CREEK FUN PARK

11011 Hwy 79 south (across from Mark Twain Cave, one mile south of downtown) **Hannibal** 63401

☐ **www.sawyerscreek.com**
☐ Hours: Open daily at 10:00am.

Sawyer's Creek is under new local ownership starting in 2010. The Fun Park features an 18 Hole Miniature Golf Course in a beautiful garden setting, Bumper Boats in the Fish Pond (feed the fish), Bounce House, Fast Pitch, Water Wars and a Too Too Twain for the little ones. Each activity has a pay to play fee or you can buy all-play wristbands. The Sweet Shop features homemade fudge and candy, ice cream, fresh caramel corn, and snacks.

- **RIVERVIEW CAFÉ** - Relaxing atmosphere featuring a "Taste of Hannibal". Enjoy a sandwich for lunch or the large Soup and Salad Bar. Dinner selections include everything from catfish to steaks. Top it off with a delicious homemade dessert or your favorite beverage. Every table has a great view of the Mississippi River...in season you can dine inside or on their river view deck.

PADDLEWHEEL POPCORN & CANDY COMPANY

Hannibal - *121 North Main St., downtown 63491. www.paddlewheelpopcorn.com. Phone: (573) 221-0880 Delicious popcorns and hard-to-find candies make Paddlewheel Popcorn the one-stop shop to satisfy that sweet tooth. What we like best about this store is they've named their gourmet popcorns after characters. For example: Becky Thatcher (vanilla sugar), Huck Finn (slingshot zing cheddar cheese), Injun Joe (hot and sweet cinnamon), or Tom Sawyer (troubly, bubbly buttery caramel).*

TOM SAWYER DAYS

Hannibal - *Downtown. www.hannibaljaycees.org. A Hannibal tradition for over 50 years. The National Tom Sawyer Days celebration focuses on family fun. Visitors can watch or join in many of the activities. The town Mark Twain grew up in plays host to the National Fence Painting Championships, the Tomboy Sawyer competition, a frog-jumping contest (you can rent a frog if you didn't bring your own), Mississippi Mud Volleyball, entertainment, food and then a big fireworks display on July 4th. (days leading to July 4th)*

CAMP RIVER DUBOIS, LEWIS & CLARK STATE HISTORIC SITE

IL 3 & New Poag Road (take I-270 over the River to IL. Then head north on IL 3) **Hartford, IL** 62048

- ☐ Phone: (618) 251-5811 **www.campdubois.com**
- ☐ Hours: Wednesday-Sunday 9:00am-5:00pm.
- ☐ Admission: FREE.
- ☐ Educators: Lesson Plans about the Lewis & Clark expedition are found on links on the For Teachers page of the website.

On May 14, 1804, Captain Meriwether Lewis wrote, "The mouth of the River Dubois is to be considered the point of departure." Visit the Lewis and Clark Interpretive Center, a replica of the 1803-04 winter encampment, and the Lewis and Clark Monument at this facility. The space tells the story of how the Corps of Discovery assembled equipment, supplies and men at Camp River Dubois. In the Convergence Theater an original 15-minute, high definition film, "At Journey's Edge," is shown every 20 minutes. Highlighting the tour is the "Cutaway Keelboat," a 55-foot long replica of the keelboat

Lewis had built in Ohio. The boat has been cut in half revealing how it was filled with "tools of every description." This is the room where kids can really explore! Be sure to ask the front desk for the scavenger/stamp hunt sheet. As you explore and log your provisions and usefulness, try to determine whether you would be able to pack and organize as well as these folks. Try it.

Finished packing? Now venture outside towards the reconstruction of the camp. The volunteers act as guides to the fort where visitors can view the sleeping quarters of the men and the main building that served as guardhouse, storehouse, and the Captain's quarters. Be sure to behave so you don't get 100 lashings. The Camp often had visitors, many who provided information about the west. Today you are invited to visit and share as many may have done before. We promise, this historic site sparks a kids' sense of adventure.

DEUTSCHHEIM STATE HISTORIC SITE & MUSEUM

109 W. 2nd Street (west of Market Street / Hwy. 19) **Hermann** 65041

- ☐ Phone: (573) 486-2200 **www.mostateparks.com/deutschheim.htm**
- ☐ Admission: The Missouri state park system does not charge entrance fees. However, there are fees associated with camping, lodging, tours, museums and certain special events.
- ☐ Tours: Tours are given daily at 10:00am, 12:30pm and 2:30pm. (April-October), Thursday-Sunday Only (November-March).

Deutschheim State Historic Site captures the culture and heritage of the German people who migrated to Missouri in the mid- to late-19th century. Tours of the Strehly and Pommer-Gentner houses, along with two period gardens, focus on the culture of German immigrants and German Americans across Missouri. Tour Deutschheim's buildings and experience the daily life of German Americana the way it really happened 150 years ago.

While the New Germany was never achieved in Hermann or any other part of the U.S., the German language has been the first one spoken by many Missourians right up into the 1950s. Before farming became industrialized, travelers always knew when they had come to a German American district by the barns and the distinctive haystacks. Workers in some industries and in dairies and gardens wore wooden shoes as recently as the 1960s. Once even windmills could be found in some places, and half-timbered buildings are still common. Other traditions have lasted: foods like home-made wurst (sausages) and the making of sauerkraut, wine, beer, and Christmas cookies like Lebkuchen and Springerle are still part of the lives of many German Americans.

MASTODON STATE HISTORIC SITE

1050 Charles J. Becker Drive (I-55 to Exit 186/Imperial/Kimmswick, heading west) **Imperial** 63052

☐ Phone: (636) 464-2976 **www.mostateparks.com/mastodon.htm**

☐ Hours: The park trails are open sunrise to sunset. The museum is the highlight of your visit, however. Open 9:00am-4:30pm Monday-Saturday and Noon-4:30pm Sunday (mid-March thru mid-November). Closed Tuesday-Thursday and opens at 11:00am other days during winter.

☐ Admission: The Missouri state park system does not charge entrance fees. However, there are fees associated with the museum (small admission for folks age 16+) and certain special events.

Archaeological excavations found Paleo-Indians hunted the American mastodon here during the ice age. Bones of mastodons and other now-extinct animals were first found here in the early 1800s. A slide show is started every half hour. The museum dioramas detail these discoveries with placards explaining the difference between animals today vs. Prehistoric times. They display a prehistoric beaver skull and a modern beaver skull. The prehistoric beaver's skull was about twice if not three times the size of the modern beaver. A full-size replica of a mastodon skeleton highlights the exhibits. The area gained fame as one of the most extensive Pleistocene ice age deposits in the country and attracted scientific interest worldwide. Archaeological history was made at the site in 1979 when scientists excavated a stone spear point made by hunters of the Clovis culture (14,000 - 10,000 years ago) in direct association with mastodon bones. This was the first solid evidence of the coexistence of people and these giant prehistoric beasts. The site's museum displays ancient artifacts, fossils and a mastodon skeleton replica. A day use area is available for picnics and hikes to explore the same land where the lives of Native Americans and mastodons once intertwined. It's like the movie "Ice Age" come to life!

CLARK COUNTY MULE FESTIVAL

Kahoka - *Route EE, Clark County Fairgrounds. The Clark Co. Mule Festival is a three day mule show. It includes crafts; a flea market; trail rides; and souvenirs. Enjoy Mule Polo and Team penning Friday, 6:00pm, Saturday and Sunday, 10:00am and a Mule Rodeo Saturday, 7:00pm. Food, drink, and camping available on the grounds. Phone: (660) 727-2490. Admission. (mid-September weekend)*

STILL NATIONAL OSTEOPATHIC MUSEUM

800 W. Jefferson Street (Museum is located inside the Tinning Education Center, which is the glass-fronted building ahead on the right as you enter the campus grounds) **Kirksville** 63501

☐ Phone: (660) 626-2359 **www.atsu.edu/museum**
☐ Hours: Monday-Wednesday & Friday 10:00am-4:00pm, Thursday 10:00am-7:00pm, Saturday Noon-4:00pm.
☐ Admission: FREE.

Home of the founding Osteopathic School. Osteopathy is an approach to healthcare that emphasizes the role of the musculoskeletal system in health and disease. Artifacts span 150 years of the evolution of osteopathic medicine and include the log cabin where Dr. Andrew Still was born and the original two-room classroom building of the American School of Osteopathy, founded in 1892. Young kids may not get too excited about a human bones museum but they are attracted to many of the tools early doctors used, the bright red manipulation table, and sensor-activated audio systems that present interpretive glimpses into the Still family's frontier life and the earliest years of the ASO. The main gallery also contains a fully-dissected human nervous system—one of only four such dissections known to exist. While it may be gross to weak stomachs, curious kids tend to *"ooh and aah"*.

THOUSAND HILLS STATE PARK

20431 State Hwy. 157 **Kirksville** 63501

☐ Phone: (660) 665-6995 or (800) 334-6946
www.mostateparks.com/thousandhills.htm
☐ Admission: The Missouri state park system does not charge entrance fees. However, there are fees associated with camping, lodging, tours, museums and certain special events.

THOUSAND HILLS STATE PARK (cont.)

Nestled in the hills of northern Missouri, this park is centered around Forest Lake. It offers cabins, a marina, dining, a beach, camping, and hiking and mountain biking trails. A shelter along one trail protects an 1000-year-old American Indian petroglyphs. The dining lodge at Thousand Hills State Park serves a wide selection of excellent foods. Water recreation is a highlight of Thousand Hills State Park's outdoor activities. The lake and its 17 miles of shoreline make it popular for fishing, water skiing, paddle boating, canoeing and motor boating. At the marina, you can rent all types of boats including paddle boats, kayaks, canoes, fishing boats and pontoons.

SHRINE PRO RODEO

Kirksville - *NEMO Fairgrounds. Largest rodeo in this part of state has barrel racing, saddle bronc riding, calf roping, steer wrestling, team roping and bull riding. (third weekend in June)*

WAKONDA STATE PARK

32836 State Park Road **La Grange** 63448

- ☐ Phone: (573) 655-2280 **www.mostateparks.com/wakonda.htm**
- ☐ Admission: The Missouri state park system does not charge entrance fees. However, there are fees associated with camping, lodging, tours, museums and certain special events.

Located on the Mississippi River flyway, this park is noted for bird-watching. It features six lakes, a rare sand prairie, hiking and mountain biking trails, Missouri's largest natural sand beach, recreational trailers and camping. The clear lake waters attract thousands of waterfowl such as Canada geese, snow geese, mallards, snowy egrets and great blue herons during the migratory seasons (note: during migratory season, Agate Lake is closed to boating. Often the trail around the lake is closed, too). The lakes also offer anglers a chance at catching largemouth bass, bluegill, crappie and catfish. Two of the lakes have boat ramps. Non-motorized jon-boats and canoes can be rented at the park office.

JACKSON COUNTRY CONNECTIONS

La Plata - *28496 Nature Lane (zip code: 63549). www.jacksoncc.info/. Good ol' family fun, country style. You'll find hayrides, corn and bale mazes, a bounce house, a corn cannon and a pumpkin patch. (September & October).*

ASL PEWTER FOUNDRY

123 South Third Street **Louisiana** 63353

- ☐ Phone: (573) 754-3435 **www.aslpewter.com**
- ☐ Gallery Hours: Daily 10:00am-5:00pm. Occasionally closed on Mondays.
- ☐ Tours: just a look during gallery hours is fine but educational tours are pre-arranged by groups. Call ahead.
- ☐ Educators: If you have a home school or other school related group, they can work with your history, business or arts curriculum. Just give them an outline of the information you want to have covered, as it relates to pewter, owning and operating a small business and/or Early America.

Pewter is one of the oldest known alloys, dating back to the Bronze Age. Since they make all of the pewter pieces in their studio in Louisiana, MO, the studio is always open. Visit them as they create a "new antique" or a piece destined to become a family heirloom. See how the crafters spin metal and cast in antique molds. Other works are turned - pushing a flat piece of pewter into shape over a wooden form using wooden tools. Afterwards the pewter pieces are assembled or altered, including soldering, cutting, pressing, polishing, and finishing - all done by hand. Learn about what pewter is made of (90% tin plus scarce amounts of silver, copper, bismuth, and antimony)

While in town, look for the 24 murals commemorating historical events from Louisiana and the United States. Visit this website beforehand (www. louisiana-mo.com) or pick up a map at the Chamber of Commerce just up the street from the pewter shop.

LONG BRANCH STATE PARK

28615 Visitor Center Road **Macon** 63552

- ☐ Phone: (660) 773-5229 **www.mostateparks.com/longbranch.htm**
- ☐ Admission: The Missouri state park system does not charge entrance fees. However, there are fees associated with camping, lodging, tours, museums and certain special events.

Located along Long Branch Lake, this park combines wooded areas and restored rolling prairie. The park offers a wheelchair-accessible fishing dock, a sand swimming beach, boat slips and ramps, a store, hiking trails, picnic sites and a campground. Near one of the picnic shelters is a one-mile trail that leads to the lake where benches await, providing a great spot to sit and watch the day go by.

AUDRAIN HISTORICAL SOCIETY MUSEUM COMPLEX

501 S. Muldrow (in Robert S. Green Park) **Mexico** 65265

- ☐ Phone: (573) 581-3910 **www.audrain.org**
- ☐ Hours: Tuesday-Saturday 10:00am-4:00pm, Sunday 1:00-4:00pm. Often closed in January.
- ☐ Admission: $5.00 adult, $3.00 child (12 and under).

The complex has an antebellum mansion named Graceland, that's fully furnished with period pieces, the American Saddlebred Horse Museum, the Audrain Fire Brick Museum, a country school, country church and stables. A unique feature of the church is the original theater-style seating. The country school is set up just like it would have been in 1903 with a slate backboard, desks, schoolbooks, and such. And, for horse lovers, the American Saddlebred Horse Museum, the oldest in the nation, was established to complement Graceland, while commemorating Mexico's longtime renown as the Saddle Horse Capital of the World. Every famous horse or rider from these parts is prominently featured. And what is "fire brick"? Audrain also became known as the "Fire Brick Center of the World." The importance of fireclay lay in its capacity to withstand extremely high temperatures without changing form or deteriorating. It was used to build industrial furnaces and became essential to many basic industries. This type of brick was the most significant industry in the counties history. It became obsolete in 2002.

BINDERS HILLTOP APPLE AND BERRY FARM
24688 Audrain Road 820 **Mexico** 65265

☐   Phone: (573) 581-1415 **www.applesandalpacas.com**

More than 50 colorful alpacas are on-site. Tour the alpaca barn and get close
to the animals. Or, come out to get some fresh produce...apples, peaches
and blackberries in July; you pick the apples. The Farm store offers organic
produce in season, apple products and alpaca apparel. You might want to
purchase a bag of apple chips to snack on the way home. Summer and Fall
are the best times to visit.

•   THE U-PICK APPLE TOUR: Tours are offered on Monday, Tuesday and
    Wednesdays, mornings or afternoons. $3.50 per person. Minimum of 10
    (or $35.00 charge is applied to smaller groups). Start in the apple orchard,
    then go to the honey bee yard. Students even get to pick an apple without
    having to climb on ladders - how? Why are bees so important to apple
    farmers? Next watch the ducks play or the guineas in their wanderings
    around the farm. Head over to the pond (in the morning, ducks take baths
    there) and finally end up over by the alpacas to learn about this unique
    creature. Kids get to pet a baby alpaca, feeling their soft fiber. Now that
    you've picked some apples, you'll get a chance to make it into apple
    juice. Surprise samples and activity sheets are sent home. (mid-August
    until mid-October).

MARK TWAIN LANDING
42819 Landing Lane **Monroe City** 63456

☐   Phone: (573) 735-9422 or (877) 700-9422 **www.marktwainlanding.com**

At Mark Twain Landing, all RV sites include a 40-foot cement pad and patio
area, full hookups with water, sewer, and electric, BBQ grill and picnic table.
All roads to and within the RV park are paved and the cabins are only one half
mile from Spalding Beach and boat ramp on Mark Twain Lake. They have
over 250 RV and tent camping sites, cabins, and even a motel. At the Playland
they have go carts, bumper boats, miniature golf and much more. Come
splash around in their Water Park where you will be able to ride the waves
in one of Missouri's largest wave pools that tops out at 500,000 gallons! You
can scream through the space bowl at speeds approaching 35 mph; then race

down any of four water flumes! You can relax a little as you float around in the Lazy River. The waterpark is an extra fee of $20.00+ per person. At night, gather around the fire ring or grab a snack at the diner.

GRAHAM CAVE STATE PARK
217 Hwy. TT **Montgomery City** 63361

☐ Phone: (573) 564-3476 **www.mostateparks.com/grahamcave.htm**
☐ Admission: The Missouri state park system does not charge entrance fees. However, there are fees associated with camping, lodging, tours, museums and certain special events.

Nestled in the hills above the Loutre River in Montgomery County, Graham Cave State Park features an unusual sandstone cave that contained evidence that rewrote history books. Once used for shelter, Graham Cave became historically significant when archaeologists discovered how long ago human occupancy had occurred. Radiocarbon dating has shown it was inhabited thousands of years ago. Graham Cave Trail is a walking trail that leads to the main feature of the park, Graham Cave, and the interpretive shelter. It also connects with Fern Ridge Trail. The paved path from the parking lot to Graham Cave has a high degree of incline. Today, visitors are allowed in the entrance of the cave, where interpretive signs point out interesting discoveries. The park also offers picnic areas, camping, Loutre River access and hiking trails.

STARLIGHT ALPACA RANCH
55105 Buffalo Lane (20 miles south of Hannibal) **New London** 63459

☐ Phone: (573) 267-3778 **www.starlightalpacaranch.com**

Home to over 100 alpacas, Starlight is a great place to interact with these gentle animals. Raised for their luxurious fiber, visitors are amazed at their softness. Every spring and fall the herd is expanding with the arrival of numerous new babies (cries). No matter when you visit you will see the young romping through fields. You may even get to feed the animals. Pack a picnic and eat at the pavilion by the lake while enjoying the beautiful scenery. Alpaca products are available at the ranch store. This is a working ranch so please call ahead so they can be watching for you. They are open year round for free tours or stop by during on-site alpaca festivals in June and September.

ROBERTSVILLE STATE PARK

902 State Park Drive (5 miles east of I-44 on Route O near the junction of
Route N) **Robertsville** 63072

☐ Phone: (636) 257-3788 **www.mostateparks.com/robertsville.htm**
☐ Admission: The Missouri state park system does not charge entrance fees.
However, there are fees associated with camping, lodging, tours, museums
and certain special events.

With the Meramec River and Calvey Creek along its border, this park
attracts many kinds of waterfowl. The 1,225-acre park features a variety of
outdoor activities for visitors of all ages, including canoeing and fishing in
the adjoining Meramec River. Facilities include a boat-launching area on
the river, a picnic area with two shelters, hiking trails, a playground and a
campground. For those wishing to spend a night or more in the park, well-
shaded basic and electric campsites are nestled among the wooded hills.

FAST LANE CLASSIC CARS

427 Little Hill Blvd. **St. Charles** 63301

☐ Phone: (636) 940-9969 **www.fastlanecars.com**
☐ Hours: Monday 9:30am-7:00pm, Tuesday-Thursday 9:30am-6:00pm, Friday
9:30am-7:00pm, Saturday 9:30am-5:00pm.
☐ Admission: FREE.

Corvettes, Cameros, Mopars, Mustangs, street rods and more. See the shine
of freshly polished chrome and smell the aroma of a Hemi warning up for a
turn around the block. See an authentic Shelby Mustang. Many of these cars
are available for auction sale so the museum for looking is FREE.

FIRST MISSOURI STATE CAPITOL STATE HISTORIC SITE

200-216 S. Main Street **St. Charles** 63301

☐ Phone: (636) 940-3322 **www.mostateparks.com/firstcapitol.htm**
☐ Tours: The Missouri state park system does not charge entrance fees.
However, there are fees associated with camping, lodging, tours, museums
and certain special events. Tour Fees $4.00 adult, $2.50 child (7-12). Tours:
Monday-Saturday 10:00am-3:00pm ends with 3:00pm tour. Sunday Noon-
3:00pm ends with the 3:00pm tour (April-October). No tours on Mondays rest
of year and Sunday & Monday in January & February.

FIRST MISSOURI STATE CAPITOL STATE HISTORIC SITE (cont.)

Missouri's first legislators met here from June 4, 1821 to Oct. 1, 1826, to reorganize Missouri's territorial government. Tours are given of the restored building, including the governmental chambers, a residence and a dry goods store. For a nominal fee, visitors can take a guided tour through the actual restored and furnished rooms where Missouri state government was created and first practiced. The Peck Bros. Dry Goods Store contains examples of merchandise needed in the 1820s, with furs on display to show visitors the importance of the once-thriving fur trade. Admission is free to the historic site's interpretive center, which offers two floors of exhibits and an orientation show. Any families with kids in grades 4+ would be recommended to take the wonderful, interesting ranger tours.

HISTORICAL CHILDREN'S FESTIVAL

St. Charles - *First Missouri State Capitol - Come live and play as children in the 1820's did. Hear interesting stories on Missouri's struggle for statehood. Learn about life in St. Charles when our first legislators were meeting. Hands on activities include: butter churning, quill pen writing, cow milking, candle dipping, baby farm animals, hearth cooking, storytelling, period games, re-enactors, sewing/quilting and much more. (third Saturday in May)*

KATY TRAIL STATE PARK
St. Charles 63301

☐   Phone: (800) 334-6946   **www.mostateparks.com/katytrail.htm**
☐   Admission: The Missouri state park system does not charge entrance fees. However, there are fees associated with camping, lodging, tours, museums and certain special events.

At 225 miles, this park is the longest rail-trail conversion in the nation and runs from St. Charles to Clinton. There are 12 different trailheads in this region, including those in Hermann, Marthasville, Augusta, and St. Charles. If hiking, biking or bird watching are more your style, head out on the Katy Trail www.katytrail.showmestate.com or any number of dozens of trails in the area for some of the most spectacular scenery in the Midwest. Towering bluffs, flowing rivers and emerald green fields define the landscape and entice the senses in the area known as America's breadbasket. The level hiking and biking paths and woodland areas are home to hundreds of species of flora, fauna and wildlife native to Missouri and the Midwest. White-tailed deer, beaver and turkey are regularly spotted. Fishing is also excellent in the area and many places sell equipment and bait for the interested angler. For the adventurous, consider camping out under the stars just like the pioneers and the Native American Indians did. Many campgrounds are in the area and cater to a variety of needs.

LEWIS AND CLARK BOAT HOUSE AND NATURE CENTER

1050 Riverside Drive (Bishop's Landing) **St. Charles** 63301

☐   Phone: (636) 947-3199 **www.lewisandclarkcenter.org**
☐   Hours: Monday-Saturday 10:00am-5:00pm, Sunday Noon-5:00pm.
☐   Admission: $4.00 adult, $2.00 child (under 17).

The Lewis & Clark Boathouse and Nature Center is situated on the banks of the Missouri River and is home to the Discovery Expedition of Saint Charles and its authentically reproduced keelboat and pirogues. The building is also home to the recently expanded Lewis & Clark museum which houses detailed dioramas of the great adventure and many hand-on exhibits of life in the area in 1804, from its wildlife to its architecture. Your kids will understand historical styles of building as they peer through windows of four half-scale buildings each showing different architectural styles of the 1700 and 1800s.

The nature trail winds through a woodland area, and a typical wetland marsh is home to a number of plants and animals. Depending on the time of the year and time of day, you might observe ducks, geese, herons, deer and other wildlife as they visit the nearby woods, river and wetlands. Also, depending on weather and river conditions at different times of the year, you can find great photo opportunities.

RT WEILER'S RESTAURANT

St. Charles - *201 N Main Street 63301. www.rtweilers.com. Phone: (636) 947-1593. . Serving lunch and dinner daily, the name of the restaurant was meant to mimic the name of a rather large breed of dog. The kids menu has PB & J, grilled cheese, chicken strips, etc. served in an authentic doggie dish. Family owned: 15 TV's, Hand Cut Steaks, Fried Chicken to BBQ and Homemade Desserts. Moderately priced and great fun for the whole family. Lunch, Dinner and Entertainment.*

FETE DE GLACE ICE CARVING COMPETITION

St. Charles - *100 to 200 blocks of North Main Street. Watch professional ice carvers bring the art to life in a competition using chain saws, power grinders, sanders, cold chisels, hand saws, and irons from 9:30am-3:30pm. This competition is judged and juried by the crowd. Coffee and hot chocolate will be available & nearby fire pits to warm up. (last weekend in January)*

LEWIS AND CLARK HERITAGE DAYS

St. Charles - *Frontier Park. www.lewisandclarkheritagedays.com. Authentic reenactment of Lewis & Clarks encampment in 1804 prior to embarking on the exploration of the Louisiana Purchase. Saturday 9:30am-5:00pm & Sunday 10:00am-4:00pm. Parade, church service Sunday, walk through encampments; plus weapon demonstrations in the afternoons, boat replicas, museum tours, crafts & foods of 1804, children's games, period music and more. (third weekend in May)*

FESTIVAL OF THE LITTLE HILLS

St. Charles - *Frontier Park and Main Street. www.festivalofthelittlehills.com. The largest festival of the year, activities include over 300 craft booths, with some demonstrations by crafts people and artisans. Also includes numerous food & beverages booths along with live music and other entertainment and Kids Corner. (third full weekend in August)*

DOUBLE KEY TREASURE HUNTS

(ordered online) **St. Louis**

☐ **www.doublekeytreasurehunts.com**
☐ Admission: $99.00-$129.00 per kit.

Double Key Treasure Hunts creates complete treasure hunt packages in a sackcloth bag using real antique items from the 1800s to the early 1900s. To solve the clues, you'll visit various places around St. Louis by decoding the treasure written instructions and artifacts. A family, kids party, extended family can all help with one hunt as it's self-contained and you don't need outside assistance. What a great way to engage your kids in historical places you might have just peeked in for a quick look before. Now the kids are motivated to explore and they notice every square inch of the building trying to solve a part of the query.

FLAMINGO BOWL

St. Louis - *1117 Washington Avenue, downtown 63101. Phone: (314) 436-6666. www.FlamingoBowl.net. Hours: Daily, Noon-6pm for children. Admission: Children (12 & under) $3.00/game everyday until 6:00pm. Reservations are available – please inquire. Shoe rental $3.00. Twelve lanes of bowling with an Art deco design and flamingo theme. During daylight hours, the place is family friendly and kids like the foods offered - mostly appetizers, sandwiches and pizza. Average sandwich is $7.00. Fun environment to bowl and snack while downtown in the big city.*

ST. LOUIS RAMS FOOTBALL

901 N. Broadway (Edward Jones Dome) **St. Louis** 63101

☐ Phone: (Dome) (314) 342-5201 **www.stlouisrams.com**

Home field of the St. Louis Rams pro football team. If the kids want to be a part of the fan club, they can join as a kids club member and receive specialty items with the Rams Kids Club logo.

DENTAL HEALTH THEATER

727 North First Street (Laclede's Landing) St. Louis 63102

☐ Phone: (314) 241-7391 **www.ddhtstl.org**
☐ Hours: Tuesday-Saturday 9:00am-3:00pm. (Showtimes) 9:30am, 11:00am, 1:30pm.
☐ Admission: $1.00 general.

The theater specializes in programs on the importance of good dental and overall health, and focuses its efforts on children and teens. Features are a three-foot-tall set of lighted teeth and age-appropriate videos. Their newest production is the Healthy Hollow state-of-the-art puppet show. FREEBIES: Every child who attends receives a "Healthy Smile Kit" filled with dental tools. Thanks to sponsors like Missouri Foundation For Health, ADA, and Old Newsboys Day, the theatre hands out Healthy Smile Kits comprised of a toothbrush, toothpaste, flossers, pencil, sticker, disclosing tablet, timer and community resource card (for parents to access a variety of dental services throughout the St. Louis area) all sealed nicely in a reusable pencil bag.

EAT-RITE DINER

St. Louis - 622 Chouteau Avenue 63102. Phone: (314) 621-9621. Hours: Breakfast, Lunch & Dinner. Miscellaneous: No reservations and no tables in this near downtown diner...you have to hope one of the dozen counter stools are open. A second diner is located South of St. Louis at 5513 South Lindbergh Blvd and a third diner is located Southwest of St. Louis at 1059 Gravois Road. There are throwbacks to old Route 66 if you look closely. The Eat-Rite Diner near the old, now closed MacArthur Bridge is one of them. The Eat-Rite Diner is a St. Louis Route 66 Tradition. This diner has been sitting on the corner of Chouteau and 7th for almost 60 years! This small classic diner has seen a lot of action in that time and it still serves up a quick meal. Their slogan, "Eat-Rite or Don't Eat At All". It's a dinky little place but a classic diner experience.

EUGENE FIELD HOUSE & ST. LOUIS TOY MUSEUM

634 South Broadway   St. Louis 63102

☐ Phone: (314) 421-4689 **www.eugenefieldhouse.org**
☐ Hours: Wednesday-Saturday 10:00am-4:00pm, Sunday Noon-4:00pm. Monday & Tuesday, by appointment. (January & February only by appointment).

For updates & travel games visit: **www.KidsLoveTravel.com**

☐   Admission: $5.00 adult (12+), $1.00 child (11 and under).

Take a trip back in time at the Eugene Field House and St. Louis Toy
Museum. A National Historic Landmark, the Eugene Field House is the
home of Roswell Field, the attorney for Dred Scott and his son, Eugene, "the
children's poet." Eugene Field was a St. Louis children's poet, famous for
such poems as 'Little Boy Blue' and 'Wynken, Blynken and Nod'. Eugene's
father Roswell was the lawyer who represented Dred Scott in the fight against
slavery, a defense that ultimately failed and at least sped up [if not led to]
the Civil War. The famous children's poet's downtown row house is filled
with antique toys and fascinating traveling exhibits. The combination of the
miniature toys museum with the displays and information on the Fields and
the Scotts really help to keep the kids interested. History is weaved in as
interactive displays show the lives of slave kids or the installation Narrative
Voices tells about the Dred Scott case.

GATEWAY ARCH
(St. Louis riverfront, last Missouri exits off Interstates) **St. Louis** 63102

☐   Phone: (877) 982-1410 **www.gatewayarch.com**
☐   Hours: Generally 8:00am-9:00pm summers. Shorter hours rest of year (close
       at 5:00pm)
☐   Admission: $10.00 adult, $5.00 child (3-15) for tram to the top. Museum
       of Westward Expansion is FREE. Movie fees apply for showings. Visiting
       the Gateway Arch in the summer? That's peak season for visits to the
       nation's tallest monument and "Journey to the Top" tram tickets sell out fast.
       Guarantee your ride for the day and time you want by ordering tickets in
       advance via online or phone number above.
☐   Security Checks: at one or more points before entering an exhibit space, you
       must allow some extra time to pass thru a security checkpoint. Note: Be sure
       to purchase tickets to ride to the observation deck at the top of the arch when
       you arrive. They sell timed tickets. You can visit the museum while waiting for
       your tram time. IMAX theatre on premises. FREEBIES: Click on the web icon:
       The Arch Experience. Then click Fun Stuff for an Arch quiz and a game to
       construct the Arch.

The imposing Gateway Arch, America's tallest monument, is a must see
attraction. The Arch and Old Courthouse sit on riverfront land where the
original Route 66 passed by - forging a trail to the American West. Take a
ride to the top of the Arch - 630 feet high over the Mississippi - which was

built as a monument to President Thomas Jefferson's dream of a continental United States. Journey to the Top is a two-part multimedia exhibit where riders board trams to the top. The south leg has When Riverboats Ruled, which offers a tour of St. Louis during the 1800s with sights and sounds of the era - including Mark Twain. The north leg has Fitting the Final Piece, which explains the history of the arch and gives you recreated echoed voices of construction workers creating the masterpiece. The ride feels like a somewhat slower version of a carnival Ferris wheel. Although the "pods" you ride on are painted soothing robin egg blue, the "ride" is like a futuristic adventure in the dark (except for your lighted pod). You'll catch the frontiersmen's sense of adventure, for sure! (Note: visitors with claustrophobia or "fear of heights" may have trouble with this ride. If in doubt, ask an attendant to let you try a pod first). From the top of the monument, you'll get a 30-mile panoramic view of the river and St. Louis far below.

As you're waiting for your timed ticket tram tour to the top, why not meander around the base of the museum - the Museum of Westward Expansion. You'll step back in time to see buffalo, covered wagons, Native American teepees, Lewis & Clark expedition dioramas and many other artifacts from America's western beginnings in St. Louis. To keep it interesting for the young-ins, look for these animatronic figures - Thomas Jefferson; William Clark; a buffalo soldier; and a 1846 Overlander woman preparing to head west. If you have more time, purchase a movie ticket to be submerged in high tech movies about westward expansion or the building of the arch.

Since this is possibly a once-in-a-lifetime family experience, be sure to bring your camera with charged batteries. We took pictures of everything - even the funky pods you ride to the top. At times, you'll get butterflies and feel so proud of America!

GATEWAY ARCH RIVERBOAT CRUISES

800 North First Street (riverfront, below the Gateway Arch) **St. Louis** 63102

- ☐ Phone: (877) 982-1410
  www.gatewayarch.com/Arch/info/act.riverboat.ss.1hr.aspx
- ☐ Admission: (Sightseeing) $14.00 adult, $8.00 child (3-15). Other tours are available. Call or see website for cruise schedule.
- ☐ Tours: (Sightseeing 60 minutes) Daily 1:30pm, Weekends Noon & 1:30pm. (March). Daily Noon, 1:30pm, 3:00pm. (April). Monday-Friday 10:30am,

Noon, 1:30pm & 3:00pm, Weekends,10:30 am, Noon, 1:30pm, 3:00pm
& 4:30pm (May). Daily 10:30am, Noon, 1:30pm, 3:00pm, 4:30pm. (June-
August). Monday-Friday, Noon, 1:30pm & 3:00pm, Weekends Noon, 1:30pm,
3:00pm, 4:30pm (September). Monday-Friday, Noon, 1:30pm, Weekends
Noon, 1:30pm & 3:00pm (October). Daily @ Noon (November). Reservations
required.

The Gateway Arch Riverboats, two replica steamboats, explore the Port of St.
Louis daily. After the boat ride, you can rent bikes on the dock and explore
the Riverfront Trail or roll through downtown to see the sights.

ST. LOUIS CARDINAL'S BUSCH STADIUM TOURS

700 Clark Street (purchase tickets at Gate 5 windows on Clark Street)
St. Louis 63102

☐   Phone: (314) 345-9565 (tour line)
    http://stlouis.cardinals.mlb.com/stl/ballpark/ballpark_tours.jsp
☐   Admission: $10.00 adult, $8.00 senior (60+), $6.00 child (<15).
☐   Tours: (During Season) Public tours will be offered at 9:30am, 11:00am,
    12:30pm, and 2:00pm. No Tours During: Dates of afternoon home games
    (tours are available during days of home night games). Dates of special
    events at the ballpark. (Off-Season) Tours will be offered daily throughout
    the off-season at 11:00am and 1:00pm. Tours depart from Gate 5 (on Clark
    Street). Tours last one hour and end at Gate 3 (near the Stan Musial statue).
    Tours normally include the following stops: a Party Room, the Redbird Club,
    the Press Box, the Cardinals Club, and the Cardinals Dugout, as well as
    other unique areas in the ballpark.

Aspiring athletes can swing away like a big league ballplayer in the Family
Pavilion at Busch Stadium. Open before and during Cardinals baseball games,
the attraction offers a batting challenge, pitching areas and other interactive
activities. Fred Bird, the Cardinals mascot, roams the ballpark to interact with
kids during their baseball adventure.

•   TOUR: Tour the Cardinals' home and host of the All-Star Game in 2009.
    The tour lasts one hour and provides an in-depth look at the Cardinals'
    home. Tours normally include the following stops: a Party Room, the
    Redbird Club, the Press Box, the Cardinals Club, and the Cardinals
    Dugout, as well as other unique areas in the ballpark. One of baseball's
    all-time greats, Hall of Famer Stan "The Man" Musical, played his entire
    career for the St. Louis Cardinals. Thirty-seven Cardinals plus the late

broadcaster Jack Buck and former Cards' broadcaster Harry Caray have been inducted into the Baseball Hall of Fame at Cooperstown, New York.

- BUDGET NOTE: It's a steal! The St. Louis Cardinals and KTRS 550-AM, the team's flagship radio station, offer "First Pitch Tickets." Starting at 9:00am on a regular season game day, the first 275 customers at the Busch Stadium Eighth Street ticket window can purchase a voucher entitling the fan to receive two tickets at $5.50 each later that day. The tickets -- a virtual grab bag of locations returned to the ticket office by Cardinals players, the visiting club, sponsors and others - may be for anywhere within the ballpark, from field or terrace level to standing room only. Ten minutes before game time - at 7:00pm sharp for a 7:10pm. game -- fans will be asked to produce their picture I.D. and voucher at the "First Pitch Tickets" sign at Gate 5 to claim their tickets and enter Busch Stadium. Tickets will be in sealed envelopes and distributed on a completely random basis.

THE OLD COURTHOUSE

11 North 4th Street St. Louis 63102

- ☐ Phone: (314) 655-1700 **www.nps.gov/jeff/planyourvisit/och.htm**
- ☐ Hours: Daily 8:00am-4:30pm. Extended summer hours.
- ☐ Admission: FREE.

St. Louis' Old Courthouse, now part of the Jefferson National Expansion Memorial, was the site of the first two trials of the Dred Scott anti-slavery case, in 1847 and 1850, which led to the Supreme Court decision that helped ignite the Civil War. Your kids might be familiar with the names from U.S. History class, but have you been to the courthouse where Scott, a slave, sat after he successfully sued to earn his freedom? Walk the halls where the Scotts' battle for freedom began (roughly 300 other people sued to earn their freedom at the courthouse, too), view a display about the trial or watch a video featuring an interview with one of the Scotts' descendants. The east steps facing the Gateway Arch were the scenes of slave auctions before the war and where, in 1859, Grant freed his only slave. If your kids have studied the slavery issues leading to the Civil War, they will find this particularly interesting and moving to be walking along the same hallways as the courageous slaves did years ago.

CITY MUSEUM
701 North 15th Street **St. Louis** 63103

☐ Phone: (314) 231-CITY (2489) **www.citymuseum.org**

☐ Hours: Monday-Thursday 9:00am-5:00pm, Friday-Saturday 9:00am-1:00am, Sunday 11:00am-5:00pm. Closed Monday & Tuesday in winter.

☐ Admission: $12.00 General (ages 3+). Additional fee for World Aquarium and The Roof.

☐ Educators: grade appropriate questions and games are found under: Group Activities/Educational. FREEBIES: Coloring Pages and Scavenger Hunts are on the Educational page at the bottom. Print them off before you arrive.

See the world's only completely recycled museum when you visit the art-filled playground of City Museum -- an intriguing mix of history, architecture and whimsy. You know you're there when you walk up to the building and see the bus...dangling about three stories above your head. Or, the giant pencil poking out of another wall of the exterior. Anyway, inside is even more bizarre than outside. With endless places for kids to climb and play, these artsy structures are irresistible to children. Everything here is made from recycled materials so nothing is uniform or "new." You'll see kids race through Enchanted Caves as parents try to keep up behind them. The City Express departs at the whim of the engineer and at the request of the kiddie crowd. At one-eighth the size of a regular locomotive, the ride takes passengers under a bridge, through a cosmic tunnel and to an even tinier train. Check out the World Aquarium. Sharks, stingrays, reptiles and fish of all kinds, from almost every ocean, sea, lake and river in the world, are found here. Next, swim through thousands of rubber balls, write your name with the world's largest pencil or climb through MonstroCity, a monstrous montage of monkey bars and unusually placed objects along the way. Swinging on a bridge hundreds of feet above the pavement was about when we (the parents) gave out and just followed the shortest path back down to the ground level benches to observe.

SCOTT JOPLIN HOUSE STATE HISTORIC SITE

2658A Delmar **St. Louis** 63103

- ☐ Phone: (314) 340-5790 **www.mostateparks.com/scottjoplin.htm**
- ☐ Admission: The Missouri state park system does not charge entrance fees. However, there are fees associated with camping, lodging, tours, museums and certain special events.
- ☐ Tours: Tuesday-Saturday tours are offered every hour between 10:00am-4:00pm. (February - last tour at 3:00pm). Monday-Saturday tours are offered every hour between 10:00am-4:00pm (March-October - last tour at 3:00pm).
- ☐ The site is closed November-January. Tour fees are $4.00 adult, $2.50 child (6-12).

While fellow African-American G.W. Carver was a pioneer in the field of science, Scott Joplin was a visionary in music. His ability to combine musical styles earned him the moniker "The King of Ragtime." The sounds of Joplin's music still fill the air at this home, where Joplin lived with his wife, Belle, and produced some of his better-known works, including the "The Entertainer" (featured in the movie, "The Sting," Oscar winner for Best Picture of 1973). Lit by gaslight, and appropriately furnished for 1902, the Joplin flat where many ragtime classics were composed awaits your visit. An antique player piano plays as you enter the modest walk-up flat for a tour. To create a feel for the times, the park has recreated what they call the new Rosebud Café, which interprets a café or music hall that would have been in existence during Joplin's era. You can sneak a peak in there. The music makes your toes tap, doesn't it?

ST LOUIS BLUES HOCKEY

1401 Clark Avenue (Scottrade Center, downtown) **St. Louis** 63103

- ☐ **http://blues.nhl.com/**

The St. Louis Blues are the only NHL team to appear in the playoffs every year during the 1980s and 1990s. Since joining the National Hockey League in 1967, the Blues have missed the Stanley Cup Playoffs only five times. Today's team takes to the ice at the 20,000-seat Scottrade Center in downtown St. Louis.

UNION STATION

1820 Market Street (Downtown) **St. Louis** 63103

☐ Phone: (314) 421-6655 **www.stlouisunionstation.com**
☐ Hours: Monday-Saturday 10:00am-9:00pm, Sunday 10:00am-6:00pm.

This landmark features more than 80 shopping venues along with a food court, street performers, paddleboats rentals on artificial lake behind station, indoor glow-dark putt putt, and a self-guided tour brochure of The Best of St. Louis memorabilia. Most of the stores and restaurants are unique and specialized - great gift shopping and fun souvenirs.

SOULARD MARKET

730 Carroll Street **St. Louis** 63104

☐ Phone: (314) 622-4180 **http://stlouis.missouri.org/citygov/soulardmarket**
or **www.soulardmarket.com**
☐ Hours: Wednesday-Friday 8:00am-5:00pm, Saturday 6:00am-5:00pm.

This open-air market, with more than 90 vendors, has been serving the St. Louis area for more than 200 years. Vendors provide fresh produce, meats, fish, poultry, baked goods and spices. There's also craft booths on Saturdays. Kids might like to try some new types of foods at the many cafes serving snacks and meals.

CROWN CANDY KITCHEN

St. Louis - *1401 Saint Louis Avenue (Old North Street neighborhood) 63106. Phone: (314) 621-9650* **http://crowncandykitchen.net/** *Hours: Daily opens at 10:30am-closing at 8:00 or 10:00pm. Sundays 11:00am-6:00pm. Crown Candy's menu features not only includes their delicious 1904 World's Fair style sundaes, but lunch and dinner options for any occasion. Whether you're in the mood for a thick stacked sandwich, chili, a giant gourmet frank, a salad or a bowl of soup - and don't forget about their desserts - exquisite selection of candy, malts and shakes. Crown Candy Kitchen also makes chocolates, including chocolate hash—marshmallows covered in chocolate and topped with pecans. Think you can drink 5 malts or shakes in 30 minutes? If you do, you, and others (Man vs. Food) get them free (plus a t-shirt). And the average price for most everything you can order? About $5.00.*

BOB KRAMER'S MARIONNETTE THEATER

4143 Laclede Avenue (Located in the heart of Saint Louis's Central West
End, just minutes west of the Arch) **St. Louis** 63108

☐   Phone: (314) 531-3313 **www.kramersmarionnettes.com**
☐   Hours: Showtimes are Monday-Saturday 10:00am and 1:00pm, Sunday
      1:00pm.
☐   Admisson: $12.00 adult, $10.00 senior & child (1-12). Holiday shows slightly
      higher. Reservations are required for all shows.

Tour the workshop, get an one hour demonstration of puppetry arts and
manufacturing and then watch a performance. Your family will learn all kinds
of things about the marionettes, how they are made, the process in which the
parts are created, assembled, and what all is required to go into a show. The
shows are a lot of fun to watch. The stories are wholesome, old-fashioned
tales like "*Peter And The Wolf*", "*Hansel And Gretel*", and "*Toyland*". The
neatest thing that happens is when their mouths open and they start to sing.
It very unique to see a wooden puppet sing as though it was on a Broadway
stage. Kids are mesmerized.

EARTHWAYS CENTER

3617 Grandel Square **St. Louis** 63108

☐   Phone: (314) 577-0220 **www.EarthWaysCenter.org**
☐   Admission: $3.00 general (13+). Children Age 12 & Under FREE.
☐   Tours: Third Saturday & Sunday of each month at 11:00am, Noon, 1:00pm,
      2:00pm. Tours sometimes have a specific theme. Call or visit website for
      details.

The Missouri Botanical Garden acquired the EarthWays Home and made
it the Gateway Center for Resource Efficiency headquarters in November
of 2000. The EarthWays Home, a three-story Victorian residence built in
1885 was renovated in 1994 to showcase practical demonstrations of energy
efficient systems, recycled products and waste reduction practices. Guided
tours of this rehabbed Victorian residence showcase affordable green options
to reduce the use of natural resources in your home. Many of these ideas you
can take home and apply to your home - even kids leave with ideas of ways
to help.

THE SHELDON

3648 Washington Blvd **St. Louis** 63108

☐   Phone: (314) 533-9900 **www.thesheldon.org**

The Sheldon introduces young people to jazz, folk, classical, blues and the American musical in weekday morning programs for school groups. Teacher packets are available for each program, for use before or after the concert, and tickets are just $3.50 each. Concerts begin at 10:00am unless noted. Call The Sheldon Education Coordinator at (314) 533-9900 for reservations or more information.

TED DREWES FROZEN CUSTARD

St. Louis - 6726 Chippewa (Rte 66) 63109. www.teddrewes.com. Phone: (314) 481-2652 Note: Across the street from Ted Drewes is the Donut Drive In, a Route 66 icon still serving up cakey glazed donuts. This is a St. Louis tradition of arguably the best custard in the world and a sweet stop along Route 66. Famed concrete shakes are so thick they're served upside down to prove the point. First timers get quite a start from that one! On any given day you might find wedding parties, television crews, tour groups, classic car clubs, journalists and visitors from all 50 states waiting in line at the Mother Road's most famous refreshment stop. Opened in 1929, Ted Drewes has served frosty "concretes" to generations of hungry travelers and long lines of loyal St. Louisans. The frozen vanilla custard shakes are blended with fruits, nuts, candies and other flavors and served so concrete-thick they're handed to customers upside down. Sample an "All Shook Up" blended with peanut butter and bananas in honor of Elvis or have a little "Cardinal Sin" mixed with tart cherries and hot fudge. Bunny-cretes-a carrot cake concoction-show up around Easter and it's not fall unless you have a Pumpkin-crete, which is custard blended with a slice of pumpkin pie. Don't let the crowds scare you away. Lines, which are longest on summer nights after Cardinals baseball games or theatre performances in Forest Park, move at an amazing pace.

FOREST PARK

Government Drive **St. Louis** 63110

☐   Phone: (314) 289-5300

Introduce the kids to Broadway musical theatre...for free. No need to spend cold cash on high-end show tickets to learn that little Annie wants to leave before intermission. Take advantage of the first come, first served free seats - there are 1,200 available for every performance -- at The Muny in Forest Park, the nation's oldest and largest outdoor theatre. Each summer, the 12,000-seat theatre offers a seven-week season of musicals starring nationally known performers, from late June until early August. Shuttle bug around park. Biking is fun on the 7.5-mile path around the park's perimeter, and the kids can pedal or paddle small boats around the park's refurbished lakes from the Boat House. In winter, the whole family can lace up their skates and take to the ice at the park's Steinberg Rink, and sledding is permitted down Art Hill when Mother Nature provides the white stuff. A favorite is climbing on the whimsical giant turtle sculptures in Turtle Playground.

GREAT FOREST PARK BALLOON RACE

St. Louis - *Forest Park - Balloon Glow on Friday night, Balloon Race on Saturday. FREE. www.greatforestparkballoonrace.com. Central Field in Forest Park. (mid-September weekend)*

MISSOURI BOTANICAL GARDEN

4344 Shaw Blvd. **St. Louis** 63110

- ☐ Phone: (314) 577-5100 **www.mobot.org**
- ☐ Hours: Daily 9:00am-5:00pm.
- ☐ Admission: $8.00 adult (13+) Age 12 and under FREE. (Children's Garden open April-October) $5.00 (ages 3-12). Adults no extra charge for Children's Garden. Resident discounts available.
- ☐ Tours: narrated tram tours offered April thru October for $3.00; guided walking tours are offered year-round and are included with garden admission.

Stroll through 79 acres of landscaped display gardens, indoor conservatories and historic structures. Check out these garden scenes in particular:

- CLIMATRON - The Climatron at the Missouri Botanical Garden, built in 1960, was the world's first climate-controlled geodesic dome designed as a greenhouse. Today, it houses a re-created rain forest filled with plants and uses E-feron glass to help it use solar energy more efficiently.

- JAPANESE GARDEN - Largest Japanese Garden in North America.

- <u>CHILDREN'S GARDEN</u> - Wander through kid-sized plantings that you can re-create back home or get temporarily "lost" inside the Garden's tall Victorian maze.

CHINESE CULTURE DAYS

St. Louis - *Missouri Botanical Garden. Annual Chinese Culture Days celebration at the Missouri Botanical Garden. The event features a Grand Parade with 70-foot dancing dragon, martial arts, Chinese calligraphy, painting and authentic regional cuisine. Enjoy T'ai Chi and tea tasting in the Grigg Nanjing Friendship Garden, where special tours focus on the symbolism of many plant species and architectural details. Admission. (second or third weekend in May)*

GARDENLAND EXPRESS

St. Louis - *Missouri Botanical Garden. One of St. Louis's most beloved holiday traditions returns with Gardenland Express, the Garden's annual holiday flower and train show. Admission. (Thanksgiving time thru New Years Day).*

ST. LOUIS ART MUSEUM
1 Fine Arts Drive (Forest Park) **St. Louis** 63110

- ☐ Phone: (314) 721-0072 **www.slam.org**
- ☐ Hours: Tuesday-Sunday 10:00 am–5:00pm, Friday open until 9:00pm.
- ☐ Admission: FREE. Admission to featured exhibitions vary.

This art museum prides itself on having more than 30,000 works from nearly every culture and time - Oceanic, pre-Columbian, Chinese, 19th-20th century European and American, and a large collection of 20th century German paintings. Kids always look for the small Egyptian room with the authentic mummy. Artsy families take note of free, hands-on art activities, family tours with complimentary guidebooks, artist demonstrations and performances every Sunday afternoon from 1:00pm-4:00pm. The family-friendly theme changes monthly.

ST. LOUIS SCIENCE CENTER
5050 Oakland Avenue St. Louis 63110

- Phone: (314) 289-4400 **www.slsc.org**
- Hours: Monday-Saturday 9:30am-4:30pm, Sunday 11:30am-4:30pm.
- Admission: General admission for many exhibits, FREE. Fees for some special rooms and shows.
- Miscellaneous: A four-story Omnimax Theater and a Planetarium are on the premises. Showtimes and fees are posted online.

The Saint Louis Science Center in Forest Park brings the world of learning to life with hands-on activities. The attraction has re-done its Ecology and Environment Gallery and transformed it into an informative and exciting playground where kids can learn about the Earth's biologic and geologic past. Visitors of all ages can explore the "gene scene" and cast their vote on the ethical issues of genetic engineering, or build a replica of the Gateway Arch. Get a feel for what it's like to live, work and play on the International Boeing Space Station, then use radar guns to clock the speed of cars zooming beneath the enclosed bridge spanning I-64. Here at the St. Louis home of the X-Prize, the James S. McDonnell Planetarium offers the state-of-the-art Boeing Space Station where kids can see what it is like to live and work in space. Watch an OMNIMAX® large screen movie, visit the Exploradome to see traveling exhibits, touch a tornado or be amazed at the roaring, life-size animatronic dinosaurs. This science center includes more than 700 hands-on exhibits and the Life Science Lab. The Discovery Room is an area just for kids aged 3-7 to explore a range of interactives with magnets, a water table, and dress up at the medical area or native American area. FREE 10-minute science demo shows run every hour.

ST. LOUIS ZOO
One Government Drive St. Louis 63110

- Phone: (314) 781-0900 or (800) 966-8877 **www.stlzoo.org**
- Hours: Daily 9:00am-5:00pm. Extended summer hours.
- Admission: FREE, but there are charges to do things like visit the children's zoo, ride the carousel or ride the train. Parking is $11.00 at the Zoo's North Lot on Government Drive and South Lot on Wells Drive.
- Miscellaneous: there are many cafes throughout the property, some sit down. Educators: Teacher Lesson Plans: www.stlzoo.org/education/forteachers/ teacherlessonplans.htm

The St. Louis Zoo is home to over 18,000 exotic animals; many are rare and endangered. Visit Fragile Forest, Penguin and Puffin Coast and the Children's Zoo. Catch a Sea Lion Show, pet a stingray or ride the Zooline Railroad. The more interactive St. Louis Zoo offers kids the chance to pet guinea pigs and goats and see naked mole rats up-close and personal. There's a large colony of meerkats -- which the kids may recognize from the TV show "Meerkat Manor" or perhaps the animated tale, "The Lion King," and an active family of small Fennec foxes with huge ears. A popular stop for zoo visitors is the Fragile Forest, a habitat for great apes that provides a refuge for endangered orangutans and chimpanzees. Don't miss the Cypress Swamp exhibit, which is housed in the refurbished 1904 World's Fair flight cage, the Penguin & Puffin Coast and the Conservation Carousel as well. At the Zoo's River's Edge, you can get an eye-to-eye view of river-dwelling hippos and the elephant family.

The Children's Zoo also has a "Just Like Me" play area where children can climb a giant spider web or dig like an aardvark in a sandbox. The indoor space is divided into desert, forest, water and backyard, and kids can crawl through the Frog Surround, climb a cool tree house or "drive" a jeep through a savannah.

The early bird at the Saint Louis Zoo rides the Conservation Carousel for free. Arrive at the Zoo between 8:00am-9:00am for a free spin aboard one of the colorful carousel's 64 beautiful hand-carved wooden animal figures. Hop off the Carousel and head to the cheerful Children's Zoo for complimentary admission through 9:00am.

DID YOU KNOW ? The Zoo, a pioneer in the use of open enclosures, placing animals in natural environments without bars, is again on the cutting edge of technology with the "The Living World" education center. "The Living World" is the first center to use live animals and high technology together to teach about the diversity of life.

MISSOURI HISTORY MUSEUM
5700 Lindell Boulevard (at Lindell and DeBaliviere in Forest Park)
St. Louis 63112

- ☐ Phone: (314) 746-4599 **www.mohistory.org**
- ☐ Hours Daily 10:00am-5:00pm. Open until 8:00pm on Tuesday.
- ☐ Admission: General admission to the Museum is FREE. Some fees are charged for special exhibits.
- ☐ Miscellaneous: Restaurant and shop are on-site.

This museum invites guests to participate in the past, present and future. The museum traces the early history of the state of Missouri and its major commercial center, St. Louis, through a variety of exhibits including "Seeking St. Louis". Check out exhibits on everything from Charles "Lucky" Lindbergh to more artifacts from explorers Lewis & Clark and a look at the storied 1904 World's Fair. You'll learn how St. Louis' McDonnell Douglas Corporation (now Boeing) designed and built the first space capsule. The Eads Bridge (nearby going over the Mississippi) was the first arched steel truss bridge in the world (naysayers said it was impossible) and the engineer who built it also built the St. Louis, the first ironclad boat built in America. This is a great place for people who are interested in American History. The Forest Park Metrolink Station is close to this museum.

MINIATURE MUSEUM OF GREATER ST. LOUIS
4746 Gravois Avenue **St. Louis** 63116

- ☐ Phone: (314) 832-7790 **www.miniaturemuseum.org**
- ☐ Hours: Wednesday-Saturday 11:00am-4:00pm, Sunday 1:00pm-4:00pm.
- ☐ Admission: $5.00 adult, $4.00 senior (62+) & student (13-18), $2.00 child (2-12). Discount coupons available on website.

The Miniature Museum of Greater St. Louis is home to permanent and rotating exhibits of dolls and dollhouse furniture. The dollhouses and miniature replicas include some historical scenes, a shopping center, the "old Cathedral," a Trading Post, a 1927 Armory, roomboxes and vignettes of all eras. What kids may notice most is the miniature figures are posed as if they are really lounging watching TV in the living room, shopping at the local grocer, eating in the kitchen or mess hall, or exchanging goods in the middle of the wilderness. A creative human approach to displaying toys.

MUSEUM OF TRANSPORTATION
2967 Barrett Station Road St. Louis 63122

☐ Phone: (314) 965-6885 **http://transportmuseumassociation.org/**

☐ Hours: Monday-Saturday 9:00am-5:00pm, Sunday 11:00am-5:00pm. (May-Early September). Tuesday-Saturday 9:00am-4:00pm, Sunday 11:00am-4:00pm (early September- April).

☐ Admission: $6.00 adult, $4.00 senior & child (5-12).

☐ Tours: Public guided tours are available on days of operation according to season and on Sundays. Summer tours are available Monday - Saturday at 10:00 am, 12:00 noon & 2:00pm and on Sundays at 12:00 noon & 2:00pm. Winter tours are available Tuesday - Saturday at 10:00am and on Sunday at 1:00pm. Children's Tours: June- early August, Wednesdays at 10:15am. Appropriate for Pre-K - 2nd Grade. There is lots of walking. No reservation needed!

☐ FREEBIES: Ask for the I Spy Scavenger Hunt at the front desk. Educators: this online page has several different games or activities that quiz transportation history knowledge: http://transportmuseumassociation.org/classroom.html

Get your kicks on Route 66 by visiting St. Louis' Museum of Transportation. It's home to more than 300 moving vehicles including locomotives, streetcars, aircraft, test cars, and automobiles. Many of the historic transportation pieces housed at the museum were experimental vehicles in their time, and several are the only examples remaining in existence. The passenger car collection includes the 1964 Bobby Darin "Dream Car" and a 1901 St. Louis car - a four-seat, single or two-cylinder engine vehicle with tiller steering. Another display features a portion of the Coral Court Motel - St. Louis' infamous Route 66 rendezvous spot that offered drive-in units. The museum includes a miniature train ride for the kids.

GRANT'S FARM
10501 Gravois Road St. Louis 63123

☐ Phone: (314) 843-1700 **www.grantsfarm.com**

☐ Hours: Saturday 9:00am-3:30pm, Sunday 9:30am-3:30pm (mid-April - early May). Tuesday-Friday 9:00am-3:30pm, Saturday 9:00am-4:00pm, Sunday 9:30am-4:00pm. Open Summer Holiday Mondays 9:00am-4:00pm (early May - mid-August). Friday 9:30am-2:30pm, Saturday & Sunday 9:30am-3:30pm (mid-August - October). Times above reflect when park entrance is open. Park closes 90 minutes after park entrance closes.

GRANT'S FARM (cont.)

☐   Admission: The admission to Grant's Farm, tram rides and all shows is
     FREE, but there is an $11.00 parking charge.

At the onset of the Civil War in 1861 Grant reported to Army headquarters
in St. Louis, beginning a wartime career that eventually would lead to the
White House. Although Ulysses S. Grant was not a farmer, he, at one time,
attempted to become a civilian and work normal jobs for a time. He soon
learned he was better suited for the military. Today the ex-President's two-
story cabin is on display at Grant's Farm, an animal preserve on the estate of
the Busch brewing family of St. Louis. A fence made of Civil War gun barrels
surrounds a portion of the estate near the cabin.

The real draw here is the farm animals. The property houses more than 1000
animals representing more than 100 different species from six continents. See
baby Clydesdales, watch amazing dogs and enjoy bird and elephant behavior
shows at Grant's Farm from April through October. A trackless train carries
families around the farm's wildlife preserve and stops at the petting zoo.
Several times each day (summer) or weekend (fall & spring), the farm hosts
Education or Encounter shows - many with elephants. Horse-lovers will be
drawn to the Clydesdales. There are also plenty of deer and zebra roaming
the grassland.

AMERICA'S INCREDIBLE PIZZA COMPANY

*St. Louis - 5254 S Lindbergh Blvd 63126. www.ipcstlouis.com. Here you'll find an
incredible all-you-can-eat buffet featuring fresh pizza, pasta, soup, salad and the
best desserts in town. Enjoy your meal in one of our four themed dining rooms: the
Gymnasium, the 50's Diner, the Family Room, and the Starlite Drive-In complete with
old movies showing. Then, hop into some fun at The Fairgrounds, where you'll find
indoor Go-Karts, Bumper Cars, Glow-In-The-Dark Mini Golf, Mini Bowling, and a
huge Game Room where you can redeem tickets for incredible prizes. All of this is
completely indoors so there's no fear of poor weather ruining the day. Open daily for
lunch and dinner until dark.*

SUSON PARK

6059 Wells Road **St. Louis** 63128

☐ Phone: (314) 638-2100 **www.co.st-louis.mo.us/parks/suson.html**

☐ Hours: Daily 10:30am-5:00pm (April-September). Closes at 3:00pm (October - March).

Country living is just around the corner at the Suson Park animal farm display. Most breeds of farm animals are represented for urban dwellers to see and enjoy, from the draft horses that helped plow our soil to examples of the modern cattle breeds. A lake on the property is available for fishing. Free admission. (goats, pigs and chickens - cows and horses are in the barn on weekends only).

OLD CHAIN OF ROCKS BRIDGE

10950 Riverview Drive (just below I-270, north of downtown St. Louis)
St. Louis 63137

☐ **www.trailnet.org/p_ocorb.php**

☐ Hours: Daily 9:00am-dusk.

☐ Note: Follow the city's Riverfront Trail, a hiking and biking path, from the Old Chain of Rocks Bridge to the Gateway Arch.

The Old Chain of Rocks Bridge, at 5,353 feet long, is one of the world's longest bicycle and pedestrian bridges. The Bridge spans the Mississippi River and provides a vital link in the bi-state trail system, connecting to the St. Louis Riverfront Trail in Missouri and the MCT Confluence Trail in Illinois. The Bridge, once part of the beloved Route 66, has a rich history and is on the National Register of Historic Places. Located north of downtown, the bridge was Route 66's original crossing over the Mississippi River at St. Louis. The span, which is one of the longest pedestrian and biking bridges in the world, is open to visitors every day. From the bridge, you'll see stunning views of downtown St. Louis and the city's whimsical castle-like water intake towers from high over the Mississippi. Route 66 themed bump-out, full-span pedestrian lighting, Missouri-side restrooms, benches, bike racks and interpretive plaques. Parking available on either side.

EAGLE DAYS AT THE OLD CHAIN OF ROCKS BRIDGE

St. Louis - *Old Chain Of Rocks Bridge. This FREE public program gives visitors the opportunity to view wintering bald eagles in a natural habitat. Educational eagle program repeated every 20 minutes; Viewing scopes on the Bridge permit close-ups of eagles Lewis & Clark re-enactors interact with the public and acquaint visitors with aspects of their 1804-06 expedition, the Corps of Discovery; View St. Louis area birds through hands-on exhibits by St. Louis Audubon volunteers; Get your photo taken in the replica of an eagle's nest. Bring your binoculars and dress to stay warm. Note: Programming is at both Bridge entrances and in the middle of the Bridge. It is about a 1/2-mile walk to the middle of the Bridge for assisted eagle viewing and programming in the warming tent.*

THE HILL

The Loop, along the St. Louis Walk of Fame **St. Louis** 63139

          www.hill2000.org

- **RIGAZZI'S RESTAURANT** - Toasted ravioli - sample the appetizer that originated on the Hill.

- **BLUEBERRY HILL** - www.blueberryhill.com/menus. Some more toasted ravioli but they also have Cheddar Cheese Balls as an appetizer. Locals name it as the place for burgers - the famous 7oz hamburger with cheddar (soft spread). Their burgers avg. under $6.00 and nothing is over $9.00. In addition to its reputation for food and music, the restaurant is known as home to the world's best jukebox and eclectic collections that range from Chuck Berry's guitar to Howdy Doody items and vintage lunchboxes. After you place your order, play some pinball or video games.

ST. LOUIS STORYTELLING FESTIVAL

St. Louis - *University of Missouri - St. Louis. http://stlstorytellingfestival.org/index. php/about. 30-40 pro storytellers converge from across nation to perform in various locations around area. FREE. (first weekend in May).*

CELEBRATE ST. LOUIS - FAIR ST. LOUIS

St. Louis - *Downtown by the Arch. http://celebratestlouis.org/Celebrate/index.cfm. This annual Fourth of July event has a Parade, Air Show, K-Town Kids Zone, Local and national entertainment and Nationally recognized fireworks displays each night. FREE. (July 3rd and 4th). Following the Fourth of July fesKviKes, the celebraKon will conKnue throughout the month of July with the LIVE on the Levee concert series. A complete line-up of entertainment for both Fair Saint Louis and LIVE on the Levee will be announced in May.*

ST. LOUIS HOLIDAY MAGIC

St. Louis - *The America's Center convention complex. Celebrate the holidays at Holiday Magic. The family-friendly show features unique shopping, dazzling holiday lights and decorations, indoor carnival rides and live entertainment. Admission. (first weekend in December).*

FAUST PARK

15185 Olive Blvd. (Located one mile north of Highway 40/64)
St. Louis (Chesterfield) 63017

☐   Phone: (314) 615-8328 **www.co.st-louis.mo.us/parks/Faust_home.html, www.stlouiscarousel.com; www.butterflyhouse.org**

This is the home of three attractions for kids: the BUTTERFLY HOUSE, the HISTORICAL VILLAGE and the ST. LOUIS CAROUSEL. While the Historical Village typically is only open to tour groups, the buildings can be viewed from the outside using a free self-guided tour booklet available at the Seed Visitor Center. The Butterfly House has more than a 1,000 live, tropical butterflies flying freely in the 8,000-square-foot glass conservatory. Watch a butterfly emerge from a chrysalis, visit the outdoor Butterfly Garden, or enjoy indoor insect exhibits. (open year-round for $4.00-$6.00 per person). Next, take a ride on a fully restored, hand-carved 1920s Dentzel carousel with 67 animals and two chariots. ($1.00/ride, open February-December).

DID YOU KNOW ? If you wear bright colors, the resident butterflies are more likely to land on you for a quick, up-close experience.

SWING-A-ROUND FUN TOWN

335 Skinker Lane St. Louis (Fenton) 63026

- Phone: (636) 349-7077 www.swing-a-round.com
- Hours: Monday-Thursday 10:00am-9:00pm, Friday-Saturday 10:00am-11:00pm, Sunday 11:00am-9:00pm.
- Admission: Pay per activity with prices ranging from $1.00-$6.50. Discount packages available.

Feel the need for speed? Swing-A-Round Fun Town is stocked with Go-Karts, bumper boats, batting cages and an arcade, and miniature golf pros will like the links at the amusement center. Fun centers are located in St. Charles and other neighboring cities, too.

CHALLENGER LEARNING CENTER - ST. LOUIS

205 Brotherton Lane (one mile north of I-70 off Florissant Road - next to McCluer South-Berkeley High School) St. Louis (Ferguson) 63135

- Phone: (314) 521-6205 www.clcstlouis.org
- Hours: Public programs are available and hours are subject to change. Please call or visit website for most updated schedule.
- Admission: $15.00 for public programs when available.
- Tours: Brief training session, 2-hour mission, recommended for ages 11 and up.

The center provides hands-on space science education programs and features a replica space station and Mission Control center. Participants partake in a simulated space mission. Advance reservations required; check online calendar.

BIG FOOT 4 X 4 INC.

6311 N. Lindbergh Blvd St. Louis (Hazelwood) 63042

- Phone: (314) 731-2822 www.bigfoot4x4.com
- Hours: (Store) Monday-Friday 9:00am-5:00pm, Saturday 9:00am-1:00pm.
- Admission: FREE.

The BIGFOOT® monster trucks have thrilled millions of fans in stadiums and arenas around the world, on television and in the movies. You can explore the world of "The Original Monster Truck®" where it all started, at BIGFOOT 4x4 Inc., the "Home of BIGFOOT," in St. Louis Missouri. The showroom also houses some truly great Bigfoot souvenirs, apparel and collectibles. Visiting Bigfoot 4x4 Inc. is an adventure in itself and includes a tour of the factory or the repair shop that makes the infamous monster trucks. It features more than 20 years of monster truck history and displays the world's largest collection of monster truck memorabilia. Before you leave, be sure to get a group picture standing in the wheel of just one monster machine.

ST. LOUIS MILLS MALL - SPORTSTREET
5555 St. Louis Mills Blvd St. Louis (Hazelwood) 63042

☐ Phone: (314) 227-5900 **www.stlouismills.com**

St. Louis Mills is a retail and entertainment destination that offers a dynamic mix of value-priced shopping and interactive experiences, unique to St. Louis. With 12 anchor stores, including Missouri's only Cabela's, and over 160 specialty retailers, restaurants and entertainment venues, a mini express trackless train, plus a children's play area, there's something for everyone.

* SKATEPARK - www.plan-nine.net
* ICE ZONE - www.icezone.com
* NASCAR SPEEDPARK - www.nascarspeedpark.com
* PUTTING EDGE - www.putting-edge.com

MAGIC HOUSE: ST. LOUIS CHILDREN'S MUSEUM
516 S. Kirkwood Road (one mile north of I-44) St. Louis (Kirkwood) 63122

☐ Phone: (314) 822-8900 **www.magichouse.org**
☐ Hours: Monday-Saturday 9:30am-5:30pm. Friday until 9:00pm. Sunday 11:00am-5:30pm (Memorial Day-Labor Day). Tuesday-Thursday Noon-5:30pm, Friday Noon-9:00pm, Saturday 9:30am-5:30pm, Sunday 11:00am-5:30pm. (Labor Day-Memorial Day).
☐ Admission: $8.50 (ages 1+).

Hands-on, the Magic House, St. Louis Children's Museum is a three-story facility set in a lovely Victorian home that tests minds and imaginations with plenty of "please touch" activities for everyone from babies to adults. Visit The Magic House to transform your silhouette into a kaleidoscope of color; lift yourself with a pulley; freeze your shadow on a wall; experiment in a water playground; make a three-dimensional impression of yourself; and zoom down a three-story slide! The static electricity ball is a favorite. Kids touch it and it makes their hair stand on end (they can even take a funny picture for a $3.00 fee). The popular attraction, which features indoor and outdoor play and learning areas, also hosts Seasonal favorites, such as Toddler Traffic Town and Sandcastle Beach, and traveling exhibits are always popular at the ever-changing Magic House. We like that each station is simple and clear and the settings for role-playing are very realistic. Formatted best for curious kids ages 1-11.

POWDER VALLEY CONSERVATION NATURE CENTER

11715 Cragwold Road (off I-44 at Geyer, then make the angled-back left onto Cragwold and follow the long winding road until you're parallel to I-270) **St. Louis (Kirkwood) 63122**

- ☐ Phone: (314) 301-1500 **http://mdc.mo.gov/areas/cnc/powder/**
- ☐ Hours: (Trails) 8:00am-6:00pm, open longer in summer. (Building) Tuesday-Saturday 8:00am-5:00pm. Gift shop closes at 4:30pm.

Most families start at the Nature Center. Kids wander around the displays about nature and bugs. They also have a big bee hive. Live animals include turtles and snakes. Three hiking trails are all good for the novice; they're paved, so you can wear your street shoes, and they start from the parking lot. Sloping rocky woods are a haven of beautiful wildflowers, towering trees and tangled vines.

LAUMEIER SCULPTURE PARK

12580 Rott Road **St. Louis (Kirkwood) 63127**

- ☐ Phone: (314) 615-5278 **www.laumeier.com**
- ☐ Hours: (Park) Daily, 8:00am to sunset with the exception of Christmas Day and the Thursday before the annual Art Fair in early May. (Museum Gallery & Shops) Tuesday-Friday 10:00am-5:00pm, Saturday-Sunday Noon-5:00pm.
- ☐ Tours: During regular Museum Shop hours visitors can rent iPods and take our new audio tour that highlights the collection. Also From Spring to Fall, free docent-led tours are available the first and third Sundays of each month from May-October. One-hour tours depart from the Museum Shop at 2:00pm.

Head west for Laumeier Sculpture Park for free art of another kind. The open air "museum" features a fascinating - and sometimes whimsical - world-class collection of more than 70 modern sculptures. The 105-acre campus includes indoor galleries and exhibitions of paintings, ceramics, glass and photography related to the outdoor sculpture program, as well as an outdoor garden. Each August the park brings in tons of sand for fantasy sand castle. Mid-December is winter solstice with fire/ice sculptures.

JEFFERSON BARRACKS HISTORIC PARK

345 North Road (End of South Broadway south of Kingston in south St. Louis County) **St. Louis (Lemay)** 63125

☐   Phone: (314) 638-2100   **www.co.st-louis.mo.us/parks/j-b.html**
☐   Hours: (grounds) 8:00am to one half hour past sunset, except when reservations are issued. (Museum buildings) open from Noon-4:00pm Wednesday-Sunday.

South of St. Louis, Jefferson Barracks was a U.S. Army military post from 1826-1946 and for many years was the most important station on the frontier. As a result, more officers who would become generals of both armies served here before the Civil War than at any other place. The museum buildings date back to the 1850s and the site is now a park operated by St.Louis County and offers a Visitors Center and many historical events.

DID YOU KNOW ? The first successful parachute jump from an airplane took place at St. Louis' Jefferson Barracks in 1912.

WORLD WAR II WEEKEND

St. Louis (Lemay) - *Jefferson Barracks - WWII Weekend is one of the largest and oldest WWII reenactment events in the St. Louis area. It has been held at Jefferson Barracks Park for more than 25 years. This event is hosted by the U.S. 2nd Ranger Infantry Battalion of St. Louis, a unit that is more than 32 years old, to honor all those who have served in the US Armed Forces. There are living history camps daily, containing up to 350 re-enactors with units representing US Rangers, US Airborne, US Armored Forces, US Infantry, Russian Infantry, British Airborne, Canadian YMCA, Canadian RCME, Italian Infantry, German Heer, German SS, German Paratroopers, and German SS Panzer forces. Three battles will be staged. http://2ndrangers.org/ wwii_weekend.php. FREE. (last weekend in April)*

LIVING HISTORY HAYRIDES

St. Louis (Lemay) - *Jefferson Barracks - Jefferson Barracks was a military base from 1826 through 1946. The hayrides will travel through the park, stopping as camps of soldiers from the Revolutionary War, Civil War, and World War II. Re-enactors help you travel through the past. Admission. (May and September weekends)*

MODEL TRAIN EXHIBIT

St. Louis (Lemay) - *Jefferson Barracks - Enjoy this exhibit displaying model trains of several scales, plus military toys. Admission: $2. (Thanksgiving weekend thru New Years)*

PIWACKET CHILDREN'S THEATER

2810 Sutton Blvd. (just south of Manchester Boulevard and approximately one mile west of I-44) **St. Louis (Maplewood)** 63143

- ☐ Phone: (314) 781-8300 **www.piwacket.com**
- ☐ Hours: Vary by performance. Call or see website for current schedule.
- ☐ Admission: $12.00 general.

Housed as the children's wing of the Black Cat Theatre, Piwacket Theatre for Children captivates young audiences with cleverly adapted fairy tales filled with catchy songs, fun dances, colorful costumes, and magical props.

AQUAPORT

2344 McKelvey Road **St. Louis (Maryland Heights)** 63043

- ☐ Phone: (314) 738-2599 **www.marylandheights.com/index.aspx?page=97**
- ☐ Hours: Saturday-Thursday 11:00am-7:00pm, Friday 11:00am-8:00pm (late May - mid-August). Only open on weekends after mid-August.
- ☐ Admission: $15.00 adult (16+), $10.00 youth (4-15). Resident discounts available.

A family fun, four-acre water park that includes six water slides, a lazy river, children's pool, family leisure pool and the Extreme Bowl. Food, refreshments, lockers and free parking available.

THIES FARM & GREENHOUSES

St. Louis (Maryland Heights) - *www.thiesfarm.com. 3120 Maryland Heights Expy. Each fall, this farm transforms itself into Pumpkinland. The farm-based play area entertains little ones with cable gliders, slides, tunnels, obstacle courses, a suspended bridge, petting zoos, a cornfield maze and wagon rides.*

FITZ'S AMERICAN GRILL & BOTTLING CO.

St. Louis (University City) - *6605 Delmar Blvd 63130. Phone: (314) 726-9555 www.FitzsRootBeer.com. Hours: Open daily at 11:00am. Closing will vary between 9:00pm and Midnight depending upon season/day of week. Educators: Field Trips: Tell your teacher about field trips that are now being offered to Fitz's. You and your class can see how root beer is made, learn about the neighborhood, and enjoy an activity that involves the unique St. Louis Walk of Fame. Wednesday, Thursday, Friday mornings by appointment. This is the place where root beer floats rule. Enjoy a meal and watch the bottling process at Fitz's, which began selling its famous root beer at Fitz's Drive-In in 1947. Noted for incredible smoothness and thick, creamy texture, Fitz's Root Beer was served in mugs and quickly became the root beer of choice among St. Louisans. The recipe is a closely guarded secret but they do reveal one secret - they still use pure cane sugar in the formula. Call ahead for bottling schedules. A full menu is offered, from 15 different gourmet hamburgers to delicious salads, pizzas and entrees. Special kids meals and treats are offered. Each Kids Meal is served up in a mini-auto. Restaurant opens daily at 11:00am. Most every plate is under $10.00.*

ULYSSES S. GRANT NATIONAL HISTORIC SITE
7400 Grant Road St. Louis (White Haven) 63123

- Phone: (314) 842-3298 **www.nps.gov/ulsg**
- Hours: Daily 9:00am-5:00pm.
- Admission: Entrance into the site is FREE. Visits inside the Main House are also FREE, however, tickets (time-specific "calling cards") are required, and are available at the Visitor Center.
- Tours: Free interpretive visits to the Main House are usually offered every 30 minutes beginning at 9:30am. Typically the last house visit of the day begins at 4:00pm. Due to preservation and safety concerns, space is limited for each time slot and tickets (which are free, and available at the Visitor Center desk) are required to reserve a place. Be sure to watch the 16-minute introductory film, A Place Called White Haven, shown in the Visitor Center theater.

ULYSSES S. GRANT NATIONAL HISTORIC SITE (cont.)

- ☐ Miscellaneous: Grant's Farm is just down the street. You can park at Grant's Farm, with plenty of parking, and walk to the Ulysses S. Grant NHS via a public walking trail. Educators: Reading History Cards (small lessons) are found here: http://www.nps.gov/ulsg/forteachers/curriculummaterials.htm

The property Grant considered his family home for four decades, White Haven, at the Ulysses S. Grant National Historic Site, commemorates the life, military career and presidency of Grant, as well as his wife, Julia Dent Grant. The 9.65-acre site contains six structures including the main house and a visitor center. There's a short movie to set the scene, a tour guide then gives you an overview about the house and then visitors can make their way around the house and grounds at their leisure. While the house is nice, kids may gravitate to the interactive exhibits in the museum (it's located in the historic stable). The displays really give you the sense he loved family life. Maybe that's because there were so many ups and downs being an important U.S. leader.

DID YOU KNOW ? After his presidency, Grant planned to retire to the home but sold it to pay off a debt just before his death in 1885.

CUIVRE RIVER STATE PARK
678 State Route 147 **Troy** 63379

- ☐ Phone: (636) 528-7247 **www.mostateparks.com/Cuivre.htm**
- ☐ Admission: The Missouri state park system does not charge entrance fees. However, there are fees associated with camping, lodging, tours, museums and certain special events.

This park encompasses much of the rugged, wooded terrain that surrounds Big Sugar Creek in the southern Lincoln Hills. A stroll through the park in the spring when many woodland wildflowers are in bloom or in the fall when the prairie grasses tower over your head is an outdoor delight. It includes a lake, a visitor center, hiking and equestrian trails, and campsites.

WORLD BIRD SANCTUARY
125 Bald Eagle Ridge Road **Valley Park** 63088

- ☐ Phone: (636) 225-4390 **www.worldbirdsanctuary.org**
- ☐ Hours: Daily 8:00am-5:00pm.

◻ Miscellaneous: While you're in town, stop at the WHITTLE SHORTLINE RAILROAD (www.woodentrain.com) for a look at the 15-foot-long train table designed so little engineers can try out the merchandise. Parents hang out on benches while the kids play with the trains.

At the World Bird Sanctuary, the kids can learn about some of the most majestic creatures of the wild - eagles, hawks and other birds of prey. Live displays feature bald eagles, owls, hawks, falcons, vultures, parrots, reptiles and more. There are hiking trails throughout the sanctuary's 305-acre wooded property. Picnic tables available. FREE.

ILINIWEK VILLAGE STATE HISTORIC SITE
(2 miles north of Wayland on Hwy. 27, take gravel roads to site)
Wayland 63472

◻ Phone: (660) 877-3871 **www.mostateparks.com/iliniwek.htm**
◻ Admission: The Missouri state park system does not charge entrance fees. However, there are fees associated with camping, lodging, tours, museums and certain special events.

This was once the site of a village inhabited by American Indians of the Iliniwek Confederacy. It is the only Illinois village site so far found in Missouri. The historic site interprets the history and daily life of the Illinois Indians and the Jolliet and Marquette expedition of 1673. The Illinois Indians were the first Native Americans that Louis Jolliet and Father Jacques Marquette encountered in present-day Missouri in 1673. At that time, the village contained 300 lodges and perhaps 8,000 people. Evidence of early European contact appears in archaeological finds through glass beads, metal objects and Jesuit trade rings. A short walking trail crosses the site, and the location of an excavated Illinois Indian longhouse is marked to show its size. Picnic sites are available.

JONES - CONFLUENCE STATE PARK
1000 Riverlands Way **West Alton** 63386

◻ Phone: (636) 899-1135 **www.mostateparks.com/confluence.htm**
◻ Admission: The Missouri state park system does not charge entrance fees. However, there are fees associated with camping, lodging, tours, museums and certain special events.

In 1804, Meriwether Lewis and William Clark began their journey up the Missouri River at the confluence of the two great rivers of North America, the Missouri and Mississippi. Today, visitors can watch as the Big Muddy and Mighty Mississippi merge into one at Edward "Ted" and Pat Jones - Confluence Point State Park. The role that both rivers played in the Lewis and Clark Expedition and the history of the rivers are interpreted at the park in outdoor exhibits. A short interpretive trail takes visitors to the confluence point. NOTE: Heavy rainfall in spring or fall temporarily close this state park so look online before you go.

BABLER MEMORIAL STATE PARK
800 Guy Park Drive Wildwood 63005

☐ Phone: (636-) 458-3813 **www.mostateparks.com/babler.htm**
☐ Admission: The Missouri state park system does not charge entrance fees. However, there are fees associated with camping, lodging, tours, museums and certain special events.
☐ Miscellaneous: The park also provides experiences for those with special needs at the Jacob L. Babler Outdoor Education Center, a barrier-free resident camp with swimming pool (exclusive to outdoor education center users), cabins and recreation and dining halls.

Located in the St. Louis area, this wooded park in the Missouri River hills features camping, hiking and equestrian trails, a paved bicycle trail, picnic areas, interpretive programs and a visitor center. A visitor center with exhibits illustrates the wonders of the park's natural communities; classrooms and an auditorium are available for special programs. Several special events are offered annually. They include Bug Day, which celebrates the wondrous world of insects.

HIDDEN VALLEY SKI RESORT
17409 Hidden Valley Drive Wildwood 63025

☐ Phone: (636) 938-5373 or Snow Report @ (636) 938-6999
www.hiddenvalleyski.com

Hidden Valley Ski Area located near Eureka, Missouri, is a resort that is fun for all levels or skiing or snowboarding, with 310 feet of vertical drop. For beginners: Hidden Valley has lessons for all ages as well as a beginner Wonder Carpet, located on the Easy Street. If you're up for something a little more challenging check out Hidden Valley's Outlaw Terrain Park.

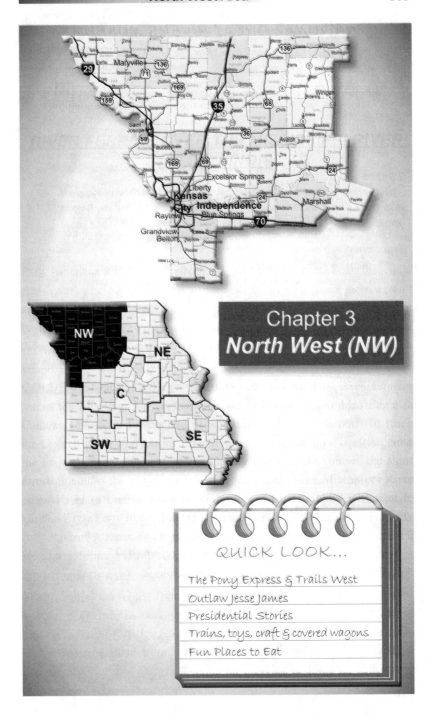

Chapter 3
North West (NW)

QUICK LOOK...

The Pony Express & Trails West

Outlaw Jesse James

Presidential Stories

Trains, toys, craft & covered wagons

Fun Places to Eat

Belton

- Belton, Grandview & Kansas City Railroad Co.

Blue Springs

- Burr Oak Woods Conservation Nature Center
- Fleming Park & Blue Springs Lake
- Dogtober Fest

Cameron

- Wallace State Park

Craig

- Big Lake State Park

Grandview

- Truman National Historic Site

Hamilton

- J. C. Penney Museum & Boyhood Home

Higginsville

- Confederate Memorial State Historic Site

Independence

- 1859 Jail, Marshal's Home And Museum
- Adventure Oasis Water Park
- Chicago & Alton Train Depot
- National Frontier Trails Center
- Pioneer Trails Adventures
- Truman Home, Museum And Information Center
- Puppetry Arts Institute
- Cool Crest Family Fun Center
- Strawberry Festival At Vaile Mansion

Jamesport

- Amish Community Of Jamesport

Kansas City

- Arthur Bryant's Barbecue
- Fiorella's Jack Stack Restaurants
- American Royal Museum & Visitor Center

Kansas City (cont.)

- Arabia Steamboat Museum
- City Hall Observation
- City Market
- College Basketball Experience
- Chips Chocolate Factory
- Coterie Theatre
- Crayola Café
- Crown Center
- Fritz's Railroad Restaurant
- Hallmark Visitor Center
- Kaleidoscope
- KC Rail Experience
- National Wwi Museum At Liberty Memorial
- Negro Leagues Baseball Museum
- Science City
- Union Station Complex
- Kemper Museum Of Contemporary Art
- Nelson-Atkins Museum Of Art
- Thomas Hart Benton Home And Studio State Historic Site
- Toy And Miniature Museum
- John Wornall House
- Kansas City Chiefs - Arrowhead Stadium
- Kansas City Royals - Kauffman Stadium
- Kansas City Zoo
- Lakeside Nature Center
- Cave Spring Historic Site And Nature Center
- Coco Key Water Resort
- Longview Lake Park
- Harley-Davidson Vehicle & Powertrain Operations Tour
- Shoal Creek Living History Museum
- Oceans Of Fun
- Worlds Of Fun
- Federal Reserve Bank Of Kansas City
- Schlitterbahn Vacation Village Waterpark
- Festa Italiana
- Kcriverfest
- Faulkner's Pumpkin Farm
- Kansas City Ballet Presents "The Nutcracker"

Kansas City (Riverside)
- Kansas City Scottish Highland Games & Celtic Festival

Kansas City (Westport)
- Battle Of Westport

Kansas City, KS
- Great Wolf Lodge
- Renaissance Festival

Kearney
- Jesse James Farm & Museum

Kingsville
- Powell Gardens

Laclede
- Gen. John J Pershing Boyhood Home State Historic Site
- Pershing State Park

Lawson
- Watkins Mill State Park & Site

Lee's Summit
- Missouri Town 1855
- Paradise Park Family Entertainment Center

Lexington
- Battle Of Lexington State Site

Liberty
- Jesse James Bank Museum
- Martha Lafite Thompson Nature Sanctuary
- Carolyn's Country Cousins Farm Pumpkin Patch

Marceline
- Walt Disney Hometown Museum

Maryville
- Mozingo Lake & Recreation

Meadville
- Fountain Grove Conservation Area

Miami
- Van Meter State Park

Mound City
- Squaw Creek National Wildlife Refuge

North Kansas City
- Chappell's Restaurant And Sports Museum

Osborn
- Shatto Milk Company

Platte City
- Pumpkins Etc.

Rushville
- Lewis And Clark State Park

Sibley
- Ft. Osage National Landmark

St. Joseph
- First Street Trolley
- Robidoux Row Museum
- Jesse James Home Museum
- Patee House Museum
- Pony Express Museum
- Society Of Memories Museum
- Remington Nature Center
- Schweizer Orchards
- Trails West Festival
- St. Joe Corn Maze

Sumner
- Swan Lake National Wildlife Refuge

Trenton
- Crowder State Park

Weston
- Snow Creek Ski Area
- Weston Bend State Park

Weston
- Weston Red Barn Farm
- Ferries Over Mississippi

Travel Journal & Notes:

_____
_____
_____
_____
_____
_____
_____
_____
_____
_____
_____
_____
_____
_____
_____
_____
_____
_____
_____
_____

Sites and attractions are listed in order by City, Zip Code, and Name. Symbols indicated represent:

 Festivals   **IOI** Restaurants   ⏳ Lodging

BELTON, GRANDVIEW & KANSAS CITY RAILROAD CO.

502 E. Walnut St. 10 miles south of the I-470, I-435, US 71 interchange (the Grandview Triangle) **Belton** 64012

- ☐ Phone: (816) 331-0630 **www.beltonrailroad.org**
- ☐ Tours: May thru Fall. $10.00 - $25.00 per person. Fares are for ages 3+. Weekends.
- ☐ Miscellaneous: only able to accept cash and checks at this time, sorry, no credit/debit cards. Train is neither heated nor air conditioned, we suggest you dress for the weather on the day of your visit.

If you're looking for a scenic ride in a full-size train, here's a place to step back in time aboard a 1920s era passenger train. 45 minute round trip train ride travels in 1920s open window coach and 1960s open air flatcar with picnic tables. The museum also offers a first-hand look at a 1950s diesel locomotive, along with a passenger car and caboose. You can even ride in the caboose with the conductor or in the cab of the locomotive with the engineer.

BELTON RAILROAD SANTA TRAIN

Belton - *Belton Railroad - This event features a real train decorated in lights, complete with cookies, hot chocolate and the chance to meet Santa. The train departs the museum at 10:00am on Saturday. Admission. (first Saturday in December).*

BURR OAK WOODS CONSERVATION NATURE CENTER

1401 NW Park Road (20 miles east of Kansas City) **Blue Springs** 64015

- ☐ Phone: (816) 228-3766 **http://mdc.mo.gov/areas/cnc/burroak/**
- ☐ Hours: (Trails) Daily 7:00am-6:00pm (until 8:00pm during DST). (Nature Center) Tuesday-Friday 7:00am-6:00pm, Saturday 8:00am-5:00pm.

BURR OAK WOODS CONSERVATION NATURE CENTER (cont.)

Nestled in the heart of this conservation area are five hiking trails, including two paved trails, which provide easy access to most parts of the area. The area is composed of woodlands, glades, native grass and forb plantings. The Nature Center features conservation exhibits including a 3,000-gallon aquarium, a wildlife viewing room and a variety of live amphibians and reptiles. Multimedia programs allow kids to make decisions about the environment and see the results. Can you balance human wants and needs with conservation of natural resources?

FLEMING PARK & BLUE SPRINGS LAKE

22807 Woods Chapel Road (2 miles east of I-470 and Highway 291)
Blue Springs 64015

☐   Phone: (816) 503-4800 **www.jacksongov.org**

Blue Springs Lake, located in Fleming Park, offers 720 acres of water excitement. Power boating, water skiing, tubing and jet skiing are all familiar sights on this popular lake, which also features a beach. The park also has a campground, nature trails, a radio-controlled model airplane and boat area, an archery range, native hoofed animal enclosure where bison and elk roam freely, and an observation tower that lets you watch the animals from up high. Tours of the animal enclosures on a hay-filled truck are available for a small fee on Saturdays. Bring apples or pears to feed the animals.

DOGTOBER FEST

Blue Springs - *Fleming Park, www.jacksongov.org/dogtober/ Kemper Outdoor Education Center. A day of dog shows, competitions and fun. Many dog breed clubs and vendors are featured. Special demonstrations by Jackson County Sheriff's K9 Unit; search and rescue; and dock diving dogs. There is a special Tails for Trails dog walk. FREE. (third Sunday in October)*

WALLACE STATE PARK
10621 NE Hwy. 121 **Cameron** 64429

☐ Phone: (816) 632-3745 **www.mostateparks.com/wallace.htm**
☐ Admission: The Missouri state park system does not charge entrance fees.
     However, there are fees associated with camping, lodging, tours, museums
     and certain special events.

Close to Kansas City, this park is a destination for bird-watchers, nature lovers
and anyone seeking tranquility away from the city. Hiking trails meander
through the wooded hills and a peaceful campground and small lake are other
features.

BIG LAKE STATE PARK
204 Lake Shore Drive (just off I-29) **Craig** 64437

☐ Phone: (660) 442-3770 or (660) 442-5432 (Lodging)
     www.mostateparks.com/biglake.htm
☐ Admission: The Missouri state park system does not charge entrance fees.
     However, there are fees associated with camping, lodging, tours, museums
     and certain special events.

The 625-acre, natural oxbow Big Lake borders the park, which lies along a
major migratory flyway. The park features fishing, a motel, snack bar, store,
camping, a pool and cabins.

TRUMAN NATIONAL HISTORIC SITE
12301 Blue Ridge Blvd **Grandview** 64030

☐ Phone: (816) 254-9929 **www.nps.gov/hstr**
☐ Hours: Friday, Saturday, Sunday 9:30am-4:00pm (Memorial Day-Labor Day).
☐ Admission: (Tour Fee) $4.00 (age 16+). Children 15 and under are FREE.
☐ Tours: 30-minute guided tours begin at 9:00am and run throughout the day.
     Each tour is limited to 6 people. Tickets are offered on a first-come, first-
     served basis and may sell out by early afternoon.
☐ Educators: Your family can take a cell phone tour of all the properties:
     http://www.nps.gov/hstr/photosmultimedia/cell-phone-tour.htm.

Located in the center of what was once an expansive 600-acre farm, this
quiet prairie home was the stomping grounds for a young Harry S. Truman,
who worked the farm into his late teens. Harry Truman's story is one of hope

and frustration, choice and chance. As President, he took the US from its traditional isolationism into the age of international involvement.

J. C. PENNEY MUSEUM & BOYHOOD HOME
312 North Davis Street Hamilton 64644

☐ Phone: (816) 583-2168
    www.ruralmissouri.coop/08pages/08MayJCPenney.html
☐ Hours: Monday-Friday 9:00am-Noon, 1:00pm-5:00pm, Saturday 9:00am-
    Noon. Hours subject to change, please call to verify.
☐ Admission: FREE.

The J.C. Penney Museum presents the life and career of the famous store chain entrepreneur. Penney grew up here and owned farmland here. The Museum tour includes a 20-minute video. Penney's home is restored to its late 19th century appearance. Parents like the fact that, weaved through most every quote or directive J.C. Penney gave, are hints of the Golden Rule. His original store was even named that. Inspirational for budding entrepreneurs in your family.

CONFEDERATE MEMORIAL STATE HISTORIC SITE
211 West First Street Higginsville 64037

☐ Phone: (660) 584-2853 **www.mostateparks.com/confedmem.htm**
☐ Admission: The Missouri state park system does not charge entrance fees.
    However, there are fees associated with camping, lodging, tours, museums
    and certain special events.
☐ Tours: Knowledgeable interpreters conduct guided tours of portions of
    Confederate Memorial State Historic Site. To get the most out of your visit
    and to better understand what occurred here, take a tour of this unique
    historic site. Each tour takes approximately 45 minutes and includes the
    chapel and cemetery. There is no charge for tours at this site.

In Higginsville, visit the Confederate Memorial State Historic Site on the grounds of the old Confederate Soldiers Home. The site contains the former home building, the restored 106-year-old chapel and historic cemetery including the grave of William Quantrill. The home was used to house dependent Confederate veterans and their families. These veterans hailed from points throughout the South and served in every major battle of the Civil

War. Foot soldiers, artillery and cavalrymen, marines, guerilla fighters and even spies found a place of rest here in their old age. The very last of these former rebel soldiers, John T. Graves, died at the home in 1950 at the age of 108, thus bringing an end to an amazing era in Missouri history. The grounds include the century-old chapel and cottage, a farmhouse, and the 1920s-era hospital building. Interpretive exhibits tell the story of the home and other historic buildings. There are picnic sites in the shade of fine old trees and fishing in one of the many lakes in the park.

1859 JAIL, MARSHAL'S HOME AND MUSEUM
217 North Main Street Independence 64050

☐   Phone: (816) 252-1892 **www.jchs.org/jail/museum.html**
☐   Hours: Monday-Saturday 10:00am-4:00pm, Sunday 1:00-4:00pm (April-October 31).
☐   Admission: $5.00 adult, $4.50 senior, $2.00 youth (5-15).
☐   Miscellaneous: Guided tours by Pioneer Trails offer covered wagon rides from the square featuring discussion of Independence's historic sites and Civil War history. Educators: a teacher's guide to the site is available here: http://www.jchs.org/education/guide.html.

Massive walls, barred windows that once housed Frank James give an authentic look at frontier justice; and mid-1800s home life. In 1907, a brick jail was added to the back of the limestone jail to house chain gangs. Chain gangs were used to build roads, sewers and other tasks assigned them. They left six days a week at sunrise and returned at sunset. One inmate spent a year on the chain gang for stealing a cow. You can see the Marshal's home from Main Street, but the two-story limestone jail and the 1901 chain gang jail joins the rear of the home. Four feet away is a federalist style house that was home for county marshal until 1920s. Everything is set up as it was at the time of the Civil War. Take a self-guided tour of the jail and museum for a first hand look at frontier justice. Tour the beautifully decorated home where the wife and children of the marshal lived. Guided tours are available upon request in advance.

ADVENTURE OASIS WATER PARK

2100 South Hub Drive (Just off 23rd Street, just west of the Rte. 291 intersection) **Independence** 64050

☐ Phone: (816) 325-6238
   www.ci.independence.mo.us/parksandrec/AdvenOasis.aspx
☐ Hours: Call or see website (Memorial Day-Labor Day)
☐ Admission: Multi-punch passes available from $24.00-$32.00. Annual passes $105.00 adult, $75.00 youth or senior, $250.00 family.

This exciting aquatic area is a state-of-the-art facility featuring a 900-foot long continuous lazy river ride with waterfall, 6,000-square-foot interactive family play pool with zero-depth entry, six-lane 25-yard lap pool with diving area, and three water slides: 210-foot open flume slide, 197-foot enclosed tube slide and 308-foot raft slide. It also contains a 30,000 square foot sun deck, modern bathhouse and full-service concessions.

CHICAGO & ALTON TRAIN DEPOT

318 West Pacific Avenue (3 blocks South of the Independence Square) **Independence** 64050

☐ Phone: (816) 325-7955 **www.chicagoalton1879depot.org**
☐ Hours: Monday, Thursday, Friday & Saturday 9:30am-4:30pm, Sunday 12:30-4:30pm. (April-October)

Independence is also home to The Chicago & Alton Train Depot - a stunning two-story depot that depicts a 1890s-era depot. As you walk through the door, you'll see the waiting room where passengers purchased tickets and an original bell from a Santa Fe train. There's also a baggage room, living quarters and an extensive display of railroad artifacts. In celebration of the holiday season, the depot hosts "A Visit from St. Nicholas" on Saturdays in December.

NATIONAL FRONTIER TRAILS CENTER

318 West Pacific Avenue **Independence** 64050

☐ Phone: (816) 325-7575 **www.ci.independence.mo.us/nftm/**
☐ Hours: Monday-Saturday 9:00am-4:30pm, Sunday 12:30pm-4:30pm.
☐ Admission: $5.00 adult, $4.50 senior (62+), $3.00 youth (6-17).
☐ Educators: Teacher Resource Packets on trails topics in history is found here: http://www.ci.independence.mo.us/nftm/TeacherResources.aspx

For updates & travel games visit: **www.KidsLoveTravel.com**

Learn what it would be like to be a 19th century pioneer family. Hear tales of those who headed west from Independence along the Santa Fe, Oregon and California Trails in covered wagons. Learn about mountain man John Coulter, who went west and why, hop aboard a covered wagon for a narrated tour of historic sites, and learn how wagon trains prepared for their trips west. Begin your visit by viewing the museum's award winning film, "West." This 17-minute film gives an overview of America's westward expansion. Look for two authentic pioneer wagons (large, hard to miss) and learn about the trades and businesses that prepared emigrants for the journey. Interactive exhibits test your knowledge of the trails and allow you to see some of the supplies that explorers and pioneers brought through this region. Do you know what brought the overland wagon trails to an end? How about what you should pack for such a long journey?

Outside: During the trails period, thousands of wagons rolled down the hill from the Courthouse Square and passed over the property where the museum now sits. Evidence of the migration can still be seen today in the form of swales, or wagon ruts, left in the field directly across the street from the museum campus. A 1/4-mile long asphalt pathway circles around the swales. Interpretive signs give information about the swales and what it was like to begin the long trail journey. Handicapped accessible.

PIONEER TRAILS ADVENTURES

533 S. Pleasant Street (Historic Independence Square)
Independence 64050

☐ Phone: (816) 254-2466 or (816) 456-4991
www.pioneertrailsadventures.com
☐ Hours: Daily 9:30am-4:30pm (April-October). By reservation only (November-March).
☐ Admission: $7.00-$25.00 depending on tour option selected.
☐ Tours: During April-October reservations are not required but helpful. Various tour options are available from a 20-minute Town Square Tour, up to a 75-minute Full City Tour.

See Independence as a pioneer would, by mule-drawn covered wagon (or sleigh in the snow). Visit the city where the journey to the Wild West began. The Historic Independence square was the host of two Civil War battles, William Quantrill and his raiders, General Sterling Price, Wild Bill Hickok, and notorious outlaws such as the James brothers. Pass by the home where one President began his march to the White House or the place where young Harry had his first job. On your wagon tour find out why: Frank James' jail cell door was never shut, why Order number 11 made Harry S. Truman emphatic about the Marshal Plan, how the painting of order number 11 destroyed a mighty General, why Missouri is the Show-Me-State and so much more. Pioneer history is explored with specific attention to the preparation for the journey west and the responsibility of each member on the wagon train, even the children. What would you pack for the journey? This is all but the perfect way to engage young kids in history without the fussy old historic town walking tours. Your family should start with this tour and then determine which historical sites you may still want to visit for a tour. Often, the young ones opt out of (or take naps) stuffy old buildings but really enjoy the covered wagon tour! You really get to feel like a pioneer sitting on a covered wagon bench…

TRUMAN HOME, MUSEUM AND INFORMATION CENTER

223 N Main St. (Take I-70 W to Noland Road. Exit and travel north about five miles to U.S. Highway 24 E) **Independence** 64050

- ☐ Phone: (816) 254-4491 **www.nps.gov/hstr or www.trumanlibrary.org**
- ☐ Hours: Visitors Center open 8:30am-5:00pm.
- ☐ Admission: Tickets on first-come first-served basis at Visitor Center, Main St. & Truman Rd. Tour Fee: $4.00, children 15 and under are free.
- ☐ Tours: Thirty minute guided tours of the Truman Home will be offered Tuesday through Sunday. Admission to the Truman Farm Home is by guided tour only. Each tour is limited to 6 people.
- ☐ Educators: Lesson Plans on Harry Truman, the Presidency and Independence, MO are on the FOR TEACHERS>Lesson Plans & Teacher Guides page.

Travelers to Independence can still experience Truman's town and follow in his footsteps on a neighborhood walking tour, smell the concord grapes ripening on his back porch, and even read the oral histories of his friends and family. Start at visitor center to view a Free 12 minute intro slide program and buy tickets or join group tours of Truman's home and farm.

The Harry S. Truman Library & Museum recounts the life of America's 33rd president, Harry S. Truman. One of only 12 U.S. Presidential Libraries, the museum's two permanent exhibits chronicle the Missourian's private life and political career — with exhibits depicting his most difficult decisions like using the atomic bomb, the Cold War and recognizing Israel. As you enter, an impressive 495-square-foot mural named "Independence and the Opening of the West" depicts three decades of Independence's history in the mid-1800s. Want to see what a president was like as a kid? The "Life & Times" section chronicles Truman's boyhood, family life and his role as "Mr. Citizen." While the younger set may not "get it," the Decision Theatres offer two interactive auditoriums that put the audience into the President's shoes to make important Oval Office decisions. Kids can help their parents vote how they would respond to Truman-era issues such as 1948 election pressures and Cold War spies. Another spot that all kids recognize - the Oval Office replica.

The **HARRY S. TRUMAN WALKING TRAIL** on Truman Road is a 2.7 mile sidewalk trail that was Truman's favorite route in Independence. The 43 plaques embedded in sidewalks along the route focus on Truman and his hometown. Brochures are available at key points.

The **TRUMAN HOME**, 219 Delaware, showcases the simple life Truman and his beloved Bess enjoyed in Independence before and after his presidency. The National Park Service offers tours every 15 minutes. Also in Independence, the Truman Depot (111 W. Pacific) served as the final stop for Truman's 1948 Whistlestop Campaign. Now a working Amtrak station, more than 8,500 admirers greeted Truman and Bess there when the pair returned to town following his second term. Don't forget to stop by Clinton's Soda Fountain, 100 W. Maple, where 14-year-old Harry earned $3 a week at his first job. You can still order ice cream treats at the counter. (closed Sundays)

DID YOU KNOW ? The sayings: "Monday morning quarterback" and "The buck stops here" are both expressions popularized by Truman.

PUPPETRY ARTS INSTITUTE

11025 East Winner Road **Independence** 64052

- ☐ Phone: (816) 833-9777 **www.hazelle.org**
- ☐ Hours: Various program and times. Call or visit website for most current schedule.
- ☐ Admission: $5.00+/person includes program and museum.

This building is home to marionettes created by renowned manufacturer Hazelle Rollins. Institute is magical with fabulous puppets from around the world. Tour the puppet museum, paint a puppet head, dress it in a costume and perform an impromptu show. Everyone gets one Free finger puppet or make-your-own puppet head. Like many other puppet factories, most are amazed at how professional and entertaining real puppetry art is - especially the shows.

COOL CREST FAMILY FUN CENTER

10735 E. US Highway 40 **Independence** 64055

- ☐ Phone: (816) 358-0088 **www.coolcrest.com**
- ☐ Hours: Vary by season and attraction. Call or check website for current schedule.
- ☐ Admission: Pricing is flexible with options ranging from individual game tokens, per ride prices, or Unlimited Fun Passes are priced per hour.

This large facility features video games and redemption games for the whole family; four 18-hole mini golf courses; an eatery featuring pizza, ice cream and such; batting cages; go-karts; and an indoor playground.

STRAWBERRY FESTIVAL AT VAILE MANSION

Independence - *1500 N Liberty. Enjoy a day of free music and entertainment, crafts, antiques, flea markets, flowering baskets, all kinds of strawberry treats, children's activities, antique cars, carriage rides, home tours by costumed guides, and concessions. Admissions to grounds is free; extra charge for home tours or carriage rides. (first Saturday in June).*

AMISH COMMUNITY OF JAMESPORT
Jamesport 64648

☐ Phone: (660) 684-6704 or (660) 684-6146 **www.JamesportMissouri.org**

☐ Hours: Most stores are open 8:00am-5:00pm. All stores are closed on Sundays, and most of the Amish businesses are closed on Thursdays as well.

☐ Tours: Various tour options from guided to self (w/CD) are available. Call or see website for details.

☐ Miscellaneous: All stores accept cash and check. Most stores in town accept Visa and Mastercard, but most Amish stores do not. Hook & Eye Tours: Rosemary Simmons gives Amish House and Farm Tours. Call (660) 684-6179 for information.

Missouri's largest Amish Community offers Amish furniture and other handcrafted items as well as baked goods and horse-churned ice cream. Spend the afternoon browsing "English" shops downtown or Amish shops in the outskirts (a map of locations is available at City Hall). Feed Jersey calves a bottle and take a break from cell phones (no service in town), credit cards, internet and movies. The Amish are welcoming and friendly but live simple lives and do not want to be interviewed or have photos taken of them. As you arrive in town, you'll notice many Amish buggies. Following is a list of Amish & Brethren businesses you'll probably want to visit to get the full experience:

SHOPPING & FUN

• **H & M COUNTRY STORE, COUNTRYSIDE BAKERY** - 21910 St. Hwy 190, (660) 684-6848. They sell eight varieties of bread, dinner rolls, homemade noodles, cinnamon rolls, cookies, and pies. At H & M, you'll see an Amish grocery with bulk spices, mixes, homemade noodles, jams, butters, farm fresh eggs, pickled vegetables, dried fruit, and snacks.

• **HOMESTEAD CREAMERY** - 2059 Liv 506, (660) 684-6970. The Flory's, a Brethren family, operate this local dairy and creamery. They raise Jersey cows and make natural rinded Farmstead cheese on site. On Tuesdays, you can watch cheese making. On Saturday, we saw cheese packaging. They provide free samples of the cheeses in their shop. Often, a family member will take the kids out to the barn and teach them to bottle feed calves.

AMISH COMMUNITY OF JAMESPORT (cont.)

- **OAKRIDGE FURNITURE & CRAFTS** - 799 SW 80th St, (660) 684-6802. The highlight of this stop was the Horse Churned Ice Cream (available seasonally on Saturdays)! Kids are absolutely intrigued to see a horse making ice cream! At Oakridge, they sell handcrafted furniture, wooden toys, and clocks. The quilt shop features quilts, lace, jams, and Amish Dolls. They also sell Christian books, Amish Cookbooks, and candles.

DINING

- **GINGERICH DUTCH PANTRY**: Intersection of Auberry Grove and Broadway, (660) 684-6212. Homemade soups, noodles, sandwiches and baked goods.

- **COUNTRY CUPBOARD**: Old Hwy 6, (660) 684-6597. Home cookin' style menu.

- **JAMESPORT TAVERN & GRILL**: (660) 684-9906. Traditional grill menu. The unique feature here? The restaurant is also a retailer of shotguns, black powder supplies, antique guns and restoration.

- **JAMESPORT CAFÉ**: 209 S. Locust, (660) 684-6700. Family dining, famous for their hand-breaded jumbo pork tenderloins.

ARTHUR BRYANT'S BARBECUE

Kansas City - *http://arthurbryants.com/. Author Calvin Trillin once declared Arthur Bryant's "the single best restaurant in the world." Kansas City's world famous barbecue is available at more than 100 area restaurants. It's a barbecue mecca where presidents, poets and paupers have dined. Some complain that Arthur Bryant's rests on old laurels; others insist that such steadfastness is a virtue. Judge for yourself. And don't forget to wipe your chin. The sauce is like nothing you can get anywhere else. It is so unique that you might not even like it so don't plan on taking finicky kids here for BBQ (order sides for them).*

FIORELLA'S JACK STACK RESTAURANTS

Kansas City - *www.jackstackbbq.com/jack-stack-barbecue/i/2/. Experience a 50-year tradition of remarkable barbecue. Each restaurant reflects its unique neighborhood: the romance of the Country Club Plaza, the history of the Downtown Freight House (Union Station area), the energy of Overland Park, and the warm welcome waiting for you at Martin City. While Gates sauce is spicy, we liked Fiorella's Jack Stack for families. Most moms will appreciate how their kid's menu doubles as an activity sheet and they offer seven different items including Sliced Meat (just like the grown-ups), ribs, chicken, grilled cheese or hot dogs. All meals are $4.95 and include milk, juice or soft drink. Adult entrees run $10.00-$25.00 and feature beef, pork, chicken, turkey and lamb slow-smoked to perfection in an authentic brick oven. They even serve the burnt ends as a specialty! And, the dry seasoning rub – served on the table – is good enough to make you want to buy some to take home.*

AMERICAN ROYAL MUSEUM & VISITOR CENTER

1701 American Royal Court, Downtown/Conv. Center area (From downtown Kansas City: Take 12th Street west to Genessee) **Kansas City** 64102

- ☐ Phone: (816) 221-9800 **www.americanroyal.com**
- ☐ Hours: Open during specific events during the American Royal season or by request. Most events are in the fall.
- ☐ Admission: Contact the Visitors Center or go online for details of event guest fees.

Started as a livestock show in 1899, the American Royal aims to educate the public about agriculture and celebrates Kansas City's heritage of equestrian sports, rodeo and livestock shows. In the Visitors Center children can sit on an English or Western saddle, weigh themselves on a livestock scale, play with farm items, see a film about the annual rodeo or train themselves to be an American Royal judge. Exhibits explain role agribusiness plays in our lives.

AMERICAN ROYAL LIVESTOCK, HORSE SHOW & RODEO

Kansas City - *One of Top 20 pro rodeos in the nation. Commercial trade show, a petting area, and a full schedule of livestock shows, competitions, rodeos, and big name entertainers. Event begins with city's largest parade and a barbecue contest. Admission. (Two month season from early October to mid-November)*

ARABIA STEAMBOAT MUSEUM

400 Grand Blvd. (located next to the City Market complex)
Kansas City 64106

- ☐ Phone: (816) 471-1856 **www.1856.com**
- ☐ Hours: Monday - Saturday first tour begins at 10:00am and last tour begins at 4:00pm (new tours start every 30 minutes). Sunday first tour is Noon and last tour begins at 3:30pm (with tours starting every 30 minutes in between).
- ☐ Admission: $12.50 adult, $11.50 senior (60+), $4.75 child (4-12).
- ☐ Educators: PDF downloads (grade appropriate) with lessons, games and quizzes are found on the >Plan Your Visit>Student & Youth Tours>PDF Downloads. These sheets are especially nice to fill out as the students explore the showcases and dioramas looking for clues to answer the questions.

The story of the shipwrecked *Arabia* and its excavation is a modern day tale of adventure, captivating all who visit the museum – especially any explorers in the family. Buried more than 132 years, the ship's cargo is on display at the museum and the "inventory" collected is often referred to as a Wal-Mart of the 1800s. Discover what the phrase "high flutant" comes from and why did parts of the boat have to have a shower 2-3 times a day. Can you identify the mystery items? If you have even an inkling of desire to treasure hunt and dig in the dirt – this place will wow you. They cleverly build the tour to peak your interest, show a film about the recovery and then hit you with the actual findings. This is unbelievable – especially the great conditions of the materials.

CITY HALL OBSERVATION

414 E 12th Street (Downtown / Convention Center Area) **Kansas City** 64106

- ☐ Phone: (816) 513-2778 **www.visitkc.com**
- ☐ Hours: Open 7:00am-3:00pm Monday-Friday. Closed during high winds.
- ☐ Admission: FREE.

View the city from the 30th floor of City Hall. City Hall is the third tallest building in the city. It measures 443 feet from the sidewalk at the north door to the top of the building. Since it's on a hill, it dominates the downtown skyline. When it was first built, it was the tallest building in the state. It remains one of the tallest city halls in the country. Security guards need to take you up so be patient as this is an extra job for them.

CITY MARKET

20 E. 5th Street (Just a few blocks north of Downtown in the River Market
district) **Kansas City** 64106

☐   Phone: (816) 842-1271 **www.thecitymarket.org/**

☐   Hours: The Saturday Farmers' Market features more than 140 local vendors
offering farm-fresh produce, plants, poultry & meats, baked goods, prepared
foods, handmade crafts and much more. 6:00am-3:00pm. Sundays offer
a more leisurely alternative with the Art of the Machine Car Series and the
popular Community Yard Sale. 8:00am-3:00pm. Most restaurants.

☐   Admission: Admission to the farmers' market is free. Concerts and special
events, plus any meals you purchase from vendors or restaurants on the
perimeter are subject to admission, parking fees or dining prices listed.

Kansas City's oldest continuously operating business, The City Market is
home to an eclectic mix of restaurants and merchants as well as the region's
largest farmers' market – many with samplings of their fresh product to try
before you buy. The smells and colors of the produce are so sensory. The
market is especially lively on weekends when more than 140 farmers bring
their goods for sale (year-round). More than 30 permanent merchants offer
fresh produce from nearby farms and around the world, specialty groceries,
meats & seafood, fresh baked pastries, desserts, floral, house wares and gift
shops that are open seven days a week, year-round, many of which are family
owned and operated.

Although kids really do love a farmers market (it is so colorful and lively), you
can really give them a taste of many cultures in one place by trying different
ethnic foods at restaurants surrounding the market booths. Venture out for a
crispy falafel or a handy Shawarma sandwich for a fast and friendly lunch
at Habashi House Middle Eastern Café or perhaps a flavorful stew, richly
seasoned at the Blue Nile. Try one of nearly 100 different Vietnamese entrees
at Hien Vuong or Indian and Pakistani cuisine at Tikka House. If something
more traditional suits your interests, try the dry rubbed, slow cooked meats at
Winslow's City Market Barbeque, a gourmet pizza at Minsky's Pizza Café,
or a grilled Panini at City Market Coffee Shop. Bo Lings Chinese Restaurant
features a wide range of Mandarin and Cantonese cuisine as well as one of
the largest Dim Sum menus in the metro area. Burrito Bros. offers fresh and
flavorful Mexican burritos, quesadillas, salads, tacos and more. Pieroguy's
Pierogies offers freshly prepared pierogies, a delicious east coast staple. You

are certain to be tempted by Bloom Baking Company's amazing selection of baked goods, pastries and sweets, which are made fresh daily, using locally grown produce and product. Stop by Lollicup Tea to see what the latest bubble drink craze is all about or to pick up a refreshingly healthy smoothie.

COLLEGE BASKETBALL EXPERIENCE

1401 Grand Blvd. (downtown/convention center area) **Kansas City** 64106

- ☐ Phone: (816) 949-7500 **www.collegebasketballexperience.com**
- ☐ Hours: Wednesday-Saturday 10:00am-6:00pm, Sunday 11:00am-6:00pm.
- ☐ Admission: $12.00 adult, $9.00 child (6-17).

Further cementing the area's reputation as a hoops hotbed, Kansas City is now home to the state-of-the-art College Basketball Experience (CBE). Connected to the new Sprint Center via a common lobby, the 41,500-square-foot entertainment facility contains hands-on, interactive basketball exhibits and houses the National Collegiate Basketball Hall of Fame. Beginning with a last-minute pep talk inside the entrance elevator, a coach's voice accompanies fans throughout the facility, guiding them through several dribble, pass and shoot stations to hone their skills. SportsCenter fans will feel right at home behind the ESPNU anchor desk, where they can call the play-by-play of college's most memorable games. We soon realized our amateur skills weren't scholarship material but boy did we have fun trying to jump high and produce free-throws at a fast pace to beat the buzzer! Sweating is almost inevitable as CBE's high-energy exhibits recreate the intensity of college basketball game-from foul-line hecklers to a last-second buzzer beater.

CHIPS CHOCOLATE FACTORY

2450 Grand Blvd., Crown Center, Level 2 **Kansas City** 64108

- ☐ Phone: (816) 421-0012 **www.kcfudge.com**

The aroma of Chocolate tickles your nose, as sweet creations of caramel apples or smooth fudge are prepared before your eyes. Call ahead for a group tour when the action is bubbling with whirlpools of chocolate. See Chip's helpers turn 20 lbs. of secret ingredients into a loaf of creamy fudge. You'll learn how every drop of chocolate starts with Cocoa Beans and you'll see their transformation from harvest through various stages of production.

COTERIE THEATRE

2450 Grand Blvd., Crown Center Shops, level 1, Ste. 144
Kansas City 64108

- Phone: (814) 474-6552 **www.coterietheatre.org**
- Hours: Matinees 5-6 days/week plus Friday evening performance.
- Admission: $10.00-$15.00 per show (shows run 60-90 minutes- just right amount of time before attention wanes).
- Educators: Curriculum and theme Resource Guide is prepared for each production with concepts outlined and follow up activities.

This KC venue of live theatre for all ages presents plays that have short stories with "touchpoints" for all ages – witty, fun, emotional. Cute lines are followed by laughter and clapping – sometimes as much from the adults as the kids. We liked the use of puppets, too.

CRAYOLA CAFÉ

Kansas City - 2450 Grand Street, Crown Center, Level 2 64108. Phone: (816) 398-4820. www.crayolacafe.com. A café so colorful, you can't pass by without resisting a peak at what each table ordered. Their regular menu has some really nice sandwich plates all around $8-9.00 but the kid's menu is all the rage ($4.00-$5.00). Guess what we tried? Peanut Butter and Banana Wrap (served warm on a whole wheat tortilla) and The Beach Pail - ice cream, Nilla wafers, chocolate sauce, whipped cream and a cherry on a sandy "beach" in a take-home sand pail. All kids entrees are served with beverage in kids souvenir cup and choice of French fries, tater tots, potato chips, carrot sticks or fruit salad. Every plate, placemat, decoration is super bright colors and everyone we saw was having so much fun eating! Next-door is the Crayola Store.

CROWN CENTER

2450 Grand Blvd. **Kansas City** 64108

- **www.crowncenter.com**

Located in the heart of downtown Kansas City, Crown Center is often called a city within a city. Three levels of great shopping and dining complement two of the city's most friendly hotels. If you're staying at the Hyatt or Westin Crown Center, you are already in the center of walkable spots especially popular with families. Crown Center, the international headquarters for

Hallmark Cards, is a must see for kids. The company's fun and creative spirit is evident throughout the entertainment complex – from the hands-on art, greeting card factory tours, water shows, play fountains, theaters, funky themed restaurants, numerous festivals and a winter ice terrace. The fountains flow year-round, but a show set to music plays spring through fall at noon each weekday then on the hour 5:00-10:00pm and weekends on the hour 10:00am-10:00pm.

You'll see listings for many unique restaurants, theatres and shops in the Crown Center throughout this chapter.

KANSAS CITY CHALK & WALK FESTIVAL

Kansas City - *Crown Center - Artists start with empty squares of asphalt and by the end of the weekend, the squares will be transformed into magnificent pieces of artwork. FREE. (third weekend in June)*

FREE FRIDAY NIGHT FLICKS

Kansas City - *Crown Center - Bring your blanket and lawn chairs, sit under the stars and take in a classic movie on a huge outdoor screen every Friday night. Concessions will be available. FREE (July and August)*

FIESTA KANSAS CITY

Kansas City - *Crown Center - Celebrate Cinco de Mayo at this tenth annual event, which features great music, food, dancing and exhibits. Sponsored by the Hispanic Chamber of Commerce of Greater Kansas City. FREE (second weekend in May).*

JIGGLE JAM FAMILY FEST

Kansas City - *Crown Center - featuring national and local entertainers and many kids activities. Admission. (Memorial Day weekend)*

FRITZ'S RAILROAD RESTAURANT

Kansas City - *2450 Grand Blvd. Suite 214, Crown Center 64108. Phone: (816) 474-4004. OK, train lovers and the families that love them – THIS IS your place to be. Fritz's inventor skills lead him to the development of a food delivery system that he designed and tested in the basement of his home. Get this – the "train" system runs below a moving train around the entire restaurant. Instead of having a server bring your order, the kitchen prepares the order and sends it along a track until it meets a STOP at your table. The train conveyor then gently releases your food down to arms length reach and you grab your selections. Kids get a conductors hat with their kids meals and the selection of food offerings is definitely kid-style = old fashioned hamburgers plain or with crazy toppings like hash browns, homemade chili, BBQ sauce, hot sauce or grilled onions. Add a milkshake on the side. Lil'engineers items are all $4.99 and include entrée, fries, and drink. Toot-toot.*

HALLMARK VISITOR CENTER

2450 Grand Blvd., Crown Center Complex (one mile south of downtown)
Kansas City 64108

☐   Phone: (816) 274-3613 **www.hallmarkvisitorscenter.com**
☐   Hours: Tuesday-Friday 9:00am-5:00pm, Saturday 9:30am-4:30pm.
☐   Admission: FREE. Free parking with validation.

Visit the place that creates ways for people to express themselves and celebrate life's seasons. Where do Hallmark artists, writers, and photographers go for inspiration? Begin a behind-the-scenes journey with a short movie viewing. Now that you're oriented, grab a Passport. As you travel through the Center, read your Passport and find six stamping stations that tell their story. Enjoy a virtual visit with hoops&yoyo, Asteroid Andy and other colorful Hallmark characters. Step inside new computer kiosks that provide all ages an entertaining, fun and high tech way to learn more about the company. Kids will be very pleasantly surprised to find out Crayola is part of Hallmark (you can even watch a video to see crayons, markers & Silly Putty being made). Or, that greeting cards are made in more than 30 languages.

But the most engaging part of the tour has to be the "crafting" area. Watch a tech make engraving dies – the metal plates that raise the 3-dimensional designs on paper or cutting dies, which work like steel cookie cutters. You can also look at artist designs to die cut machines where real cards pile up at the end of the line. Try your hand at crafting yourself at one station where you make a souvenir bow to take home. Once you've completed your Passport, don't forget to collect a small prize. Everyone leaves this center with a huge, endearing smile on his or her face! This place is really that warm & fuzzy fun!

KALEIDOSCOPE

2500 Grand Street, Crown Center Complex (right next to Hallmark Visitors Center) **Kansas City** 64108

- ☐ Phone: (816) 274-8300 **www.hallmarkkaleidoscope.com**
- ☐ Hours: vary from day to day, so call ahead. Closed holidays and Sundays. 40-minute Saturday Family Art Sessions from 9:30am-3:30pm (timed FREE tickets). Open sessions some school year weekdays and most summer weekday afternoons. Best ages 5-12.
- ☐ Admission: FREE.

Be prepared to be wowed! Put your creative juices in full throttle as you walk through the dark tunnel hallway into the most colorful whimsy land any kid could imagine. Parents, stand back and watch as children use their imagination to make art with paper, ribbon, melted crayons and tons of bright, shiny, wiggly, sparkly, fluffy, puffy stuff. Your sense of touch, sight and hearing are peaked in each space. You may start at a crazy country house, then to an under-the-sea world and on to far out outer space. Kids use Crayola art supplies and recycled materials to make take home projects such as puzzles, hats or books. It's like walking into a storybook where you get to create the props!

KC RAIL EXPERIENCE

30 West Pershing Rd **Kansas City** 64108

- ☐ Phone: (816) 460-2020 **www.unionstation.org/railexperience.html**
- ☐ Admission: $7.00 per person (age 3+).

This is a hands-on journey through the exciting history of the American railroad. "Talking characters" speak to you around every corner. Climb aboard several trains including one giant "moving train" with sound and motion. Sit at the controls, blow the whistle or pull the train out of the station and speed through tunnels. This is probably our favorite indoor train museum because of the multiple interactive stations. Amazing wows from your "little conductor".

NATIONAL WWI MUSEUM AT LIBERTY MEMORIAL
100 W. 26th Street (across the street from Union Station)
Kansas City 64108

- Phone: (816) 784-1918 **www.theworldwar.org**
- Hours: Tuesday-Sunday from 10:00am-5:00pm. The exhibits and tower close at 4:30pm. Open some holiday Mondays.
- Admission: $12.00 adult, $10.00 senior or student (18+ w/ID), $6.00 youth (6-17). Active Duty Military, Career Military (20+ years service) and kids five and under are free. Tickets allow guests access to all galleries, special exhibits and the Liberty Memorial Tower. Tickets may be used on two consecutive days. If purchased Sunday, the second day is Tuesday.
- Miscellaneous: "Over There" Café with menu items named for people and places of the Great War. Songs of the era can be heard throughout the dining area. Educators: you can order a Free Lessons of Liberty CD on their website under>Education>For Teachers>Lessons of Liberty.

President Calvin Coolidge dedicated the Liberty Memorial to World War I veterans in 1926. The new National World War I Museum opened beneath the monument in 2006. It is the only museum in the country dedicated to WWI. Walk up to the huge tower and statues. Why do you walk over a battlefield of poppies at the entrance? You'll need to begin with the 12-minute video to engage the kids in the time period. Now, explore. Look through the clever peep-holes. Would you like to be in those trenches? What did the soldiers carry in their pockets? (cards and Bibles). The various audio stations react with conversation once you enter. The audio and viewing holes are at different levels so every size kid can participate without being held or needing a stool. Other discovery stations allow you to "play" at interactive tables using light pointers. Now go outside and travel to the top of the 217-foot tower for a bird's eye view of the city. Because the theme of the museum is war, kids who have studied some American War History engage the most and really interact with the discovery station technology.

NEGRO LEAGUES BASEBALL MUSEUM

1616 E.18th Street (In the Historic 18th & Vine Jazz District, I-70 Paseo exit)
Kansas City 64108

- Phone: (816) 221-1920 **www.nlbm.com**
- Hours: Tuesday-Saturday 9:00am-6:00pm, Sunday Noon-6:00pm.
- Admission: $8.00 adult, $3.00 for children under 12. Free for children under 5. Discount tickets with the Jazz Museum.
- Miscellaneous: if you want to grab a KC authentic lunch, the original Arthur Bryant's Barbecue (1727 Brooklyn Ave.) is a few blocks to the east.

The museum is laid out as a timeline of the Negro Leagues and American history. Exhibits include hundreds of photographs, historical artifacts and several interactive computer stations. A documentary film narrated by actor James Earl Jones tells the story of the leagues with vintage film footage. Baseball fans will love the many baseball facts and computer trivia kiosks and parents will be touched by the stories of injustice during the 60s. At the end of all that reading and listening, you come upon the dynamic Field of Legends. 10 statues are positioned on the Field of Legends, a mock baseball diamond, where this mythical all-star team looks to be engaged in an epic battle. Visitor's are welcomed to walk onto the field. Bring kids along who are in to the history of baseball and its legends. Otherwise, children may be bored until the sculpture field at the end.

SCIENCE CITY

Union Station 30 West Pershing Rd **Kansas City** 64108

- Phone: (816) 460-2020 **www.unionstation.org**
- Hours: Tuesday - Saturday 10:00am-5:00pm, Sunday Noon-5:00pm. Extended hours during some school breaks and holidays.
- Admission: Tickets for Science City are $10.00 (age 3+). Visit more than one attraction and SAVE! Purchase a ticket to Science City and visit the Extreme Screen, Rail Experience or Planetarium for just $5.00!

Science City is the city's first science center and features dozens of hands-on exhibits. Parents and kids can solve a crime (like a murder mystery), dig up fossils and defy gravity on a bike that's 30 feet in the air! Then, they can publish a newspaper; go into Echo Cave or watch paleontologists working in the Dino Lab. The "city" is set up like a real city with "shops", a train depot, hotels and even unique areas like: The Physics of Golf mini-golf course teaching you the science of the green or Make your Own Slime in the Test Kitchens. While it's very busy and noisy in the main "city" scape, the parents stand on the perimeters while the kids totally immerse themselves in the science playground.

UNION STATION COMPLEX
30 W Pershing Road **Kansas City** 64108

☐   Phone: (816) 460-2020 **www.unionstation.org**

The nation's second-largest train station, Union Station was restored to its original grandeur. The complex is filled with restaurants, shops, theaters, traveling exhibits, special events, a science center called SCIENCE CITY, and a permanent exhibit on railroads called the KC RAIL EXPERIENCE. Once the home of the historic Fred Harvey Restaurant and Lunchroom, The Harvey House Diner serves up a full breakfast menu all day long, as well as Blue Plate lunch specials, burgers, sandwiches, hand-dipped shakes and malts and fresh-baked pies seven days a week. Union Station's Theater District has a giant-screen 2D and 3D movie theater, a domed planetarium and a live-stage theater. The building features a 95-foot ceiling in the Grand Hall, three 3,500-pound chandeliers and a six-foot-wide clock hanging in the Station's central arch. Millions of people went through Union Station and there are old pictures placed around the hallways to depict that. Admission to the Union Station building is FREE, but there is a charge for the attractions.

THE NATIONAL ARCHIVES AT KANSAS CITY is adjacent at 400 W. Pershing Road. Some of the most important documents in the country now have a new home in KC. The new, state-of-the-art facility adjacent to Union Station houses more than 60 million pages of historical records-including photos, maps, letters and other items dating back to 1815. Visitors can research family trees, replicate famous signatures or view rare documents from around the region, such as the original complaint from Brown V. Board of Education, the court case which ended school segregation. Admission is free. (Open 8:00am-5:00pm. closed Sunday, Monday and Federal holidays).

KEMPER MUSEUM OF CONTEMPORARY ART

4420 Warwick Blvd., (At 45th Street and Warwick Boulevard, just north of the Country Club Plaza) **Kansas City** 64111

- ☐ Phone: (816) 753-5784 **www.kemperart.org**
- ☐ Hours: Tuesday-Thursday 10:00am-4:00pm, Friday-Saturday 10:00am-9:00pm and Sunday 11:00am-5:00pm.
- ☐ Admission: FREE.

The acclaimed Kemper Museum of Contemporary Art boasts a rapidly growing permanent collection of modern and contemporary works by artists from around the world. The Kemper's permanent collection is virtually a Who's Who among contemporary artists — including works by Jackson Pollock, Andy Warhol, Chihuly glass, and Georgia O'Keeffe. Offered throughout the year, the museum's free Family Days feature hands-on activities, Scavenger Hunt Saturdays, live music, storytelling, docent-led tours, gallery games and dance and theatrical performances. Each exhibition has gallery games to engage kids and adults into the art form. Have lunch at Café Sebastienne. It's hard to miss the café's colorful walls where 110 paintings called the History of Art fit together like a puzzle. Don't forget to snap a photo of the Kemper outdoor sculptures - the 1600 pound bronze Spider on the front lawn or the "baby" spider crawling up the outside of the museum building.

NELSON-ATKINS MUSEUM OF ART

4525 Oak Street (Take I-35 to Hwy 71 South. Exit at Emanuel Cleaver II Boulevard) **Kansas City** 64111

- ☐ Phone: (816) 751-ART **www.nelson-atkins.org**
- ☐ Hours: Wednesday 10:00am-4:00pm, Thursday-Friday 10:00am-9:00pm, Saturday 10:00am-5:00pm and Sunday Noon-5:00pm.
- ☐ Admission: FREE. There may be a charge for special exhibitions. Parking is $3.00.
- ☐ Miscellaneous: Rozzelle Court Restaurant is fashioned after an open-air Italian courtyard and offers buffet-style service of gourmet main dishes, salads, soups, breads and desserts. On select Fridays, enjoy live jazz music.

Imagine a 67-story office building lying on its side, and you'll get an idea of how large the expansion of Kansas City's premier art museum is. But what really draws the kids in are the sculptures: no one can miss the main building lawn as four giant badminton shuttlecocks are positioned on the front lawn or, even the parking garage is topped by a site-specific sculpture in a large reflecting pool that allows light to filter through the water into the garage area below. Once inside the museum, a series of galleries connect by stairs and ramps and five stunning, translucent and transparent glass "lens" emerge from the space beneath. With a permanent collection that contains more than 34,500 works of art, the Nelson-Atkins is best known for its Asian art, European paintings and modern sculpture. Kids remember the knight in full parade dress, an authentic Chinese temple and many of the sculpture pieces most.

THOMAS HART BENTON HOME AND STUDIO STATE HISTORIC SITE

3616 Belleview (I-35 to Southwest Trafficway or Rainbow Blvd. Exit. Follow signs) **Kansas City** 64111

☐   Phone: (816) 931-5722 **www.mostateparks.com/benton.htm**
☐   Hours: Monday and Thursday-Saturday 10:00am-4:00pm, and Sunday 11:00am-4:00pm. (November-March). Monday and Wednesday-Saturday 10:00am-4:00pm, and Sunday Noon-5:00pm. (April-October).
☐   Admission: The Missouri state park system does not charge entrance fees. However, there are fees associated with camping, lodging, tours, museums and certain special events. $2.50-$4.00 admission for house tour (ages 6+).
☐   Educators: you will find Teacher's Guides covering pre-and-post visit activities, vocabulary and more background on Benton on their Teacher's Guide page.

Missouri's most noted 20th century artist lived in this late Victorian style house from 1939 until his death in 1975. He had been working on a mural for the Country Music Hall of Fame, called The Sources of Country Music, which was nearly complete. The house and the carriage house, which Benton converted into an art studio, contain many of his personal belongings.

TOY AND MINIATURE MUSEUM

5235 Oak Street (just a few blocks from Country Club Plaza - University of Missouri-Kansas City) **Kansas City** 64112

☐   Phone: (816) 333-2055 or (816) 333-9328 **www.toyandminiaturemuseum.org**
☐   Hours: Wednesday-Saturday 10:00am-4:00pm, Sunday 1:00pm-4:00pm.
☐   Admission: $7.00 adult, $6.00 senior (65+) and full-time student, $5.00 child (5-12). Additional fees may apply for special programming and events.

TOY AND MINIATURE MUSEUM (cont.)

Housed in a renovated 1911 mansion on the University of Missouri-Kansas City campus, the Toy & Miniature Museum features 38 rooms filled with antique toys, dollhouses, marbles and scale miniatures dating from the mid-1800s to the present. It's the largest collection of nostalgic toys in the Midwest. Near the beginning of the tour a mechanical man explains the difference between toys we play with and miniatures we place on shelves. The collection features tiny versions of decorative artifacts adorning exquisite homes and palaces from various eras – past and present. Examples of intricate miniature pieces are the Noah's Ark and the Palace of Versailles. One million marbles are in the Marble Games Gallery. Visitors can try their hand at the game in a real marble ring, or become mesmerized by colorful marbles looping and winding through the intricate marble maze stationed in the middle of the room. In an another area, kids will rave over the play food and kitchen utensils. Some French pastries look good enough to eat. If you like dolls or toy history, this place has more to look at than it seems from the outside. Girls - there are dollhouses in practically every room!

DID YOU KNOW ? The museum's oldest doll is Georgiana, an English wooden doll circa 1750. Georgiana stands just over 26 inches tall and has a wig made from human hair.

JOHN WORNALL HOUSE

6115 Wornall Road **Kansas City** 64113

- ☐ Phone: (816) 444-1858 **http://wornallhouse.org/**
- ☐ Hours: Tuesday-Saturday, First tour begins at 10:00am - last tour begins at 3:00pm. Sunday: First tour begins at 1:00pm - last tour begins at 3:00 p.m. Closed on Monday.
- ☐ Admission: $6.00 adult (13-60), $5.00 senior (60+) & child (5-12).
- ☐ Tours: All tours of the Museum are guided and last approximately 1 hour. Reservations are welcome but not necessary.
- ☐ Miscellaneous: Easter Egg Hunt on the Lawn weekend before Easter. Small admission.

When one steps inside the John Wornall House Museum, they enter another century. In 1858, Kentuckian John B. Wornall built this elegant home in the Greek Revival style. Accurately restored to the period, its interior spaces and authentic furnishings demonstrate why the house was called the most pretentious house in the section. The house was used as a hospital during the Civil War and has lots of stories. Staff provides group tours, ghost tours, living history, hands-on workshops and other activities.

- OPEN HEARTH COOKING DEMONSTRATIONS - The Wornall House offers open hearth cooking demonstrations on some Saturdays of each month. Come see how Mrs. Wornall prepared meals during the 1850s. Even if you have toured before, this new experience will be worth your while. These demonstrations will be offered with any standard tour between 12:00pm and 3:00pm. Check the calendar of events for exact dates.

KANSAS CITY CHIEFS - ARROWHEAD STADIUM

One Arrowhead Drive (East on Interstate 70. Exit at Blue Ridge and Arrowhead Stadium will be located on the right) **Kansas City** 64129

- ☐ Phone: (816) 920-9300 **www.kcchiefs.com**
- ☐ FREEBIES: This kids zone page has online games you can play: www.kcchiefs.com/fan-zone/kids/games.html. Another link has coloring pages.

Arrowhead Stadium, the home to the Kansas City Chiefs, has just undergone its first major renovation in 40 years. The new state-of-the-art sports and entertainment destination received many fan improvements, including a new stadium club, an expanded memorabilia store and a Hall of Honor which commemorates more than 45 years of Chiefs memories. Nowhere does football quite like Kansas City, home to one of the NFL's loudest stadiums.

Arrowhead Stadium is also home to the KANSAS CITY WIZARDS - www.kcwizards.com. Outdoor soccer team plays from April thru October.

KANSAS CITY ROYALS - KAUFFMAN STADIUM

One Royal Way **Kansas City** 64129

- ☐ Phone: (816) 921-8000 **www.royals.com**
- ☐ Tours: Kauffman Stadium tours to the public run April thru October. Tickets for the Classic 75-minute tour (recommended tour for kids-note: lots of walking) run $7.00-$10.00 (ages 4+). Tours are not available on game days. Can be scheduled by calling (816) 504-4222 or going online: http://kansascity.royals.mlb.com/kc/ballpark/ballpark_tours.jsp.

KANSAS CITY ROYALS - KAUFFMAN STADIUM (cont.)

☐ Educators: When you go on the tour page, go to the bottom of the page for more info about Educational Tours: The $10.00 student fee includes a ballpark tour and 3, 20-minute units of instruction dealing with Science, Math, Social Studies, Language Arts, Character Education, History and Health & Physical Education.

The Kansas City Royals' new Kauffman Stadium has reestablished its place as one of the best ballparks in Major League Baseball. In addition to wider concourses, more restrooms and added concession stands, other new amenities include a 9,500-seat, open-air pavilion; 1,500 fountain view seats; a new Fan Walk; a sports bar-restaurant; a Royals Hall of Fame; Interactive Kids Area; and there are special events and promotions planned all summer long including Fireworks Fridays presented by Hy-Vee & Pepsi and Sprint Fun Runs on Sundays (when all fans can run the bases following the game). And, of course, many vendors selling barbeque. The Kansas City Royals play more than 80 home games each year at Kauffman Stadium. Tickets as low as $7.00 each.

TOURS: Kauffman Stadium's unique features include 104' high video board and a 322-foot wide water spectacular. A tour of this "Crown Jewel" of baseball stadiums will take you to areas of the ballpark not normally open to the public including the Royals Dugout, Press Box, Royals interview room, and Visitor's locker room. Tickets for all public tours can be purchased in advance or on the day of your tour at the main ticket office located behind home plate at Kauffman Stadium.

KANSAS CITY ZOO

6800 Zoo Drive (I-70 W, merge onto I-435 S via Exit 8A. Then take Exit 66, Blue Parkway/MO-350 E. Take the 63rd Street ramp towards Raytown)
Kansas City 64132

☐ Phone: (816) 513-5700 **www.kansascityzoo.org**
☐ Hours: Daily 9:30am-4:00pm. The Zoo is closed only on Thanksgiving, Christmas and New Year's Day.
☐ Admission: $11.50 adult, $10.50 senior, $8.50 child (3-11). Tuesday is discount day. FREE parking.

☐ Miscellaneous: IMAX Theater. Five transportation options to explore the Zoo. Golf cart and Segway tours, as well as boat, train and tram rides are available to the public seasonally. Located throughout the park, the zoo's three restaurants and six snack bars offer everything from cotton candy and Dip-N-Dots to larger meals. Picnic areas are also available. FREEBIES: Downloadable Word Search and games are on the Education Programs>Student & Teacher Programs>Classroom Activities, Zoo Visit page. Also on that page: themed self-guided Scavenger Hunts. Educators: on the FREEBIES page are also activities aligned with science standards.

The Kansas City Zoo features an impressive collection of animals in naturalistic settings-all stretched across 200 acres in Swope Park. The Zoo's exhibits are organized by continent with major sections for Africa and Australia. Check out the North American river otter exhibit just inside the zoo's entrance. Two of the Zoo's most recent animal additions are critically endangered Sumatran tigers, Langka and Manis. Also newer are the polar bears-the best polar bear exhibit between Chicago and the west coast. Less than 250 are thought to exist in the wild. If you love monkeys, this zoo has one of the largest chimpanzee environs in North America. In the Tropics area are adorable, yes really, porcupines. While visiting the porcupines, look overhead and you may see white-cheeked gibbons swinging over the Asian small-clawed otters. Children can get up-close with lemurs, meerkats and squirrel monkeys in the indoor Discovery Barn. A free, year-round activity lets Kansas City Zoo visitors feed and interact with small lorikeet birds. These brightly-colored Australian parrots fly right onto a visitor's hands, arms or head to get a sample of fruit nectar.

DID YOU KNOW? The Kansas City Zoo has five black rhinos, 1 percent of the species' world population.

LAKESIDE NATURE CENTER

4701 E. Gregory Blvd., Swope Park **Kansas City** 64132

☐ Phone: (816) 513-8960 **www.lakesidenaturecenter.org**
☐ Hours: Tuesday through Saturday, 9:00am-4:00pm.
☐ Admission: FREE.
☐ FREEBIES: a Scavenger Hunt is available here:
  www.lakesidenaturecenter.org/Edu_Scavanger%20Hunt.pdf

Wildlife education programs for all ages with live animals. Nature Center is free, has a hiking trail, picnic pavilion and native Missouri wildlife exhibit.

The nature center is one of Missouri's largest wildlife rehab facilities and typically houses about 75 animals including two bald eagles, two turkey vultures, three barred owls, and many hawks and falcons. The Center even has a box turtle named "Wilma" that is thought to be about 76 years old. The Mother Nature Reads storytime and crafttime is free but there is a small fee for events like Breakfast with the Beasts.

MAGIC WOODS

Kansas City - *Lakeside Nature Center. Watch the forest come alive at Lakeside Nature Center's annual Magic Woods for a safe, family-friendly event. Admission is $5; children 3 and under are free. Activities include face painting, tattoos, games, crafts and live animal presentations, actors from Coterie Theatre and Eco Elvis. (second weekend in October)*

CAVE SPRING HISTORIC SITE AND NATURE CENTER

8701 E Gregory Blvd. **Kansas City** 64133

- ☐ Phone: (816) 358-CAVE (2283) **www.cavespring.org**
- ☐ Hours: (Park & Trails) Trails are open daily, year round.
- ☐ 9:00am-sunset. (Nature Center) Tuesday-Friday 10:00am-4:00pm.
- ☐ Admission: $2.50 adult, $1.50 child.

The easily traveled hiking trails combined with the natural features of a cave and wildlife habitat pond allow many opportunities to pursue ecological studies. Visit the interpretive center with its history and nature exhibits. Learn why Cave Spring was an important part of the westward movement. Take a nature hike to learn which plants and trees were important to Pioneers and how they used them. See the cave and spring just like the Pioneers did in the mid-1800's. Come and enjoy the beauty of the natural surroundings while taking a trip along the Sante Fe Trail. Cave Spring provides trail directions, and scavenger hunt booklets for each student, if you ask.

COCO KEY WATER RESORT

9103 East 39th Street (Holiday Inn Kansas City Sports Complex-across the street from Arrowhead & Kauffman Stadiums) **Kansas City** 64133

- ☐ Phone: (816) 737-0200
  www.cocokeywaterresort.com/Locations/kansascity/index.aspx
- ☐ Hours: Monday-Thursday 4:00-9:00pm. Friday-Saturday 10:00am-9:00pm and Sunday 10:00am-8:00pm.
- ☐ Admission: Splash Packages start at $139 (includes waterpark passes and room). Day Pass only - $12.00-$15.00 per person, per day. Online and local coupons are available. Coupons are not accepted during holidays and school breaks.

The Hotel Sports Complex now has a new look and name -- complete with a 65,000-square-foot indoor waterpark, the largest in Missouri. The year-round CoCo Key Water Resort features body slides, tube slides - including the Barracuda Blast two-person raft slide - an adventure river, and the Palm Grotto indoor/outdoor spa. It also offers Parrot's Perch interactive play island with a 300-gallon tipping bucket. Younger children love the Dip-In Theatre, a shallow pool with a constant display of movies and cartoons. Inside, it is always a comfortable 84 degrees. Dry off and head on over to Key Quest Arcade, their interactive game room filled with state-of-the-art video games. The hotel's 374 guest rooms were also renovated. Amenities such as a 32-inch flat screen television and a leather chair and ottoman will make your stay even more comfortable. The Tradewinds Restaurant is inside the property and a Pizza Hut express / A&W service counter is too.

LONGVIEW LAKE PARK

11100 View High Drive (Take the Raytown Road Exit #4 off I-470 and turn south. Go 1 mile) **Kansas City** 64149

- ☐ Phone: (816) 503-4800 **www.jacksongov.org**

The centerpiece is Longview Lake - good for powerboating, waterskiing, jet-skiing, or pontoon boating (with full service marina and fishing). Lake has a sand beach, playground, picnic, a 6 mile asphalt lakeside bike path and another 4-mile nature trail, plus a campground with tent and RV sites (spring thru September).

CHRISTMAS IN THE PARK

Kansas City - *Longview Lake Park. The park campgrounds host an elaborate drive-through lighted display with more than 225,000 lights and 175 animated scenes. Donations requested. (Thanksgiving thru December)*

HARLEY-DAVIDSON VEHICLE & POWERTRAIN OPERATIONS TOUR

11401 N Congress Avenue (I-29 to 112th St. exit, heading east. Left on Congress) **Kansas City** 64153

- ☐ Phone: (816) 270-8023 **www.harley-davidson.com/wcm/Content/Pages/Factory_Tours/kansas_city.jsp?locale=en_US**
- ☐ Admission: FREE.
- ☐ Tours: Tours begin at regular intervals between 9:00am-1:30pm Monday-Friday. Tours last approx. one hour. Children under the age of 12 are welcome in the Tour Center, but are not allowed on the factory tour. Visitors under the age of 18 must be accompanied by an adult at all times. Tickets are distributed on a first-come, first-served basis. Tours are not offered on weekends, major holidays, or during production changes and year-end maintenance. You must wear totally enclosed flats for the factory floor tour.
- ☐ Miscellaneous: The gift shop is open until 3:00pm each weekday the factory is open.

What little traveler hasn't seen (or better, heard) a Harley-Davidson motorcycle pass by? Founded in 1903, Harley-Davidson has become a passion of the American dream. Inside the Tour Center, view displays of models made here, including the Sportster, Dyna and VRSC families of motorcycles, including the liquid-cooled Revolution powertrain for the VRSC V-rod. The center also features exhibits that guide you through the various manufacturing and assembly processes. You'll also have the chance to sit on current production motorcycles and visit the gift shop, which features tour-related souvenirs.

Your tour experience begins with an introductory video. Then it's on to the factory floor where you'll witness a wide range of operations from welding, laser-cutting and frame-bending, to polishing and assembly. You'll see the fabrication area, where sheets of steel go into a press and out pops a fender or a fuel tank. Another station is laser-cutting. Polishing is done with a robotic arm. Other machines bend steel tubes into the frames and workers fuse tubes together. Now that the parts are ready, assembly of the pieces/parts occurs. Each station has the chore of adding a different component from the handle bars to the kickstand. You'll also see the Revolution® powertrain assembled from crankcase to cylinder heads. Finally, have some fun watching the new machines get placed in the "testing booth" for simulated riding tests.

What does a doctor, a lawyer, machine operator, actor, business owner, and pastor all have in common…a Harley-Davidson motorcycle!

SHOAL CREEK LIVING HISTORY MUSEUM

Hodge Park, 7000 NE Barry Road (I-435, take Highway 152 east. Go 1/2 mile, then turn north onto Shoal Creek Parkway) **Kansas City** 64156

- ☐   Phone: (816) 792-2655 **www.kcmo.org/CKCMO/Depts/ ParksandRecreation/ShoalCreekLivingHistoryMuseum/index.htm**
- ☐   Hours: Daily, dawn to dusk
- ☐   Admission: FREE to just walk around property. Most events are $5.00 per person (age6+).

Shoal Creek Living History Museum is a village of more than 20 authentic 19th century buildings. The buildings date from 1807-1885 and include log cabin and clapboard structures to an antebellum brick mansion home. You can take a self-guided tour of the park but honestly the best time to come for kids is during special events (ex. Reenactments) to get more insights from costumed interpreters showing you the ways of 1800s people and lifestyles.

HARVEST FESTIVAL

Kansas City - *Shoal Creek Living History Museum. Are you yearning for a simpler time? Join them for an old fashioned County Fair. Bring your baked goods, sewing, handcrafts for judging or participate in the buffalo chip throwing or sack races! (second Saturday in October)*

A VISIT WITH ST. NICHOLAS

Kansas City - *Shoal Creek Living History Museum. Experience Christmas as it was meant to be in the 19th century. Visit log cabins of 1825 and 1835, a school, church, mercantile and then St. Nicholas, resplendent in green velvet robes. Ride the horse drawn sleigh and take the walking tour through 17 historic buildings. (first Saturday in December)*

OCEANS OF FUN

4545 Worlds of Fun Avenue (10 minutes northeast of downtown Kansas City
on I-435 exit 54) **Kansas City** 64161

- Phone: (816) 454-4545 **www.worldsoffun.com**
- Hours: Oceans of Fun is open seasonally from May through September. Daily
  operating hours vary; call or visit the Web site for more details.
- Admission: Regular (guests 48" or taller) is around $29.00. About half price
  for younger guests and seniors. Twilight (after 4:00pm) reduced regular rates.
  Ride and Slide admission discounts. Buy online discounts. Parking $10.00.
- Miscellaneous: With several different food locations throughout the park,
  Oceans of Fun has everything from hometown barbecue to old-world
  traditional pizza.

The waterpark's attractions include a million-gallon wave pool, an 800-
foot lazy river and a family kayaking/canoeing area. Paradise Falls is the
Midwest's largest family water playhouse with several interactive areas to
explore. A gigantic bucket sits atop the playhouse, dumping 1,000 gallons
of water onto its guests every five minutes. The newest of the waterpark's 18
water slides is Hurricane Falls, a family raft ride boasting a 680-foot flume.
"Superpool" Coconut Cove features 20,000 square feet of fun, including
floating characters, water obstacles and other challenging activities. Young
guests will love Crocodile Isle, a "sprayground" just for small children and
their parents. Those who prefer pure relaxation can float along the Caribbean
Cooler, an 800-foot gently flowing lazy river. Worlds of Fun is next door. For
easy access, use the Ride & Slide Gate that links the two parks.

WORLDS OF FUN

4545 Worlds of Fun Avenue (10 minutes northeast of downtown Kansas City
on I-435 exit 54) **Kansas City** 64161

- Phone: (816) 454-4545 **www.worldsoffun.com**
- Hours: Worlds of Fun is open seasonally from April through October. Daily
  operating hours vary; call or visit the Web site for more details.
- Admission: Regular (guests 48" or taller) is around $41.00. About half price
  for younger guests and seniors. Twilight (after 4pm) reduced regular rates.
  Ride and Slide admission discounts. Buy online discounts. Parking $10.00.

☐ Miscellaneous: The Worlds of Fun Village resort features 20 cottages, 22 log cabins and 82 deluxe RV sites. Park visitors can choose from more than 40 different food locations including three dine-in restaurants: All Stars Grill, Coasters Drive-In and Zarda Bar-B-Q. Concession options range from light snacks to meal-sized entrees. Annual Festivals are held in the park. Example: HeartFest - contemporary Christian music concerts (mid-May).

Worlds of Fun offers more than 170 acres of wild rides, unique food and live entertainment in five themed continent areas: Americana, Africa, Europa, the Orient and Scandinavia. The wooden Prowler zig-zags its way through the deep woods of the theme park's Africa section. The smooth, "bobsled-like" ride has an initial drop of 85 feet and peaks at a speed of 51 mph. The Prowler is the first wooden coaster constructed at Worlds of Fun since the park favorite Timber Wolf debuted almost two decades ago. Another mammoth thrill ride is the Patriot. The Patriot is the longest and tallest inverted roller coaster in the region. Camp Snoopy at Worlds of Fun offers kids the chance to meet Peanuts characters and ride "kid-sized" rides similar to the big thrill rides-scaled down on the wild factor. Peanuts Playhouse is a three-story interactive funhouse with more than 5,000 foam balls plus slides, geysers, catapults and blasters. Visitors can use the Ride & Slide Gate to access the adjacent waterpark, Oceans of Fun.

FEDERAL RESERVE BANK OF KANSAS CITY
1 Memorial Drive (Crown Center Area, adjacent to the Liberty Memorial)
Kansas City 64198

☐ Phone: (816) 881-2683 **www.KansasCityFed.org/MoneyMuseum**
☐ Hours: Open Monday - Friday 8:30am-4:30pm excluding bank holidays.
☐ Admission: FREE.

Visit the Federal Reserve Bank of Kansas City's Money Museum – a billion dollar experience! Free and open to the public, the Money Museum offers guests the opportunity to watch millions of dollars in currency be processed in a giant vault, lift a gold bar worth nearly $400,000 and enjoy fun, interactive exhibits while learning about the economy. Compare real and counterfeit money or learn to use an automated teller machine that spits out real receipts. At the end of your self-guided tour (only takes one-half hour), each guest receives a free souvenir bag of real money - shredded - sorry! Still, a wonderful free souvenir that kids can show-and-tell to friends when they get home.

SCHLITTERBAHN VACATION VILLAGE WATERPARK

9400 State Avenue west loop of I-435 at Exit 13. just east of Kansas
Speedway and Village West) **Kansas City** 66112

- ☐ Phone: (913) 312-3110 **www.schlitterbahn.com/kc/**
- ☐ Hours: Starting weekends mid-May and daily all summer, hours are generally
  10:00am-7:00pm with later closing times mid-summer.
- ☐ Admission: $25.00-$33.00 per person (ages 3+). Online and two-day
  discounts. Many hotels in the area offer discount ticket overnight packages.
- ☐ FREEBIES: FREE parking, use of inner tubes, use of life jackets and guests
  are permitted to bring their own food and beverages INSIDE THE PARK!

Schlitterbahn Vacation Village will eventually be one of the world's largest
tubing parks with miles of interconnected rivers plus the current signature
attractions--Torrent River and the Master Blaster, a six-story uphill water
coaster. The outdoor waterpark features a thrilling uphill water coaster, two
mammoth tubing rivers including the world's longest tidal wave river, three
huge slides, a white water tube chute, 13 mini slides for kids, three relaxing
beach areas and a giant hot tub with swim-up refreshment bar.

The year-round resort will also feature 1,800 hotel rooms including waterfront
cabins and "treehaus" accommodations. Plans also include a mile-long River
Walk with destination shopping, dining and entertainment options in a
covered, year-round environment. A large Interactive Marine Park will feature
salt water lagoons for snorkeling, helmet diving and touch pools. The park's
entertainment venues will be connected by a state-of-the-art Transportainment
River System. A fusion of transportation, sport and entertainment, man-made
rivers will carry guests between lodging units and attractions.

FESTA ITALIANA

Kansas City - *Zona Rosa. www.zonarosa.com. One of Kansas City's favorite festivals,
Festa Italiana, the unique celebration of Italian traditions and Italian-American
culture, will be hosted once again at Zona Rosa this year! This longtime local ethnic
festival draws visitors from across metropolitan Kansas City and beyond. This popular
family event has free admission and showcases Italian food booths, live Italian music,
dancers, a kids play area, firework display and more. FREE. (first weekend in June)*

KCRIVERFEST

Kansas City - *Riverfront Park, 5th St. and Grand Blvd. KCRiverFest is Kansas City's Premier Independence Day Festival. The annual KCRiverFest features the largest fireworks display in Downtown Kansas City, great bands, crafts, a Children's Zone with rides and entertainment, river boardwalk, a variety of foods, exhibits and more. Discount advance tickets available online at www.KCRiverFest.com. Admission. (July 4th weekend)*

FAULKNER'S PUMPKIN FARM & RANCH

Kansas City - *10600 Raytown Rd. (Conveniently located just 1/4 mile South of I-470 on West side of Raytown Rd). Phone: (816) 763-4644 www.faulknerspumpkinfarm.com. Take home the perfect pumpkin, bump along on the hayride and meet the barnyard friends in the petting farm at their beautiful new farm and ranch located right by Longview Lake! Try the new Pumpkin Cannon - target shooting with pumpkins. Farm train rides. Wild West playground. Duck races and pony rides. Field maze, pedal karts and moonwalks. Croquet games with brooms or ranglin' on steel horses. Organized games with prizes every hour. Admission. (entire month of October)*

KANSAS CITY BALLET PRESENTS
"THE NUTCRACKER"

Kansas City - *Music Hall, 301 W 13th Street. www.kcballet.org. Holiday magic sparkles as the curtain goes up for Kansas City Ballet's enchanting presentation of "The Nutcracker" with the music of Tchaikovsky accompanied by live orchestra. Featuring elaborate scenery, stunning choreography and vibrant costumes, Clara's magical adventure captures the imaginations of all ages. KCB's "The Nutcracker" is the largest production in an eight state region and lasts approximately two hours. Admission. (two weeks leading up to Christmas)*

KANSAS CITY SCOTTISH HIGHLAND GAMES &
CELTIC FESTIVAL

Kansas City (Riverside) - *EH Young Park, 1001 NW Argosy Pkwy. Kansas City Scottish Highland Games and Celtic Festival includes: athletic competition; highland dancing; pipes and drums; Irish dancing; Irish and Scottish musical entertainment; kids events; clans; history and culture; highland wrestling; animals; great food;*

drink; archery; birds of prey; a British car show, merchandise vendors. Friday night is a full musical entertainment evening with Tartanic, Mother Grove, Tullamore and Highland Reign opening up for Enter The Haggis. Lots to do for all family members. Come be a Scot, even if you're not. Admission. www.kcscottishgames.org. (second weekend in June)

BATTLE OF WESTPORT

6601 Swope Parkway **Kansas City (Westport)** 64111

- ☐ Phone: (913) 345-2000
- ☐ **http://www.battleofwestport.org/pdf/Battle%20of%20Westport%20Self-Guided%20Auto%20Tour%20Map.pdf.**

The most important Civil War battle in the Kansas City area was the Battle of Westport, known as the "Gettysburg of the West." On Oct. 23, 1864, the ragtag brigades of Gen. Price's Confederate army met Union armies that outnumbered him two to one. Westport was a Union victory, but Price was spared a total disaster when Brig. Gen. "JO" Shelby's Iron Brigade made a last stand on the site of present-day Forest Hill Cemetery, where Shelby was buried long after the war. Information about the Battle of Westport and a map of a self-guided auto tour of more than 20 marked and interpreted sites can be obtained at the Harris-Kearney House Museum in Westport.

GREAT WOLF LODGE

10401 Cabela Drive (I-435 exit 13) **Kansas City, KS** 66111

- ☐ Phone: (913) 299-7001 **www.greatwolf.com/kansascity/waterpark**
- ☐ Admission: Lodge room suites include 4-6 waterpark passes. Rooms vary from $169-$499 per night but off-peak and seasonal specials are always being updated online.
- ☐ Miscellaneous: all suites: family, KidCabin (log cabin in room with bunk beds) have a microwave and small refrigerator. Check out the wonderful holiday theme packages they offer for Easter, Fall Harvest, Thanksgiving and Christmastime.

Serving as Kansas' Year-Round Family Resort, Great Wolf Lodge provides a comprehensive package of destination lodging amenities, including 281 family-sized suites; featuring a grand scale waterpark; arcade with ticket redemption; children's craft and activity room; Aveda® Concept Spa; fitness room; northwoods-themed restaurant; confectionery café; spacious outdoor pool; gift emporium and a performing Great Clock Tower. Whether it's 10 degrees below or raining cats and dogs, it's always a balmy 84 degrees inside the resort's huge, 38,000 square-foot indoor waterpark. Bear Track Landing puts the emphasis on fun with 8 waterslides, three pools and a four-story treehouse waterfort. Bear Track Landing is an ideal escape for both parents and kids, offering an environment that allows for both bonding together-time and safe, supervised yet independent kid-friendly fun that gives parents time to relax with children in sight. Two areas for the 10 and under crowd are the nightly Storytime by the lobby fireplace (come in your pajamas) or the craft room, Cubs Cabin. Each month they change the seasonal theme of the crafts offered and most are free. The staff and quality of craft always receive high ratings from our crew. This "safe" waterpark and dry activity environment is probably the key factor for recommendation to young families - especially with kids age 10 and under.

RENAISSANCE FESTIVAL

Kansas City, KS - *Adjacent to Sandstone Amphitheater. www.kcrenfest.com. Come explore the 16th century village as it comes to life for seven spectacular autumn weekends. The Festival, now in its 30th year, provides an enchanting escape within nearly 16 acres of shaded lanes. Experience the joust, where knights in armor duel on horseback to win the Queen's honor. Interact with over 500 costumed characters and listen to the soothing music of the dulcimer, mandolin and harp. If you prefer, catch exhilarating shows like fire eating and zany comedy on one of 13 stages. Feast on food fit for a king such as giant turkey legs, roasted corn on the cob, Scotch eggs and chocolate covered cheesecake on a stick. For the perfect day, join them for the Feaste of Fooles! In addition, there are over 162 shops to explore brimming with fine goods including jewelry, glass, leather goods, and more. Explore unique games and rides like the Crows Nest and Slay the Dragon. Kids will also enjoy their Children's Realm filled with games, shows and crafts and Knightings by the King each day in the Children's Realm! Admission. (weekends starting Labor Day thru Columbus Day in October)*

JESSE JAMES FARM & MUSEUM

21216 James Farm Road **Kearney** 64060

- ☐ Phone: (816) 736-8500 **www.jessejames.org**
- ☐ Hours: Daily 9:00am-4:00pm (May-September), Monday-Saturday 9:00am-4:00pm, Sunday Noon-4:00pm (October-April).
- ☐ Admission: $7.50 adult (16+), $6.50 senior (62+), $4.00 child (8-15).

In Kearney, tour the Jesse James Farm and Museum, the birthplace and family home of Jesse James. The museum offers displays relating to the famous Missouri outlaw and his brother, Frank, and the role the Civil War played in their lives. On display are Jesse James and James family artifacts including three of Jesse's guns, the boots he was wearing when he was killed, a pair of boot spurs, and the family Bible, with inscriptions written in Zerelda's own hand. Even the picture Jesse was straightening on the wall when he was shot is on display. Inside the log cabin home, you'll see the bedroom Jesse was born in and the bedroom where Frank died of a stroke. Most every object in the home is original and of 1875 era vintage. Was his gang member a coward or a hero for ending Jesse's life? Each Jesse James historical attraction may have a different viewpoint.

DID YOU KNOW ? James was influenced as a young, impressionable youth watching Civil War raids through town.

POWELL GARDENS

1609 NW US Hwy 50 (30 miles east of KC) **Kingsville** 64061

- ☐ Phone: (816) 697-2600 **www.powellgardens.org**
- ☐ Hours: Daily, 9:00am-5:00pm (until 6:00pm April-October).
- ☐ Admission: $9.50 adult, $8.50 senior, $4.00 child (5-12) (April-October). Discounted rates November-March. Rates for special events vary.
- ☐ Miscellaneous: Powell Gardens' Café Thyme offers a wide variety of menu options for brunch, lunch and snacks. (The café is closed Mondays and Tuesdays during January and February.)

Kansas City's botanical garden features 915 acres of beautiful, ever-changing gardens, nature trails, and year-round events. The 3.25-mile Byron Shultz Nature & Hiking Trail leads visitors past frog-filled ponds, through woods of honey locust and into a field of meadow flowers. There's also lakeside gardens, the secluded Island Garden and a 600-foot "living" rock wall, the largest of its kind in North America.

Powell Gardens has unveiled what may be the first garden of its kind in the country. The 100-percent-edible, 12-acre Heartland Harvest Garden shows the path of food from seed to plate. The new area includes a demonstration kitchen, education garden and four acres of intricate quilt gardens that visitors can view from the top of a 45-foot silo. The view from high in the silo vs. ground level is worth the trip. The Heartland Harvest Garden is a delicious garden designed to satisfy all of your senses. The Menu Garden offers an appetizer of thumbnail plantings to highlight what lies ahead. In the Seed to Plate Greenhouse, sprouting seeds illustrate the beginning of the botanical miracle that ultimately leads to the foods on our dinner plates. Down the path, the Apple Celebration Court showcases Missouri's finest apple varieties. Last but not least is the youth education garden and Fun Foods Farm, where children can dig in for hands-on learning about plant science, water conservation and nutrition using curriculum tied to Missouri and Kansas education standards. The children's garden features a tutti-fruitti maze, a fun garden that explores the origin of candy flavors (yum), sculptures for climbing and a pioneer day sod house.

FESTIVAL OF BUTTERFLIES

Kingsville - *Powell Gardens. Get up close and personal with hundreds of live butterflies in our free-flight conservatory exhibit. Enter through our butterfly breezeway where native species abound, then take a turn through the conservatory to view the Blue Morpho, Gulf Frittilary, Mexican Bluewing and other special exotics. Children can catch and release butterflies and enjoy butterfly-related arts and crafts; all ages can learn how to grow a butterfly garden, buy butterfly-attracting plants and much more. Admission. (first two weekends in August)*

GEN. JOHN J PERSHING BOYHOOD HOME STATE HISTORIC SITE

1100 Pershing Drive **Laclede** 64651

- ☐ Phone: (660) 963-2525 **www.mostateparks.com/pershingsite.htm**
- ☐ Admission: The Missouri state park system does not charge entrance fees. However, there are fees associated with camping, lodging, tours, museums and certain special events.

GEN. JOHN J PERSHING BOYHOOD HOME (cont.)

- ☐ Tours: Monday-Saturday 10:00am-4:00pm and Sundays Noon-6:00pm (April-September). Tuesday-Saturday 10:00am-4:00pm (October-March). $4.00 adult (13+), $2.50 child (6-12).

General John J. Pershing, one of the highest-ranking military officers in U.S history, grew up in Laclede. Tour his boyhood home and Prairie Mound School, with exhibits of the many obstacles he walked through during his boyhood and military career. Walking tours originate at the visitor contact point and depart for the boyhood home, which is located nearby. Visitors will be taken inside the two-story house that has been furnished to reflect its appearance when Pershing was growing up here from 1866 to 1882. What was the famous General like as a kid? The Prairie Mound School Museum is open to the public for self-guided tours at no charge. John Pershing taught in this one-room school before departing Missouri for West Point in 1882. Themes in the museum reflect the doorways that Gen. Pershing passed through in his lifetime. From the doorway of the Prairie Mound School as a young adult, to the doorway of Walter Reed Hospital in Washington D.C., where he passed away on July 15, 1948 at age 87.

PERSHING STATE PARK

29277 Hwy. 130 **Laclede** 64651

- ☐ Phone: (660) 963-2299 **www.mostateparks.com/pershingpark.htm**
- ☐ Admission: The Missouri state park system does not charge entrance fees. However, there are fees associated with camping, lodging, tours, museums and certain special events.

This park is an example of a pre-European settlement landscape of northern Missouri. A hike down the 1.5-mile boardwalk or 6.5-mile Riparian Trail allows visitors to glimpse a slice of pre-settlement Missouri. Along Locust Creek are forested bottomlands, shrub swamps, marshes and a wet prairie. The park also offers small fishing lakes, hiking trails and campsites.

WATKINS MILL STATE PARK & HISTORIC SITE
26600 Park Road North **Lawson** 64062

☐ Phone: (816) 580-3387 **www.mostateparks.com/wwmill/index.html**

☐ Hours: (Visitor Center, Museum Exhibits, Grounds) Monday-Saturday 9:30am-5:00pm, Sunday 10:30am-5:00pm. (Tours of Watkins Woolen Mill and the Watkins House - See admission fee below) Monday-Saturday 10:00am-4:00pm, Sunday 11:00am-4:00pm. Mill tours are given on the even hours (10:00am, Noon, 2:00pm, 4:00pm) and house tours are on the odd hours (11:00am, 1:00pm, 3:00pm). Visitors must be with a tour guide to enter the house or mill.

☐ Admission: Entrance to the park, historic site and visitor center is free. There are fees for guided tours of the historic buildings, camping and reservation of the shelter house and church.

☐ Tours: Admission $2.50-$4.00. Tours are one hour and focus on the house and mill properties.

☐ Note: The mill and house are not heated or air-conditioned. Educators: if you send them an email, they have Teachers Guides they can send you.

WATKINS WOOLEN MILL STATE HISTORIC SITE - The Visitor's center focuses on life in the region in the 1870s. Tours of the house and mill are offered. This site interprets the landholdings of Waltus Locket Watkins. Tour his house and woolen mill, the only 19th century American woolen mill with its original machinery still intact. You'll see original machinery, Watkins home, a church, a school, and several smaller buildings. Tours of the home include the first two floors of the home, the dairy cellar, summer kitchen, icehouse, smokehouse, fruit dryhouse, garden and poultry coops.

In addition to tours, the site offers a 25-minute orientation film that is recommended for all ages. The park also has a lake for fishing, swimming and boating; camping, hiking and equestrian trails; and a paved bicycle trail.

CHRISTMAS OPEN HOUSE

Lawson - *Watkins Mill. Plantation decorated for the season and costumed re-enactors perform the music, crafts, and another activities as well as serve refreshments that were popular in the 1870s. (mid-December)*

MISSOURI TOWN 1855

8010 E. Park Road (located in Fleming Park) **Lee's Summit** 64064

- ☐ Phone: (816) 503-4860 **www.jacksongov.org/historicsites**
- ☐ Hours: Tuesday-Sunday 9:00am-4:30pm (March - mid-November). Weekends only 9:00am-4:30pm (mid-November - February).
- ☐ Admission: $5.00 adult, $3.00 senior (62+) and child (5-13).
- ☐ Educators: a thorough and easy to follow Teachers Guides is available off the main page under "Teachers Guides."

Missouri Town 1855 is composed of more than 25 buildings dating from 1820 to 1860. This living history museum uses original structures, furnishings and equipment. Also depicting the 19th-century lifestyles are interpreters in period attire, authentic field and garden crops, and rare livestock breeds. Find out what clothing from the 1850s was like, see and touch lye soap or pet one of the Missouri Town 1855 oxen. With the 1800s demonstrations going on (especially events and weekends), kids feel like they're walking around the "Little House" set.

CHILDREN'S DAY AND NATIONAL TRAILS DAY

Lee's Summit - *Missouri Town 1855 comes alive with a full offering of activities just for kids. Time honored games, such as sack races, tug-of-war and pie eating contests are just a few of the many special activities that will provide your children with a unique day. Missouri Town will be presenting information about the Jackson County trail system as part of National Trails Day. Admission. (first Saturday in June)*

INDEPENDENCE DAY

Lee's Summit - *Missouri Town takes you back to 1855 and shares how this important date was celebrated. Experience hearth cooking, enjoy period music and engage in special speeches which will be made commemorating the anniversary of independence. Guests are invited to join in a noon-time parade through Missouri Town 1855, a recreated antebellum community. Admission. (July 4th)*

CHRISTMAS CELEBRATION

Lee's Summit - *At Missouri Town 1855, experience how our ancestors prepared for Christmas in the 1850s. Interpreters share the customs of French, English and German settlers. Carolers provide a musical backdrop. Hot cider will warm you as you stroll through the antebellum structures. As day turns into night, lanterns and luminaries light your way as you reflect on a Christmas of simpler times. Admission. (second Saturday in December)*

PARADISE PARK FAMILY ENTERTAINMENT CENTER

1021 NE Colbern Road **Lee's Summit** 64086

- ☐ Phone: (816) 246-5224 **www.paradise-park.com**
- ☐ Admission: Priced per area or attraction. From $0.25 for gameroom tokens to Unlimited Indoor/Outdoor attractions for $24.95/person.

Paradise Park has three activity areas - The Family Entertainment Center, The Children's Edutainment Center, and indoor meeting/party rooms, in addition to an outdoor picnic pavilion. The park is a clean environment and the staff like to work here. The Family Entertainment Center offers a mix of indoor and outdoor attractions for all ages, including go karts, miniature golf, batting cages, bumper cars, rock climbing, a game room, and the foam factory. The Children's Edutainment Center caters to younger children and their parents with a variety of age-appropriate indoor activities, much like a children's museum, and an outdoor children's play garden.

BATTLE OF LEXINGTON STATE HISTORIC SITE

1101 Delaware Street (I-70 exit Hwy 13 north for 19 miles) **Lexington** 64067

- ☐ Phone: (660) 259-4654 **www.mostateparks.com/lexington/**
- ☐ Admission: The Missouri state park system does not charge entrance fees. However, there are fees associated with camping, lodging, tours, museums and certain special events.
- ☐ Tours: Interpreters conduct guided tours of the historic house and battleground on the hour. Cost is $2.50-$4.00 per person (age 6+). Tours run Wednesday - Saturday 10:00am-4:00pm and Sunday Noon -5:00pm.
- ☐ Educators: Comprehensive Lesson Plans are on that Additional Information page of the website.

BATTLE OF LEXINGTON STATE HISTORIC SITE (cont.)

Explore the 100-acre battlefield preserved in Lexington walking a one half mile self-guided trail around the battlefield. A visitor center explains why the "Battle of the Hemp Bales" lifted Southern spirits and further dampened Northern hopes of an easy victory in the struggle for Missouri. They have exhibits and an audio-visual program. Tour the Anderson-Davis House, used by both sides as a field hospital. The house changed hands three times, and soldiers met their death in the downstairs hallway. Probably the most interesting part of the tour for kids are the bullet holes in the walls and the story of the cannon ball shot through the attic.

JESSE JAMES BANK MUSEUM

103 North Water Street (Located on the northeast corner of the historic Liberty Square) **Liberty** 64068

- ☐ Phone: (816) 736-8510
  www.claycogov.com/county/county.php?section=PR&page=45
- ☐ Hours: Monday-Saturday 10:00am-4:00pm.
- ☐ Admission: $5.50 adult (16+), $5.00 senior (62+), $3.50 child (8-15).

This bank in Liberty was the site of the first daylight bank robbery during peacetime, which was attributed to the James gang. The original safe (where the money was taken from) is still there to see. The rest of the museum is set up to look as the bank did back then and it is furnished with period pieces of furniture. It gives you a feel of a boom town's quaint feeling and images of bandits demanding money are easily recalled from movies you may have watched. If you are planning on visiting his farm and house in Kearney this is on the way. It is about a 25-minute ride from both Kansas City and Independence.

MARTHA LAFITE THOMPSON NATURE SANCTUARY

407 North La Frenz Road **Liberty** 64068

- ☐ Phone: (816) 781-8598 **www.naturesanctuary.com**
- ☐ Hours: (Nature Center) Monday-Saturday 8:00am-5:00pm. Same hours for trails except the trails are also open Sunday.
- ☐ Admission: FREE.

The 100-acre nonprofit nature sanctuary offers four miles of trails, while the center features several exhibits and has live animals and a gift shop. See the live animals, view the fossil display or sit and relax at the bird feeding station. Other exhibits are designed for touch and feel (animal pelts game, leaf identification). Most of the trails are less than a mile in length.

CAROLYN'S COUNTRY COUSINS FARM PUMPKIN PATCH

Liberty - 17607 N.E. 52nd Street (just 15 minutes from downtown Kansas City). Phone: (816) 781-9196 **www.carolynscountrycousins.com.** *Hours: Daily, 10:00am-7:00pm. Admission: $8.00/person. Additional fees apply for railroad $3.00/person or gem mining $5.00/person. Open seasonally, everyday activity options include making a scarecrow, touring the animal barn, peddling along the trike path, romping in the play yard and riding Little Bud's Railroad. On weekends, Uncle Lester's pig races, the Antique Pedal Tractor Carousel and Uncle Earl's Mining Camp add to the fun. Take a hayride to the pumpkin patch or ride on Little Bud's Railroad. Dig around in the Colossal Fossil House or grab a bite to eat at Aunt Kate's Kitchen. (begins mid-September thru October)*

WALT DISNEY HOMETOWN MUSEUM
120 East Santa Fe Avenue **Marceline** 64658

☐ Phone: (660) 376-3343 **www.WaltDisneyMuseum.org**
☐ Hours: Tuesday-Friday 10:00am-4:00pm, Saturday 10:00am-4:00pm, Sunday 1:00pm-4:00pm. Closed Monday. (April-October)
☐ Admission: $5.00 adult (11+), $2.50 child (6-10).

One city where pop culture and history meet is Marceline, the childhood home of Walt Disney. By his own account, Walt's happiest childhood memories were of his time in this town. Disney spent part of his youth in this railroad town, which retains its ties to the animation pioneer through the WALT DISNEY DREAMING TREE AND BARN, located on the old family farm, and the Walt Disney Hometown Museum. Be sure to catch the photo op with your kids standing by the Dreaming Tree.

The Walt Disney Hometown museum is the recipient of a unique collection of family effects, never seen anywhere else in the world. Housed in the restored train depot, the Hometown Museum will excite young train buffs when they hear the real, live trains whizzing by the museum (more than 70 trains pass through town daily). The museum contains letters written by Disney. Museum guests will be thrilled to find a Midget Autopia car still in its original condition. Walt Disney retired the ride in Disneyland and sent it to his hometown Marceline in 1966. Because Walt Disney premiered the Midwest showing of the Great Locomotive Chase in Marceline's Uptown Theatre in 1956, the museum now houses a display of memorabilia from the movie. And don't worry, the museum gift shop is well stocked with Disney items.

MOZINGO LAKE AND RECREATION AREA

32348 East 245th Street (4 miles east of Maryville on Hwy. 136 then 1 mile north on Liberty Road) **Maryville** 64468

- ☐   Phone: (660) 562-8001 **www.maryvillemo.org/html/mozingo_lake_park.html**
- ☐   Admission: FREE.

This facility includes 26 miles of shoreline around a 1,006 acre lake and offers fishing, swimming, walking trails, a beach, cabins, a 70-site RV park, primitive campsites and five boat docks.

FOUNTAIN GROVE CONSERVATION AREA

32988 Blackhorn Drive **Meadville** 64659

- ☐   Phone: (660) 938-4124 **www.mdc.state.mo.us/areas**
- ☐   Hours: Daily 4:00am-10:00pm.

Fountain Grove Conservation area sits in the floodplain of the Grand River and serves as an important migration stop for a variety of wildlife. It also plays an important role as a wintering habitat for Canada geese. Here you'll find diverse wetland habitats including marshes, bottomland forests, grain fields, oxbow lakes and sloughs. Bald eagles are commonly seen in the area throughout the winter. Things to Do: Fishing, camping, hiking, wildlife viewing, picnicking and, the kids favorite - frogging.

DID YOU KNOW ? Nearby Chillicothe is the Home of Sliced Bread. (the Grand River Historical Society Museum & the Murals of Chillicothe, downtown, tell the story)

VAN METER STATE PARK

32146 N. Hwy. 122 **Miami** 65344

- Phone: (660) 886-7537 **www.mostateparks.com/vanmeter.htm**
- Admission: The Missouri state park system does not charge entrance fees. However, there are fees associated with camping, lodging, tours, museums and certain special events.

The state of Missouri and its principal river were both named after a tribe of Native Americans, known by the French explorers as the "Oumessourit" or Missouri Indians, that once lived in the area of Van Meter State Park. Today, the park provides outdoor recreational opportunities and interprets the area landscape and the Native Americans who found it to be bountiful. A hand-dug earthwork, known as the Old Fort, and several burial mounds lie within park boundaries. This park features Missouri's American Indian Cultural Center, which interprets the history of nine tribes that once inhabited Missouri. Many of the artifacts on display were found on the property. The large wall mural gives you a real sense of the ancient Indian landscape. Beneath black walnut and oak trees, visitors can find a campground, picnic area, hiking trails and a fishing lake.

SQUAW CREEK NATIONAL WILDLIFE REFUGE

(just off of Interstate 29. Take exit 79, & drive 3 miles west on Highway 159) **Mound City** 64470

- Phone: (660) 442-3187 **www.fws.gov/midwest/SquawCreek/**
- Hours: (Refuge Headquarters) Monday-Friday 7:30am-4:00pm, (Visitor Contact Station) Monday - Friday 7:30am-4:00pm (year-round) and 10:00am-4:00pm weekends (Mid-March to early May) and (Mid-October to early December). (Wildlife Drive/Outdoor Facilities) - Open daily, dawn to dusk (year-round).
- Admission: FREE.

Located in northwest Missouri and in the Missouri River flood plain, this large refuge was established as a resting, feeding and breeding ground for migratory birds and other wildlife.

EAGLE DAYS

Mound City - *Squaw Creek National Wildlife Refuge. During this time you can view 100s of bald eagles and learn about the comeback of our national symbol. Guided eagle tours, a movie about eagles, captive eagles on display. (December or January)*

CHAPPELL'S RESTAURANT AND SPORTS MUSEUM

323 Armour Road **North Kansas City** 64116

- ☐ Phone: (816) 421-0002 **www.chappellsrestaurant.com**
- ☐ Hours: Monday-Thursday 11:00am-10:00pm, Friday-Saturday 11:00am-11:00pm.

Filled floor to ceiling with sports items from the present to nearly 100 years ago, Chappell's is home to the nation's largest collection of sports memorabilia displayed in a restaurant. Can you count all 1,000 football helmets or find the dozens of autographed Hall of Fame baseballs? They offer typical American fare at moderate prices. Try Chappell's Cheese Fries (topped with zesty cheese queso or blue cheese sauce?), championship steaks (even steak soup), huge sandwiches or low carb and lite items.

SHATTO MILK COMPANY

9406 N. HWY. 33 **Osborn** 64474

- ☐ Phone: (816) 930-3862 **www.shattomilkcompany.com**
- ☐ Hours: Visitors can stop by the farm to look around on their own and visit the country store 365 days a year (during business hours).
- ☐ Tours: Tours of the dairy, bottling facility and farm are available by appointment, Tuesday through Saturday throughout the year. Tours typically last one and a half hours from start to finish. There is a modest $4 charge per person, and children ages two and under are free.
- ☐ Miscellaneous: The farm has an annual Easter Egg Hunt and Family Day at the Farm in June.

Shatto Milk Company is a small family owned dairy farm just north of Kansas City that makes milk more fun than ever. The Shatto Family offers tours of their farm year-round. It starts with the cows. Get a first-hand look at where

120 cows live, what they eat, and how they are milked. Try milking a live cow or bottle feeding baby calves. Next, learn how their milk is bottled in the processing plant. Your visit includes a tour of the processing plant and viewing the actual process, along with a description of each step their milk goes through before it ends up on your table. Things get really interesting when flavors are mixed in. The choices? Banana, orange, strawberry, chocolate, root beer and eggnog - each in glass bottles so cute you'll be tempted to not return them for the deposit. Watch the bottle wash station and then the filling station. At the end of your tour, sample many of Shatto Milk Company's tasty products.

DID YOU KNOW ? Shatto raises Holstein Cows for milking as they tend to produce more milk than cream.

PUMPKINS ETC.

Platte City - *10701 Farmer Lane. Phone: (816) 858-5758 www.pumpkins-etc.com. Visitors play in the mazes, jump on the haystacks and steer wheelbarrows toward their favorite pumpkins. FREE. KARBAUMER FARM HAYRIDES is also in town offering wagon rides through the countryside. Call for details and rates. (mid-September thru October, daily)*

LEWIS AND CLARK STATE PARK
801 Lake Crest Blvd. **Rushville** 64484

- Phone: (816) 579-5564 **www.mostateparks.com/lewisandclark.htm**
- Admission: The Missouri state park system does not charge entrance fees. However, there are fees associated with camping, lodging, tours, museums and certain special events.

This park is dedicated to explorers Meriwether Lewis and William Clark, who visited the area July 4, 1804, on their westward journey. On the border of the Lake, the park offers picnic sites, camping, fishing, a boat ramp and a beach.

FORT OSAGE NATIONAL HISTORIC LANDMARK
107 Osage Street **Sibley** 64088

- ☐ Phone: (816) 650-3278 **www.fortosagenhs.com**
- ☐ Hours: Tuesday-Sunday 9:00am-4:30pm (March - mid-November). Weekends Only 9:00am-4:30pm (mid-November - February).
- ☐ Admission: $7.00 adult, $4.00 youth, $3.00 senior, Under 5 free.

The Fort Osage National Historic Landmark was built in 1808 under the direction of William Clark, co-leader of the Lewis & Clark expedition. The site was deemed an excellent place for camp. Clark came back in 1808 and built the fort. Overlooking the Missouri River, the Fort served as both a military garrison and trade center. This historic site has been reconstructed to portray Fort Osage as it was in 1812. Today, you can tour the blockhouses, officers' quarters and soldiers' barracks that frequently come to life in living history programs of the period. Authentically attired interpreters provide living-history insights into the daily life of both the military and civilian populations.

COALITION OF HISTORIC TREKKERS NATIONAL GATHERING AT FORT OSAGE

Sibley - *Fort Osage. Experience the lifestyles of the early 1800s as re-enactors from across the country converge on Fort Osage for their national gathering. A variety of activities engage the visitors, offering a better understanding of how early explorers manage daily life. Special guided hikes introduce guests to the flora and fauna of the region. (mid-April weekend)*

INDEPENDENCE DAY AT FORT OSAGE

Sibley - *Fort Osage. The year is 1812. The soldiers and residents of Fort Osage are commemorating the anniversary of their independence against the rumors of another impending war with Great Britain. Toasts are made and speeches are given. Don't miss the firing of the cannons and muskets along with military drills. Be a witness to history and reflect upon how our contemporary celebrations contrast with those of our ancestors. Admission. (July 4th)*

GRAND FESTIVAL OF CHEZ CANSES

Sibley - *Fort Osage. Enjoy a glimpse of late 18th century American culture at Fort Osage National Historic Landmark. Volunteers demonstrate the lifestyles of our colonial ancestors. From period appropriate clothing to arts and crafts, you will share this rich segment of our heritage. Special displays of everyday objects appropriate to Colonial America will help you better understand life of the period. Admission. (second full long weekend in September)*

FIRST STREET TROLLEY
702 S. 5th Street **St. Joseph** 64501

☐   Phone: (816) 233-6700
☐   Hours: Season runs May-October.
☐   Admission: $1.75+

Getting around St. Joseph is easy aboard the popular First Street Trolleys. These reproductions of turn-of-the-century streetcars wind their way through the city with frequent stops at some of St. Joseph's most popular and historically significant attractions.

ROBIDOUX ROW MUSEUM
3rd & Poulin **St. Joseph** 64501

☐   Phone: (816) 232-5861 **www.stjomo.com/robidouxrow_museum.aspx**
☐   Hours: Tuesday-Friday 10:00am-4:00pm, Saturday & Sunday 1:00pm-4:00pm (May-September). Tuesday-Friday Noon-4:00pm. Closed Sunday and Monday. Closed January and Holidays. (October-April)
☐   Admission: $2.50 adult, $2.00 senior, $1.00 student, 12 and under free.

The city served as a starting point for wagon trails filled with pioneers heading west. Commercial growth included meat packing companies, drug companies, wholesalers and bankers. As the pioneers headed west, they occasionally stopped a while to reload and repair their wagons. This museum consists of living units (lined in a row) built in the 1840s by city founder Joseph Robidoux. How much better do you think these small dwellings were for pioneer families? Were they spoiled, maybe not wanting to go on?

JESSE JAMES HOME MUSEUM

1202 Penn Street **St. Joseph** 64503

- ☐   Phone: (816) 232-8206
  www.ponyexpressjessejames.com/index.php?pid=jesse
- ☐   Hours: Monday-Saturday 10:00am-5:00pm, Sunday 1:00-5:00pm. (April-October). Weekends only (November-March).
- ☐   Admission: $3.00 adult, $2.00 senior, $1.50 student.

Of all the worlds' legendary characters, few have attracted world-wide fascination like the outlaw, Jesse James. Some call him America's Robin Hood, while others see him as a cold-blooded killer. Perhaps he was all of these things. See the house where Outlaw Jesse James was shot in the back and killed by a friend for reward money. The place doesn't exaggerate his lifestyle nor do you want to glorify it to your kids, but this was a significant time in "Wild West" history. If you'd rather, focus on the science of DNA testing that occurred in 1995 when they exhumed the body to determine if it was truly THE Jesse James and not a fake. The DNA testing results showed a 99.7% certainty that it really was Jesse James in the grave and this is where it happened.

PATEE HOUSE MUSEUM

1202 Penn Street **St. Joseph** 64503

- ☐   Phone: (816) 232-8206   **www.ponyexpressjessejames.com**
- ☐   Hours: Monday-Saturday 10:00am-5:00pm, Sunday 1:00pm-5:00pm (April-October). Weekends Only (November-March)
- ☐   Admission: $5.00 adult, $4.00 senior, $3.00 student. Kids 5 and under are admitted FREE.

The town's focal point is the Patee House. This National Historic Landmark was a pioneer hotel and headquarters for the Pony Express in 1860. Visit the "Streets of Old St. Jo," enjoy western art, antique toys, telephones and cars. Climb aboard an 1860 train, ride a vintage carousel and stroll the streets of 1860s St. Joseph to visit a general store, a dentist's office or a jail. In the Buffalo "Saloon" volunteers occasionally serve soft drinks and popcorn. The BEST part about is you can get UP CLOSE to almost all of the objects. The museum is not only housed in the restored Pony Express headquarters office but it was also home to where the Union Army held war trails. It is one block away from the home of infamous outlaw Jesse James, where he was shot and killed by Bob Ford. After his death, the James family stayed and were interviewed in the hotel.

PONY EXPRESS MUSEUM
914 Penn Street **St. Joseph** 64503

- ☐ Phone: (816) 279-5059 or (800) 530-5930 **www.ponyexpress.org**
- ☐ Hours: Monday-Saturday 9:00am-5:00pm, Sunday 1:00pm-5:00pm.
- ☐ Admission: $5.00 adult, $4.00 senior (60+), $3.00 student (7-18).
- ☐ Educators: Ask the front desk (or call ahead) for the scavenger hunt and several worksheets the attraction has developed for school groups. Even families engage more when there's a fun scavenger hunt to do.

On April 3, 1860, a young man named Johnny Fry took off from St. Joseph on horseback, the first of a relay of riders on a new mail service to California. The museum is located on the site of the original stables and opens with a diorama of Fry on his horse, eager for the stable door to open so he can begin his ride into history. The route ran from St. Joseph through Kansas, Nebraska, Colorado, Wyoming, Utah and Nevada to Sacramento, California…almost 2,000 miles in 2 weeks…by horseback. Buffalo Bill Cody was one famous rider. Rider's horses were changed every 10 to 15 miles, and new riders mounted every 75 to 100 miles. The delivery service was set up because folks on the West Coast were eager for news from back East, where a new president was about to be elected and the country was edging toward civil war. You can imagine the quickest run ever was the delivery of President Abraham Lincoln's inaugural address (took seven days and 17 hours to complete).

Begin your tour watching a 15-minute Pony Express video. Next, move around the museum but plan to spend the most time in the interactives areas such as the "Family Life on the Frontier," where kids are able to dress up as a pioneer and experience life in the 1800s. There are plenty of hands-on activities for kids to understand the time period. Pump water from the same well that was used to water the horses. Ride a wooden sawhorse equipped with a saddle. Do you feel cavalier? Did you know saddlebags (that carried the mail) were called mochilas? Walk inside a desert air, mountain cold, and experience some of the smells encountered along the riders' trips between Missouri and California. Do you know how to choose horses that can endure the elements and the fast pace? Finally, tap out messages on a telegraph - the invention that put the Pony Express operation out of business.

PUMPKINFEST

St. Joseph - *Pony Express Museum. The spirit of the fall harvest is celebrated here with family arts festival featuring live entertainment, a children's costume parade, festival rides, pumpkin games, food, and the lighting of the Great Pumpkin. The Great Pumpkin Mountain - part of the annual PumpkinFest, is giant racks and tiers of decorated pumpkins lined to form a "tree". FREE. (second weekend in October)*

SOCIETY OF MEMORIES DOLL MUSEUM

1115 S. 12th Street **St. Joseph** 64503

- ☐ Phone: (816) 233-1420 **www.stjosephdollmuseum.com**
- ☐ Hours: Wednesday, Thursday, Friday, and Saturday 11:30am-4:30pm (June-September). Friday & Saturday 11:30am-4:30pm (May and October).
- ☐ Admission: $2.50 adult, $2.00 senior (65+), $1.00 child (6-16).

The doll museum is housed in a quaint building that is over 100 years old. It was first used as a church, but has been remodeled to display over 1,000 antique dolls, toys, and doll furniture. The items are shown in an array of interesting scenes. More of a museum to *look* at dolls rather than learn about their history.

REMINGTON NATURE CENTER

1502 MacArthur Drive (I-29 to I-229, exit on Highland Avenue (Exit 7). Go west on Highland Avenue. Right on MacArthur Drive) **St. Joseph** 64505

- ☐ Phone: (816) 271-5499 **www.stjoenaturecenter.info/**
- ☐ Hours: Monday-Saturday 10:00am-5:00pm, Sunday 1:00-5:00pm.
- ☐ Admission: $1.00-$3.00 per person (age 4+)
- ☐ Miscellaneous: Gift shop and snack shop. Friday Fish Feeding at 10:30am. FREEBIES: the website "JUST FOR KIDS" page has a Scavenger Hunt sheet, coloring pages and links to national wildlife sites for kids.

Upon entering the Nature Center guests are greeted by a life-sized Mammoth and calf along with the only mammoth bones excavated in Missouri, which happen to have been found in Buchanan County. As you walk down the hallway, or dine in our concession area, you will have the opportunity to observe native Missouri River fishes in a 7,000 gallon aquarium. Stand shoulder to shoulder with a bison, see a black bear weighing over 600lbs (an average bear weighs 200 lbs.) and get closer to a wolf than you every thought you would as you take in the vast collection of taxidermy animals that are found throughout the Center. Kids, and kids-at-heart, can explore a beaver dam, watch a functioning beehive, and gaze out the expansive windows to the Missouri River and the wildlife found there. Watch as several Missouri animals make tracks in the sand right before your eyes. You can then go outside to see the Mighty MO up close or walk down the riverwalk and view the bluffs.

The historical part of the museum takes you back to BC to the turn of the 20th century. Walk along the city streets of the 1800s, learn unique farming techniques Indians used to produce food, and go back further to the Woodlands Period and the pottery native women produced. Camp in the fur trapper tent and shop for goods in the trader cabin. Stop by the theater to watch a film about Westward Migration, the California Gold Rush, Oregon Trail and ancient Indian tales.

You can tell this attraction is newer as the developers created fresh, interactive spaces spattered with ancient artifacts. In other words, the kids are engaging in learning without really knowing it. We would say this site is both a Natural Science and History activity.

SCHWEIZER ORCHARDS

5455 FF Highway (exit 44, the Hwy 169 South exit, off I-29 and head east)
St. Joseph 64507

- ☐ Phone: (816) 232-3999 **www.schweizerorchards.com**
- ☐ Hours: (Market) Monday-Saturday 9:00am-5:30pm, Sunday 1:00-5:00pm.
- ☐ Tours: Fall field trips cost $1.50 per student and include story, walking tour of orchard and a special treat.

Peeking out from the bluffs overlooking the Missouri River is an orchard that has grown apples for more than four generations. Schweizer Orchards boasts a variety of apples and offer pick-your-own strawberries in the spring and several types of both yellow and white peaches in the summer. Each season offers a new fruit. A fall field trip extends your visit with the playground area and a stroll through the hay maze. Have you tried their apple and cherry cider slushies?

TRAILS WEST FESTIVAL

St. Joseph - *Civic Center Park, downtown. Phone: (800) 216-7080. Festival has musical entertainment, melodramas, rousing historical reenactments, food booths, and children's activities, including an art tent with hands-on art projects and performances by jugglers and magicians. Admission. (third weekend in August)*

ST. JOE CORN MAZE

St. Joseph - *5521 NE Riverside Rd. (North of Cook Rd.). Phone: (816) 273-6755 www.stjoecornmaze.com. Mazes include an Advanced Corn Maze & Beginner Corn Maze. Other activities include Hay Rides, Pumpkin Patch, Pedal Tractors, Corn Bins and much more. Light concessions. Groups welcome. Admission. (weekends and Fridays 2:00pm-6:00pm)*

SWAN LAKE NATIONAL WILDLIFE REFUGE

16194 Swan Lake Avenue **Sumner** 64681

☐ Phone: (660) 856-3323 **http://midwest.fws.gov/SwanLake/**

The primary purpose of the refuge is to provide nesting, resting, and feeding areas for waterfowl, primarily ducks. An important secondary purpose was to preserve a remnant flock of prairie chickens. Unfortunately, adequate grassland habitat to maintain a viable population of the birds was not available. So, now they expanded efforts to include Canada geese each winter. This refuge still has one of the largest concentrations of Canada geese in North America and is now the primary wintering area for the Eastern Prairie Population. Folks say you'll see more deer and geese here than you would have imagined.

DID YOU KNOW ? Nearby in Sumner Community Park is a big goose statue standing 40 feet tall, weighing three tons and has a wingspan of 61 feet.

CROWDER STATE PARK

76 NE State Highway North **Trenton** 64683

☐ Phone: (660) 359-6473 **www.mostateparks.com/crowder.htm**
☐ Admission: The Missouri state park system does not charge entrance fees. However, there are fees associated with camping, lodging, tours, museums and certain special events.

The rolling hills of northern Missouri serve as a memorial to Maj. Gen. Enoch H. Crowder, a Missourian who founded the Selective Service System. The park offers a lake, a beach, camping and hiking, mountain biking and equestrian trails. A couple of the trails run along the Thompson River.

SNOW CREEK SKI AREA

1 Snow Creek Drive **Weston** 64098

☐ Phone: (816) 640-2200 **www.skisnowcreek.com**

Snow Creek Ski Resort is located in Weston, Missouri, with 12 ski trails, served by 6 lifts. Trails: 30% beginner, 60% intermediate, 5% advanced. Snow Creek Ski Resort is located in Weston, MO, about 40 minutes from Kansas City, MO, and St. Joseph, MO. They have a SnowMonsters clubhouse and mascot for kids. Snowboarding, too.

WESTON BEND STATE PARK

16600 Hwy. 45 N **Weston** 64098

☐ Phone: (816) 640-5443 **www.mostateparks.com/westonbend.htm**
☐ Admission: The Missouri state park system does not charge entrance fees. However, there are fees associated with camping, lodging, tours, museums and certain special events.

Near Kansas City, this park features picnic tables and shelter houses, a campground, a three-mile paved bicycle trail and hiking trails. A scenic overlook, accessible to persons with disabilities, provides visitors with a view of the Missouri River, Fort Leavenworth and beyond. A hiking trail that meanders through the woods and along the edge of the bluff also provides great views of the river.

WESTON RED BARN FARM

16300 Wilkerson Road **Weston** 99909

☐ Phone: (816) 386-5437 **www.westonredbarnfarm.com**

This educational farm showcases baby animals in the spring and has a peach harvest from July to August. You can pick pumpkins, apples and blackberries (when in season), go through the corn maze, shop in the country store or take a wagon ride.

Travel Journal & Notes:

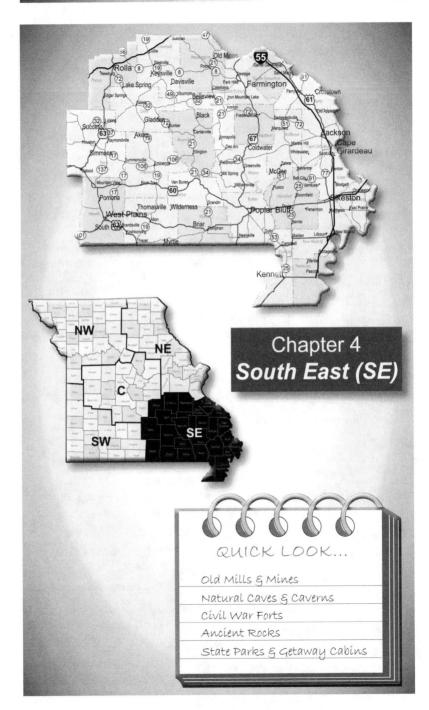

Chapter 4
South East (SE)

QUICK LOOK...

Old Mills & Mines

Natural Caves & Caverns

Civil War Forts

Ancient Rocks

State Parks & Getaway Cabins

Black
- Koinania Cottages & Cabins

Bonne Terre
- Bonne Terre Mine

Burfordville
- Bollinger Mill State Historic Site

Cape Girardeau
- Cape Girardeau Conservation Nature Center
- John Wesley Powell's Fort D
- Lazy L Safari Park
- My Daddy's Cheesecake
- Port Cape Girardeau Restaurant
- Red House Interpretive Center
- Cape Girardeau Storytelling Festival
- Cape Girardeau Air Festival

Chester, IL
- Popeye Statue And Park

Davisville
- Dillard Mill State Historic Site

Doniphan
- Civil War Days

East Prairie
- Big Oak Tree State Park
- Towosahgy State Historic Site

Ellis Grove, IL
- Fort Kaskaskia & Kaskaskia Bell State Historic Site

Eminence
- Alley Spring Grist Mill Historic Site
- Crystal Creek Ranch

Graniteville
- Elephant Rocks State Park

Jackson
- Rocky Holler USA
- St. Louis Iron Mountain & Southern Railway
- Trail Of Tears State Park

Leasburg
- Onondaga Cave State Park

Malden
- Bootheel Youth Museum

Marble Hill
- Bollinger County Museum Of Natural History

Middlebrook
- Taum Sauk Mountain State Park
- Johnson's Shut-Ins State Park

New Madrid
- New Madrid Historical Museum

Park Hills
- Missouri Mines State Historic Site
- St. Joe State Park

Patterson
- Sam A. Baker State Park

Pilot Knob
- Fort Davidson State Historic Site

Poplar Bluff
- Dunlap Pumpkin Farm

Potosi
- Sayersbrook Bison Ranch

Prairie Du Rocher, IL
- Fort De Chartres Historic Site

Puxico
- Mingo National Wildlife Refuge

Rolla
- Mineral Museum

Salem
- Bo's Hollow
- Montauk State Park
- Ozark Natural & Cultural Resource Center

Sikeston
- Lambert's Café: Home Of The Throwed Rolls
- Beggs Family Farm

St. James
- Maramec Spring Park

Stanton
- Jesse James Wax Museum
- Meramec Caverns

Ste. Genevieve
- Bolduc House Museum Complex
- Felix Valle State Historic Site
- Great River Road Interpretive Center

Ste. Genevieve (cont.)
- Hawn State Park
- Ste. Genevieve Museum
- Jour De Fete

Sullivan
- Meramec State Park

Thayer
- Grand Gulf State Park

Van Buren
- Ozark National Scenic Riverways Headquarters

West Plains
- West Plains Motor Speedway

Wickliffe, KY
- Wickliffe Mounds

Williamsville
- Lake Wappapello State Park

Winona
- Heritage Day At Twin Pines

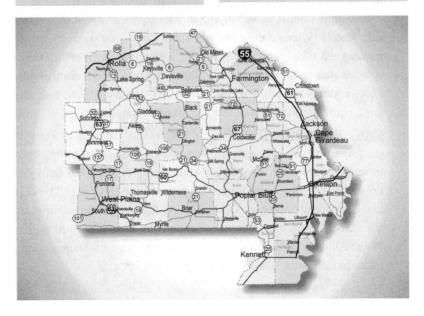

Sites and attractions are listed in order by City, Zip Code, and Name. Symbols indicated represent:

🏃 Festivals	🍽 Restaurants	🛏 Lodging

RIVER FERRIES OVER THE MISSISSIPPI RIVER INTO ILLINOIS

☐   **www.greatriverroad.com/SecondaryPages/ferries.htm**

Early American ferries consisted of rafts, rowboats and horse boats that could cross rivers where demand for transportation existed but where there weren't any easy crossings. The advent of railroads and bridges put most ferries out of business and motorized vessels replaced the earlier forms of transportation of those that survived. For modern travelers, the remaining ferries in operation can save time as well as providing scenic river views.

*   **STE. GENEVIEVE-MODOC FERRY** - N. Main Street. Follow N. Main Street about 1 1/2 miles from the Historic District of Ste. Genevieve to the Little Rock Landing on the Mississippi River. The Modoc Landing is accessible from IL-3 and IL-155 in Randolph County on the Illinois side. The ferry runs during daylight hours approximately every fifteen minutes and a fee is charged. This is the easiest way to get to the French colonial sites on the Illinois side of the river. (ex. Pierre Menard Home, Fort Kaskaskia Historic Site, and Fort de Chartes State Historic Site - the huge, partially restored stone fort kids can climb around.

*   **CANTON, MISSOURI FERRY** - Riverfront. The Canton Ferry is the longest continually operating ferry on the Mississippi having been in service since 1853. The ferry operates south of Lock and Dam #20 between the landing on the Canton Riverfront in Lewis County, Missouri to the landing at Meyer, in Adams County, Illinois. The ferry carries all size vehicles from bicycles to semi trucks. The Canton Ferry runs from 8:00am-5:00pm during the winter months and 8:00am-7:00pm during the summer months. The Canton Ferry is a toll ferry.

KOINANIA COTTAGES & CABINS

1231 County Road 66 (I-55 exit 174B -Rte. 67 south to 32 west. For rest of directions, refer to website) **Black** 63625

- ☐ Phone: (573) 269-4544 **www.koinaniacottage.com**
- ☐ Admission: Three units-Lodging fees start at $145.00 per night up to $225.00 per night with discounted weekly stays. The units available: Cottage 3 BR-2B, Ranch House Duplex 6 BR-3B-2 kitchens-2 living rooms, Cabin on Lake-sleeps 4. Full kitchens-includes linens-deck furnishings-grills.

Just 2 hours southwest of St. Louis, on 110 private acres in the beautiful Arcadia Valley in the Ozarks surrounded by Mark Twain National Forest, the folks at Koinania offer cottages and cabin lodging near the Black River. The 1/2 mile of private river frontage is a child's paradise of nature discovery an swimming fun . This isn't just a place to overnight, this is a property designed for days and days of wholesome family fun and adventures around their stocked fishing lake, hiking trails, enjoying a campfire at night, or playing in the rustic playhouse next to a small stream. This country destination has a *"Little House On The Prairie"* feel the children love. The owners have equipped closets with dress up clothes, toys, games, books, DVDs and the family friendly dogs and lovable cats top off the joy of your stay. Can you imagine catching little lizards, tree frogs, and turtles and making them your pets for a week and then letting them return to the forest? Or, early evening playing board and card games together and then watching movies, eating popcorn and staying up late?

While you could just stay on the property and explore for days, many families go horseback riding at a nearby stable, swim and play on the rocks at Johnson Shut Ins State Park or hike the trails and climb the rocks at Elephant Rocks State Park. Many families enjoy a visit to the Civil War State Historic Site at Fort Davidson and top it all off with ice cream at Pilot Knob or Caledonia.

BONNE TERRE MINE

39 North Allen Street (Hwy 47 & Allen Street) **Bonne Terre** 63628

- ☐ Phone: (573) 358-2148 **www.2dive.com/bandwtours.htm**
- ☐ Hours: Daily (Boat Tours - includes walking tour), 9:30am- 3:30pm (hourly).
- ☐ Admission: Boat tour (includes walking tour) all ages $23.00. Walking tour only $18.00 adult, $9.00 child (under 11).
- ☐ Tours: Diving Tours (certification required) are available. See website or call for complete list of available packages.

A cool way to learn more about Missouri's mine heritage takes place 80 feet below the earth's surface in Bonne Terre Mine, formerly the world's largest lead mine. One day the miners walked out and the mine began to fill with water, forming the Billion Gallon Lake and 17 miles of remote shoreline. The fact the mine is man-made makes it even more amazing, especially when you have the opportunity to see the tools used by the men who created it. The Lake is illuminated with 500,000 watts of lighting. A total of 24 dive trails have been laid out for divers to explore. For those who prefer to keep their heads above water, walking and boat tours are available (recommended for families as you must be a certified diver to go underwater).

The Walking Tour and the Boat Tour are completely different tours and views.

- WALKING TOUR - Take a one hour guided walking tour through the first and second levels of the mine along the "Old Mule Trail". Along this tour, you will see Huge Pillar Rooms, Grand Canyon, Billion Gallon Lake, Trout Pond, Underground Flower Gardens, Beautiful Calcite Falls, and ancient Abandoned Mining Tools and Rail Systems.

- BOAT TOUR - See the No. 1 Elevator, Submerged Ore Carts, Wrapped Pillars, and Ancient Abandoned Overhead Wooden Cat Walks suspended 50-100 feet above the lake.

It's a little spooky down there but you'll have tons of other tourists and a knowledgeable guide to comfort you and lead the way through an unusual tour of Missouri history.

BOLLINGER MILL STATE HISTORIC SITE

113 Bollinger Mill Road (off Hwy 34) **Burfordville** 63739

- ☐ Phone: (573) 243-4591 **www.mostateparks.com/bollinger.htm**
- ☐ Hours: grounds open daily from dawn to 10:00pm.
- ☐ Admission: The Missouri state park system does not charge entrance fees. However, there are fees associated with camping, lodging, tours, museums and certain special events.
- ☐ Tours: Typically Monday-Saturday 10:00am-4:00pm, Sunday Noon-4:00pm. Call ahead during off season to confirm. Tours run $2.50-$4.00 per person.

Bollinger Mill State Historic Site is unusual in featuring both a working mill and a covered bridge, side by side. The present mill, dating back to the Civil War period, is a massive four-story stone and brick building where visitors can still observe corn being ground into meal by water power - just as it was done long ago. The Burfordville Covered Bridge standing alongside stretches its 140-foot span across the Whitewater River, which power the mill. Begun in 1858, it is the oldest of only four remaining covered bridges in Missouri. You can tour the mill and view exhibits about how the process of milling has changed over the years and how those changes affected the mill. The 43-acre site also has a tree-shaded picnic area, and a quarter-mile of stream bank. Great lazy afternoon activity.

CAPE GIRARDEAU CONSERVATION NATURE CENTER

North County Park, 2289 County Park Drive **Cape Girardeau** 63701

- ☐ Phone: (573) 290-5218 **www.mdc.mo.gov/areas/cnc/cape/**
- ☐ Hours: Tuesday-Saturday 8:00am-5:00pm.
- ☐ Admission: FREE
- ☐ Miscellaneous: Nature Center gift shop.

The Nature Center features a 160-seat auditorium, three classrooms, hands-on exhibits for all ages, a scientific research laboratory, freshwater aquariums, and an indoor wildlife viewing area. Native American artifacts by viewing primitive tools that were used to harvest plants and animals hundreds of years ago. Interactive exhibits encourage exploration of the forest, marsh, swamp, and big river habitats of Southeast Missouri by crawling through a beaver dam or watching local fish. Outside, help a child learn how to fish at the "Kids Only" fishing pond near the nature center's entrance. Or, view sinkholes and explore ravines during a two-mile hike through White Oak Trace trail. The trails also connect to Wood Duck Swamp and Maple Hollow Trail. Kids think it's pretty cool to walk alongside a swamp. Native plants featured in the nature center's landscape provide habitat for hummingbirds, butterflies and other wildlife species. Add to this their many indoor/outdoor nature programs and you've got a great resource for free natural science.

JOHN WESLEY POWELL'S FORT D

(4 blocks south of SR 74 & Sprigg Street, just west of the Miss. River
Bridge) **Cape Girardeau** 63701

In the summer of 1861 at the beginning of the Civil War, four forts were built around the strategic city of Cape Girardeau. Fort D was designed by German-American engineers from St. Louis. The forts were built by soldiers, Engineers and local militia under the direction of Illinois Lt. John Wesley Powell. Powell, who would later gain fame as the explorer of the Grand Canyon, was detached from his regiment by a newly appointed general... Ulysses S. Grant, in order to raise a local company to man the forts. This Powell did, and his new Battery F served the forts until leaving for the Battle of Shiloh. Fort D featured as many as five cannons, the largest of which could fire a 32-pound cannon ball. The fort was manned throughout the Civil War. Of the four earthen forts only Fort D still exists, an intact survivor thanks to civic action in the 1930's. The fort grounds, featuring interpretive signs, are open free to the public dawn to dusk.

LAZY L SAFARI PARK

2763 County Road 618 **Cape Girardeau** 63701

- ☐ Phone: (573) 243-7862 **www.lazylsafari.com**
- ☐ Hours: Daily 10:00am-6:00pm (Memorial Day-Labor Day), Weekends (April, May, & September, October). Admission Gate closes at 6:00pm but Zoo closes at 7:00pm.
- ☐ Admission: $5.00 per person (ages 2+).

Lazy L Safari Park is a Walk-Thru Zoo, not a drive-thru. The park features exotic animals from around the world in a comfortable and natural setting. Visitors can walk through the park grounds in their own time and at their own pace. Take a stroll along the creek while gazing into the fields to watch zebras or antelope graze. Go on "safari" and feed the pygmy goats, watch baby animals, peer into the reptile aquariums, or check out the emu eggs in their incubator. You'll find several benches for quiet reflection or animal watching, a gift shop, a picnic shelter, and a snack shack. Be sure to visit the Petting Zoo area where you can pet and feed the animals and you won't want to miss viewing baby animals in the Animal Nursery.

MY DADDY'S CHEESECAKE

Cape Girardeau - *63701. www.mydaddyscheesecake.com. Mississippi Mud and Turtle are among the most popular cheesecake served but kids gravitate to the Gooey Louie cookie wedge - chocolate, pecans and graham crackers, or the frozen cheesecake on a stick - covered in chocolate. My Daddy has a great big brand new Bakery & Cafe and a delicious NEW all day dining menu! Start your day off right with breakfast at My Daddy's! Enjoy fresh baked Biscuit, Sourdough or Croissant Sandwiches, Breakfast Wraps, Biscuits & Gravy, Fruit Parfaits and Omelets. For lunch or dinner enjoy the "best" wraps, sandwiches and salads, like The Daddy Reuben, Quesadillas, Chicken Ciabatta, Greek Salad, Citrus Salad, Sourdough Club, Roast Beef on Wheatberry Bread, Grilled Chicken Caesar Wrap, Philly Cheese Steak, Southwestern Salad, and Veggie Deluxe Wrap.*

PORT CAPE GIRARDEAU RESTAURANT

Cape Girardeau - *19 North Water Street 63701. Phone: (573) 334-0954. During the civil war, this historic 1830s building on the riverfront housed general Ulysses s. Grant's headquarters. The building is one of the oldest standing structures west of the Mississippi River. Lunch or dinner with menu offering great BBQ, catfish, pork and a kids menu. Price Range: $7.00-$25.00.*

RED HOUSE INTERPRETIVE CENTER
128 S. Main Street **Cape Girardeau** 63701

☐   Phone: (573) 334-0757 or (573) 335-1631.
     www.orgsites.com/mo/redhouseinterpretivecenter/
☐   Hours: Saturday 10:00am-4:00pm (April-November). Open additional days in
     summer. Call or visit website for current schedule.
☐   Admission: $3.00 adult, $1.00 child.

RED HOUSE INTERPRETIVE CENTER (cont.)

☐   Educators: there are clever Scavenger Hunt Questions at the bottom of this
    Teachers Page: http://www.orgsites.com/mo/redhouseinterpretivecenter/_
    pgg2.php3.

The Red House Interpretive Center commemorates the visit of Meriwether
Lewis and William Clark in November 1803.   Louis Lorimier, Cape
Girardeau's founder, welcomed the expedition members at his home, the Red
House. The Interpretive Center houses an early 1800's exhibit that reflects the
lives of the early settlers of the "Old Cape Girardeau District." In addition,
a rendering of the Louis Lorimier Trading Post displays authentic items that
would have been sold during the early 1800's. The trading post was Cape's
main business at the time when Lewis and Clark arrived. What would you
trade for some new skins?

CAPE GIRARDEAU STORYTELLING FESTIVAL

Cape Girardeau - *Riverfront. www.capestorytelling.com. Miscellaneous: The
Mississippi River Tales Mural covers 18,000 square feet, is 1,100 feet long and
provides an energetic backdrop for the downtown business district.   Created by
Chicago artist Thomas Melvin in 2004, the mural and at least a dozen more along
Broadway have become an attraction for Cape residents and visitors alike. Join us
on the banks of the mighty Mississippi River for another unforgettable weekend as
we host some of the nation's best storytellers, along with outstanding regional tellers.
Admission. (second weekend in April)*

CAPE GIRARDEAU AIR FESTIVAL

Cape Girardeau - *Cape Girardeau Regional Airport. Military and civilian aircraft
are on display and take part in aerobatics. Food booths. Admission. Additional fee for
airplane, helicopter and simulator rides. (mid-July weekend)*

POPEYE STATUE AND PARK
(off IL 3, Great River Road) **Chester, IL** 62233

☐   Phone: (618) 826-2326

The towering Popeye Statue in the Elzie C. Segar Memorial Park is found by crossing the Mississippi River, the Chester Bridge. The monument honors Elzie Segar, creator of Popeye who was born in Chester. There's more Popeye than spinach at Spinach Can Collectibles inside Chester's historic 1875 Opera House building. Popeye merchandise and a mini-Popeye museum fill the space and headquarters of the Popeye Fan Club.

DILLARD MILL STATE HISTORIC SITE
142 Dillard Mill Road **Davisville** 65456

☐   Phone: (573) 244-3120 **www.mostateparks.com/dillardmill.htm**
☐   Admission: The Missouri state park system does not charge entrance fees. However, there are fees associated with camping, lodging, tours, museums and certain special events.
☐   Tours: Monday-Saturday 10:00am-4:00pm with the last tour beginning at 3:00pm. Sunday Noon-5:00pm. The last tour of the day starts at 4:00pm. (March-November). As of press time, tour times during the winter season were under review. Please call or visit website for details. $2.50-$4.00 per person to tour the mill. The mill is not heated. Please be sure to bring a jacket during cooler weather.

One of Missouri's best-preserved water-powered gristmills is tucked between Ozark hills and pine-topped bluffs next to the Huzzah Creek. Today, most of the original machinery is still intact and operational. Visitors can see the remaining machinery come to life during a tour of the mill. With the turn of a wheel, the mill begins to operate as it did years ago, grinding grain into flour. The sound of the water gushing over the dam outside the mill is replaced with the sounds of the belts and rollers turning. Tour the mill (built in 1900), have a picnic lunch and take a hike in this picturesque setting.

CIVIL WAR DAYS

Doniphan - *Heritage Homestead, 201 Franklin Street. Phone: (573) 996-5298 www.doniphanmissouri.org/coming_events. Join the Festivities at the Heritage Homestead in Doniphan. Craft demonstrations, music, food, fun with a strong dose of living history. Spring of 1861. Men have answered Governor Jackson's call to join the Missouri State Guard and repel the invading Federal forces. The men have gathered at Camp Burrows in Ripley County to organize and drill. The men are poorly equipped and trained; much of the time around camp is spent drilling. The novelty of war has yet to be replaced by the horror that will follow. The men are excited and looking forward to the opportunity to quickly whip their foe and return home with stories to tell their families. Women and children have gathered around the camp to watch the activities. Merchants and settlers appear, trying to capitalize on the needs of the men and spectators. FREE. (last full weekend in April)*

BIG OAK TREE STATE PARK
13640 South Hwy. 102 **East Prairie** 63845

- ☐ Phone: (573) 649-3149 **www.mostateparks.com/bigoak.htm**
- ☐ Admission: The Missouri state park system does not charge entrance fees. However, there are fees associated with camping, lodging, tours, museums and certain special events.

Majestic trees tower above the rich delta around the park. A boardwalk gives a close-up view of the swamp forest that once covered Missouri's Bootheel. Large, stately oaks and stands of giant cane give way to enormous cypress trees in the swamp. Several former state and national champion trees and two present state champions, a pumpkin ash (also a national champion) and a black willow, are labeled along the boardwalk. The boardwalk is accessible to people with disabilities. A nature center, picnic area and small lake are available. The center features the history of the logging and drainage of Missouri's bootheel; changes in the Mississippi River floodplain; and the New Madrid earthquake. Other displays focus on the park's champion trees, wildlife and unique plants (open Tuesday-Saturday 10:00am-4:00pm, April thru September). After a nature hike through the forest, visitors can enjoy a picnic lunch under the open shelter or at one of many picnic tables nestled beneath the lofty trees.

TOWOSAHGY STATE HISTORIC SITE

County Road 502 (East Prairie/Matthews exit off I-55 (Exit 58), east on Hwy.
80, south on Hwy. 77, 1 mile west on County Road 502, Mississippi County)
East Prairie 63845

- ☐ Phone: (573) 748-5340 **www.mostateparks.com/towosahgy.htm**
- ☐ Admission: The Missouri state park system does not charge entrance fees.
  However, there are fees associated with camping, lodging, tours, museums
  and certain special events.

This site preserves the remains of a once fortified Indian village, which was
an important ceremonial center. Indians of the Mississippian Culture lived
here between AD 1000 and AD 1400. The name, Towosahgy, was borrowed
from the Osage Indians and means "old town." Visitors to the 64-acre tract
of land can see remnants of past activities in the form of earthen mounds
constructed for ceremonial, residential and religious purposes. Visitors can
envision the lifestyle of a people who lived in a far distant time in Missouri
pre-settlement history. A kiosk with exhibits interprets the history.

FORT KASKASKIA & KASKASKIA BELL STATE HISTORIC SITE

4372 Park Road (take MO 51 Bridge over to IL. Take IL 3 north & follow
signs to Fort) **Ellis Grove, IL** 62241

- ☐ Phone: (618) 859-3741 **www.illinoishistory.gov/hs/fort_kaskaskia.htm**
- ☐ Hours: Daily 8:00am-4:00pm.
- ☐ Admission: FREE

Fort Kaskaskia State Historic Site preserves what's left of the old fort-one of
the first built on the Mississippi River. The fort was built to protect Kaskaskia
from British attack during the American Revolution. Lewis and Clark's boats
landed here, establishing a recruitment base and post office. All that remains
today are the earth works around the perimeter. A scenic overlook offers
views of the Mississippi and Kaskaskia Rivers and of Old Kaskaskia.

ALLEY SPRING GRIST MILL HISTORIC SITE

State Highway 106 (6 miles west of Eminence) **Eminence** 65466

- ☐ Phone: (573) 226-3945
  www.eminencemo.com/springscaveshistoricsites.html
- ☐ Hours: Daily 9:00am-4:00pm (Memorial Day - Labor Day).
- ☐ Admission: FREE (donations accepted).
- ☐ Miscellaneous: still on Hwy 106, see the vivid blue water at one of the state's prettiest springs, BLUE SPRING. It's a half-mile walk from the parking area. The steep approach ride is not recommended for large vehicles like buses. (www.nps.gov/ozar). Several canoe, raft and tube rental providers are in town. Many offer lodging or camping, too.

In 1894, this roller mill and one-room schoolhouse was the focal point of the Alley Spring community. Visit the historic 1894 Alley Mill to learn about life in those days. Park rangers in period costume show you how the mill worked, and how school was taught in the one-room schoolhouse. They offer a variety of historic programs.

CRYSTAL CREEK RANCH

County Road 414 (HCR 3 Box 55) **Eminence** 65466

- ☐ Phone: (573) 226-2222 **www.crystalcreekranch.com**
- ☐ Hours: Overlook deck, self-guided ranch tours, walking trails, labyrinth, outside primitives, and horse drawn equipment open Daily until dusk (April-October).
- ☐ Admission: Many activities are FREE and are open to all. These include the museum, self guided ranch tours, walking trails, field trips, our small animal area, the "lookout" deck, labyrinth and special seasonal activities. See website for complete offerings.

Turn off the pavement onto the one mile gravel road to the Ranch, and travel thru an Ozark forest, down the rolling hills and past the creek to the Ranch Headquarters. This ranch has lodging, free self-guided ranch tours, four-level look-out deck, a small animal area, walking trails, labyrinth and farm primitives museum. (April -October). FREE just to stop by.

ELEPHANT ROCKS STATE PARK

Route 21 (4.2 miles from 21 and "221" via 21 North) **Graniteville** 63656

☐   Phone: (573) 546-3454 **www.mostateparks.com/elephantrock.htm**

☐   Admission: The Missouri state park system does not charge entrance fees.
     However, there are fees associated with camping, lodging, tours, museums
     and certain special events.

A train of circus elephants dance trunk-to-tail to form an awe-inspiring sight
to the young and to the young at heart. This is the appeal of Elephant Rocks
State Park, named for a train of gigantic pink granite boulders perched atop
a hill, just like circus elephants! There is no record of the actual number of
"elephants" inhabiting the park. Old ones erode away and new elephants wait
beneath the cracks and joints of the granite hillside. The park's pink patriarch,
Dumbo, is 27 feet tall, 35 feet long and 17 feet wide, weighing in at a colossal
680 tons! The park's one mile circular interpretive trail was the first state park
trail in Missouri designed for visitors with physical and visual handicaps.
Known as the Braille Trail, signs written in Braille and regular text, guide
visitors along a paved, handicap-accessible trail which allows visitors to see
the huge rocks and seven acres of the park's over 131 acres. Camping is not
allowed in the park, but thirty picnic sites and a playground area provide
families with the opportunity to explore the park.

ROCKY HOLLER USA

Route 303 (five miles north of Cape Girardeau. I-55 exit 105, take 61 south
to Rte 303) **Jackson** 63755

☐   Hours: Weekends Only (May-September).

☐   Admission: $10.00 (age 5+).

Pony-drawn wagon rides, fishing, a tram, petting zoo, panning for gold,
blacksmith shop and food.

ST. LOUIS IRON MOUNTAIN & SOUTHERN RAILWAY

(Intersection of Highway 61 & 25) Jackson 63755

- ☐ Phone: (573) 243-1688 or (800) 455-RAIL (7245) **www.slimrr.com**
- ☐ Hours: Saturday Tour @ 1:00pm (May-December). Jackson to Gordonville and back (10 miles - 2 hours).
- ☐ Admission: $16.00 adult (13+), $9.00 child (3-12).
- ☐ Miscellaneous: NOTE: The steam engine is not currently available for service. The diesel engine will be running on all trips.

Hear the stories of a Jesse James Gang robbery, learn how hobos traveled the rails and see first-hand what a real diesel locomotive looks like at the St. Louis, Iron Mountain and Southern Railway. Known as the state's only full-sized passenger train, it will take you back to the 1950s and the era of passenger rail transportation. Watch out, while on your ride you may experience a James Gang robbery, magic show and Bonnie and Clyde.

ST. LOUIS RAILWAY SANTA EXPRESS

Jackson - *St. Louis Railway. Passengers can enjoy the magic of the season on December themed rides. While onboard, children can hear the story of "The Polar Express" and enjoy a visit from Santa. Admission. (December weekends)*

TRAIL OF TEARS STATE PARK

429 Moccasin Springs Road Jackson 63755

- ☐ Phone: (573) 290-5268 **www.mostateparks.com/trailoftears.htm**
- ☐ Hours: the Visitors Center is generally open 9:00am-5:00pm weekdays and 10:00am-4:00pm weekends.
- ☐ Admission: The Missouri state park system does not charge entrance fees. However, there are fees associated with camping, lodging, tours, museums and certain special events.

The tragic history that gives Trail of Tears State Park its name provides a sharp contrast to the peaceful, serene setting and the abundance of recreational opportunities enjoyed by visitors today. Walk through 3,000 acres of what serves as a memorial to the Cherokee Indians. A portion of this wooded park was part of the Trail Of Tears. Camping, a lake, a beach, fishing, a visitor center, an overlook, and hiking and equestrian trails are offered. An overlook provides a view of the Mississippi River. The park's visitor center features exhibits that interpret the forced relocation, as well as the park's many natural features. Dioramas show a peaceful people who were forced to abandon homes and lands preparing for the journey.

ONONDAGA CAVE STATE PARK
7556 Hwy. H **Leasburg** 65535

☐ Phone: (573) 245-6576 or (573) 245-6600 (Cave Tours)
www.mostateparks.com/onondaga.htm

☐ Admission: The Missouri state park system does not charge entrance fees. However, there are fees associated with camping, lodging, tours, museums and certain special events. Admission for Onondaga Cave Tours: $12.00 adult (13+), $10.00 senior (65+), $7.00 child (6-12). Admission for Cathedral Cave Tours: $8.00 adult (13+), $7.00 senior (65+), $6.00 child (6-12).

☐ Tours: Onondaga Cave - Tours leave from the visitor center and are available from March-October. Tours are offered at the minimum every 2 hours from 10:00am-4:00pm. They are walking tours, just less than one mile long, and last about one hour and 15 minutes. The cave's temperature is 57°F (13°C) year-round, so, bring a jacket and comfortable shoes. Cathedral Cave - Tour every Saturday at 10:00am-1:00pm and Sunday at 10:00am (Memorial Day-Labor Day). Tours are given on Saturdays at 1:00pm and Sundays at 10:00am (April, May, September & October). It is a lantern tour that lasts approximately two hours. The tour begins at the campground showerhouse and includes a short one-third mile walk up Deer Run Trail to the cave's entrance. The cave tour itself lasts about 90 minutes.

☐ Miscellaneous: across the river from the park is the OZARK OUTDOORS RIVERFRONT RESORT offering canoe, raft, tube rentals to float the rivers or camping/RV sites, a swimming pool, sport courts and a restaurant on site. (www.ozarkoutdoors.net)

Bordering the Meramec River, the park offers fishing, a visitor center, a store, picnicking, camping, a boat ramp, a lake and scenic hiking trails.

• **ONONDAGA CAVE** - Features some of the nation's best cave formations including towering columns and intricately woven draperies of rock. Learn about geologic wonders such as the King's Canopy, the Twins and other unusual speleothems. Guided tours point out massive stalagmites that rise like peaks from the floor of the Big Room, said to be large enough to hold a football stadium. This cave even has a river flowing through it.

ONONDAGA CAVE STATE PARK (cont.)

• **CATHEDRAL CAVE** - The cave is currently being shown as a lantern tour on weekends by the park staff.

There is also plenty of natural beauty to enjoy above ground at the park. Vilander Bluff Natural Area provides visitors with a panoramic view of the Meramec River. Come and take a hike through the Meramec River valley, canoe or fish in the Meramec River or enjoy a picnic lunch. Learn about the park's natural resources above and below the earth's surface through exhibits inside the visitor center. The park's campground offers both basic and electric/ water campsites, many of which are reservable.

BOOTHEEL YOUTH MUSEUM

700 North Douglass Street **Malden** 63863

- ☐ Phone: (573) 276-3600 **www.bootheelyouthmuseum.org**
- ☐ Hours: Tuesday-Saturday 10:00am-4:00pm, Sunday 1:00pm-4:00pm.
- ☐ Admission: $3.00 adult (18+), $5.00 child (3-17).

A hands-on discovery museum with large spaces focused on science, math, human relations, natural resources and the arts. Includes Children's Village, This Island Mars, Lewis and Clark, and a children's theater. Some workshop areas deal with gooey or acidic messes. Simple Machines is a large area where students can actually use a lever, pulleys, wheels and gears. What ratios do you need to make work easier?

BOLLINGER COUNTY MUSEUM OF NATURAL HISTORY

207 Mayfield Drive **Marble Hill** 63764

- ☐ Phone: (573) 238-1174 **www.bcmnh.org**
- ☐ Hours: Thursday-Saturday Noon-4:30pm.
- ☐ Admission: $2.00 adult, $1.00 child (18 and under).
- ☐ FREEBIES: Dino coloring pages and games are found under the website's KIDS PAGE.

Home of the Missouri dinosaur, this museum also showcases Civil War artifacts, American Indian exhibits, natural history specimens from around the world and regional historic exhibits. Kids are floored at the giant dino and crater greeting. What then grabs them is the story of how the bones were found by a farming family by accident. Dinosaur Dan was the first scientist to investigate. A new breed of dinosaur was named Parrosaurus missouriensis, and described as probably being a sauropod - a large plant eating dinosaur with a massive body, long tail, long neck and small head - such as Brontosaurus (Apatosaurus) or Diplodocus. To this day, the Chronister farm site continues to yield significant fossils of dinosaurs, turtles, amphibians and fish.

Besides the dino exhibit, there is also one on the Wreck of the Montana, the largest stern wheel steamboat that ever traveled the Missouri River. Fossil lovers will enjoy the Ozark Fossils exhibit and adventuresome kids will love the displays of real items Lewis & Clark took on the Voyage of Discovery.

DID YOU KNOW ? That the birds in your back yard are related to dinosaurs and that Velociraptors were covered with feathers?

TAUM SAUK MOUNTAIN STATE PARK
(Highway 21 to Highway "CC") **Middlebrook** 63656

☐   Phone: (573) 546-2450 **www.mostateparks.com/taumsauk.htm**
☐   Admission: The Missouri state park system does not charge entrance fees.
     However, there are fees associated with camping, lodging, tours, museums
     and certain special events.

Want to hike to the top of a mountain? Just park in the lot of Taum Sauk Mountain State Park and walk a mere 1,000 feet on a paved path to Missouri's highest point. Here, an elevation marker sits, guiding visitors to the mountain's 1,772 foot summit. If that's not enough, the hike to Mina Sauk Falls will take your breath away.

Just down the road lies the overlook which allows visitors a wide, incomparable view of the mountains to the north, and a guide to help identify and distinguish them. Nearby, a small camping area offers 12 basic campsites ($9 per night) and a picnic area which gives visitors a chance to enjoy a relaxing picnic under the trees.

JOHNSON'S SHUT-INS STATE PARK

148 Taum Sauk Trail (Highway 21 to Highway "N") **Middlebrook** 63658

- ☐ Phone: (573) 546-2450 **www.mostateparks.com/jshutins.htm**
- ☐ Admission: The Missouri state park system does not charge entrance fees. However, there are fees associated with camping, lodging, tours, museums and certain special events.

Years ago, violently explosive volcanoes hurled hot gasses and ash into the air. The ashes and gas fell and cooled, forming rhyolite rock. Many years later, shallow inland seas swallowed the ancient, worn-down mountains, burying the igneous rock under thousands of feet of sedimentary rock such as limestone, sandstone, shale and dolomite. The result is a grand mixture of beautiful multi-colored pools, unique rock formations and even giant holes in the middle of huge rocks.

Johnson's Shut-Ins State Park has reopened for day use and overnight camping. Although the campground was pummeled by the broken reservoir atop Profitt Mountain several years ago, some parts of the park reopen as they are cleared and safe. Johnson's Shut-Ins Campground, which is being built in the Goggins Mountain area of the park, was completed in spring 2010. The new campground includes basic, electric, sewer/electric/water, equestrian and walk-in campsites plus camper cabins.

New for 2010 is a Visitors Center with Child friendly museum displays. The shut-ins area of the park is once again open for swimming and splashing. A new boardwalk provides easy access to the shut-ins for viewing or swimming. Visitors can also access the East Fork of the Black River at various locations throughout the park for swimming, wading or fishing. At the north picnic area, there is easy access to the river and a gravel bar.

DID YOU KNOW ? Why the park name, Shut-ins? The swift Black River runs around huge exposed boulders to create gorges, or "shut-ins".

NEW MADRID HISTORICAL MUSEUM

1 Main Street **New Madrid** 63869

- ☐ Phone: (573) 748-5944
  http://mo-newmadrid.civicplus.com/index.aspx?NID=133
- ☐ Hours: Monday-Saturday 9:00am-5:00pm, Sunday Noon-5:00pm (Memorial Day-Labor Day). Monday-Saturday 10:00am-4:00pm, Sunday Noon-4:00pm (December, January & February). Schoolhouse only open summertime.

☐   Admission: $1.00-$2.00 per person for each museum.

☐   Miscellaneous: Each December the site offers Christmas Candlelight Tours (second weekend) in the evening.

Located on the Mississippi River in a former saloon at the foot of Main Street, the New Madrid Historical Museum reflects the history of this river town from the Mississippian period up through the early 20th century. You'll see some ancient Indian artifacts and a home set up in early 1900s. The real draw to this town is the tragic quakes of 1811 and 1812 rang church bells as far as distant Boston, Massachusetts. The epicenter of New Madrid Seismic Zone is a web of earthquake faults that reach into five states. The 1811 quake is the strongest earthquake ever recorded in North America. Shocks occurred over eight weeks, crevasses swallowed buildings, enormous trees were uprooted and the Mississippi river even ran backward for a short time. The seismograph on the premises gives evidence of continuing activity along the New Madrid fault.

Just down the street is the **HIGGERSON ONE ROOM SCHOOLHOUSE**. This one-room schoolhouse displays rural American education practices. Experience the typical school day of youngsters attending all eight grades in one room with one teacher. Relive the days of playing "Wolf Over and River" and "Caterpillars," a trip to the outdoor facility and crossing the fence on the stile.

MISSOURI MINES STATE HISTORIC SITE

Hwy. 32 (south side of Hwy. 32 at Flat River Drive overpass, 1.5 miles west of US Hwy. 67) **Park Hills** 63601

☐   Phone: (573) 431-6226 **www.mostateparks.com/momines.htm**

☐   Admission: The Missouri state park system does not charge entrance fees. However, there are fees associated with camping, lodging, tours, museums and certain special events.

☐   Tours: fee.

You'll feel small next to the St. Joe shovel at Missouri State Mines Historic Site. Located in Federal Mill No. 3, the largest mill in the old Lead Belt, the museum presents Missouri's mining history and contains mining machinery, a film on lead mining and the milling process, and an expansive mineral collection. Step outside and you'll notice the ghost town quality of the site. Photographers will appreciate the opportunity to capture weathered mine buildings on a stark landscape.

ST. JOE STATE PARK
2800 Pimville Road **Park Hills** 63601

☐ Phone: (573) 431-1069 **www.mostateparks.com/stjoe.htm**
☐ Admission: The Missouri state park system does not charge entrance fees. However, there are fees associated with camping, lodging, tours, museums and certain special events.
☐ Miscellaneous: Be sure to call or visit website for complete list of rules that apply to all off-road vehicles and riders using this area.

St. Joe State Park offers more than 8,000 acres for recreational purposes including at least 2,000 acres designated as the state's premier off-road vehicle riding area. The heart of the "Old Lead Belt" now pulses with several modes of transport, from ATVs to hooves to hiking boots.

SAM A. BAKER STATE PARK
Hwy. 143 (4 miles north of Patterson) **Patterson** 63956

☐ Phone: (573) 856-4411 **www.mostateparks.com/baker.htm**
☐ Admission: The Missouri state park system does not charge entrance fees. However, there are fees associated with camping, lodging, tours, museums and certain special events.

Set in the unspoiled wilderness of the scenic St. Francois Mountains, this park has a nature center, campsites (including equestrian), trails, cabins, float trips, dining and a clear stream for splashing. Several miles of hiking, backpacking and equestrian trails provide glimpses of the area as the early settlers found it. To explore the natural and cultural history of the park, visit the park's visitor/nature center. Visitors can spend the night in either the rustic cabins or one of two large campgrounds. The shaded picnic area is equipped with a playground, covered shelters and picnic tables. If guests prefer to eat indoors, the dining lodge overlooking Big Creek features excellent country cooking.

FORT DAVIDSON STATE HISTORIC SITE
(Hwy 221 to Pilot Knob/Ironton/Arcadia. Just before you reach Hwy 21) **Pilot Knob** 63663

☐ Phone: (573) 546-3454 **www.mostateparks.com/ftdavidson.htm**
☐ Admission: The Missouri state park system does not charge entrance fees. However, there are fees associated with camping, lodging, tours, museums and certain special events.

☐   Miscellaneous: on site are a playground and picnic area.

In September 1864, an army of Confederate soldiers 12,000 strong marched into Missouri from Arkansas, led by Major General Sterling Price. Headed north toward St. Louis, this massive cavalry soon arrived at the southern terminus of the St. Louis and Iron Mountain Railroad in Pilot Knob. There, a federal fort, Fort Davidson, stood, garrisoned by only 1,500 Union soldiers led by Brigadier General Thomas Ewing Jr. Re enactments are held every 3 years.

The earthworks of the fort are mostly intact and visitors can explore this aspect of the battle as well as a portion of the original battlefield. Maps for this self-guided tour are available at the Visitor's Center and Museum that are also on the site. This free interpretive center provides detailed information about the battle, offering visitors an opportunity to see artifacts found just outside the museum's walls as well as from the war in general. It seeks to interpret the battle and Major General Price's raid with a diorama of the battle. Visitors also have a chance to view a 25 minute film or a 15 minute fiber optic show that demonstrates the troop movements during battle. Do you know who retreated? Who evacuated?

DUNLAP PUMPKIN FARM

Poplar Bluff - *1189 Township Line Road. Phone: (573) 686-4375. Shop the patch of pumpkins already gathered from the field, take a train ride, run through a bale maze, and see a variety of farm animals. (October)*

SAYERSBROOK BISON RANCH
11820 Sayersbrook Road **Potosi** 63664

☐   Phone: (573) 438-4449 or (888) 854-4449 **www.sayersbrook.com**
☐   Tours: Open tours are conducted most Saturdays at 10:00am (April-November). It includes the video, Q&A, the herd tour and a visit to the country store. The Open Tour requires no reservations, however please call ahead to check availability, as the ranch is sometimes closed for private events.
☐   Miscellaneous: Looking for campsites nearby? COUNCIL BLUFF RECREATION AREA: Route 8. Camping, swimming, a beach, fishing and hiking ops. Also several federal recreation areas with scenic hiking trails are around town.

SAYERSBROOK BISON RANCH (cont.)

You can tour the ranch, view a video about bison and the history of the ranch, watch Skip feed the herd from the tour wagon, and enjoy fishing, boating and hiking on the property. The ranch's country store has souvenirs and more than 70 bison products.

DID YOU KNOW? **HUGHES MOUNTAIN NATURAL AREA**: Cedar Creek Road in town is an amazing stop for anyone interested in geology: The Precambrian rock outcrops on the mountain are among the oldest exposed rocks in the United States. FREE. www.mdc.mo.gov.

FORT DE CHARTRES HISTORIC SITE

1350 State Route 155 (at Ste. Genevieve, take the toll ferry over the River. Follow signs north) **Prairie Du Rocher, IL 62277**

- ☐ Phone: (618) 284-7230 **www.illinoishistory.gov/hs/fort_de_chartres.htm**
- ☐ Hours: Wednesday-Sunday 9:00am-5:00pm.
- ☐ Admission: FREE. Donations accepted.

This great stone fort, formerly one of the strongest forts in North America, was built in 1753 as the seat of government for the French colony in America. Fort de Chartres' limestone gateway, guardhouse, and some of the outer walls have been rebuilt atop original stone foundations. The chapel, priest's room, commander's office and ammunition storage room (complete with cannon balls and weaponry) have been restored. The storehouse is home to the Piethman Museum, which uses discovered artifacts to interpret life in Illinois during the colonial period. What your kids like best? Climbing around the fort walls.

FORT DE CHARTRES TRAPPERS AND TRADERS RENDEZVOUS

Prairie Du Rocher, IL - *Fort De Chartres Historic Site. Hundreds of military and civilian re-enactors set up camp and present authentic cooking, crafts, dancing, and other activities from the French Colonial period. (first weekend in June)*

MINGO NATIONAL WILDLIFE REFUGE

24279 State Highway 51 **Puxico** 63960

☐   Phone: (573) 222-3589 **www.fws.gov/midwest/mingo**

The largest remaining tract of bottomland hardwood forest in southeast Missouri features the Mingo Swamp and adjacent hills, which are nestled in a basin of the Mississippi River.

* **DUCK CREEK WILDLIFE AREA** - Route 51. This area contains 2,400 acres of wetland in addition to forest and some cropland. Facilities include four boat ramps, boat rentals, boat dock, primitive camping, six fishing jetties and an 1,800 acre lake. FREE admission.

MINERAL MUSEUM

125 McNutt Hall (UM - Rolla campus) **Rolla** 65409

☐   Phone: (573) 341-4616 **http://mining.mst.edu/research/depexpmine.html**
☐   Hours: Monday-Friday 8:00am-5:00pm.
☐   Admission: FREE.
☐   Tours: The mine is open to the general public for guided tours by special arrangement with two weeks notice by calling (573) 341-6406 or contact the Department at (573) 341-4753.
☐   Miscellaneous: A half-scale replica of Stonehenge was created at Missouri University of Science and Technology using water-jet technology. (14th Street and Bishop Ave)

On Rolla's main campus, look for the world's largest university mineral collection (approximately 3,500 specimens) at McNutt Hall in the Minerals Museum www.mst.edu. Many of the minerals exhibited at the World's Fair in St. Louis from 1904 lie encased here including gold, diamonds and meteorites.

At the Experimental Mine, students, staff and faculty of Missouri University of Science and Technology work underground in a mine founded in 1921, one of the only working mines on a university campus in the world. Students also compete in international events for mine rescue and mucking teams.

BO'S HOLLOW

22516 Bo's Hollow Lane (2 miles south of Montauk State Park)
Salem 65560

- ☐ Phone: (573) 548-2429 **www.bohollow.com**
- ☐ Hours: Friday & Saturday 10:00am-4:00pm (March-May & September-October), Thursday, Friday & Saturday 10:00am-4:00pm (June-August) plus Memorial Day & Labor Day Weekends.
- ☐ Admission: To visit Bo's Hollow you need a $5.00 Wooden Nickel. You can get your Wooden Nickel at the Wooden Nickel Sales. You may trade your wooden token for a Model A Ride, BBQ Lunch or Jerky.

Travel the last mile to this place on a gravel road. It gets you in the mood to explore this 1930s style village with a fully functional service station, a feed and hardware store, a post office and a restoration barn. Sneak a peak inside the buildings and look around. Then, take a ride in a Model A and have a picnic lunch near Ashley Creek. Their BBQ meal is one of the $5.00 options. Jerky is another.

MONTAUK STATE PARK

RR 5, Box 279 (located at the headwaters of the Current River)
Salem 65560

- ☐ Phone: (573) 548-2201 or (573) 548-2434 (Lodging)
  www.mostateparks.com/montauk.htm
- ☐ Admission: The Missouri state park system does not charge entrance fees. However, there are fees associated with camping, lodging, tours, museums and certain special events.

Offering some of the finest trout fishing in the Midwest, Montauk State Park is located at the headwaters of the famed Current River. The park's springs combine with tiny Pigeon Creek to supply 43 million gallons of water to the river each day. The cool, clear stream is an ideal home for rainbow trout, and the scenic valley is the perfect setting for camping, hiking and other outdoor pursuits. When traveling by river on the upper Current, you can see Cave Spring, where you can paddle inside the cave for approx.100 feet; Welch Spring and ruins of a 19th century hospital; and historic Akers Ferry, which takes visitors across the river. Other features include an old gristmill, camping, lodging, dining, trails and a store.

OZARK NATURAL & CULTURAL RESOURCE CENTER

202 South Main (Hwy 19) **Salem** 65560

☐   Phone: (573) 729-0029 **www.oncrc.org**
☐   Hours: Monday-Friday 9:00am-5:00pm, Saturday 9:00am-1:00pm.
☐   Admission: Most exhibits FREE. Donations appreciated.
☐   Miscellaneous: Several Canoe and Campground companies dot the area.
     Their brochures and contact info are available on the center's website and by
     visiting the info center in person.

A complete center for information on the nature and culture of the area with
local and touring exhibits featured. During your visit, you might find musicians
playing or an artist creating. People in the Missouri Ozarks developed certain
life skills as a way of survival which still blends in modern practices. Some
still practiced in the original manner are blacksmithing, spinning, weaving,
quilting, traditional soap making, pottery making, beekeeping, cooking
sorghum molasses, and home canning. Many hand crafted and one-of-a-kind
Ozark Gifts, as well as educational and entertaining books, audio CDs, and
video DVDs are available for sale at the ONCRC.

LAMBERT'S CAFÉ: HOME OF THE THROWED ROLLS

Sikeston - *2305 E. Malone 63801. Phone: (573) 471-4261 www.throwedrolls.com.
Hours: Daily, 10:30am-9:00pm. Good food and tableside entertainment. During your
meal, fresh-baked rolls are thrown to you and you can choose from "pass-around"
side dishes that change daily and are FREE of charge when you purchase an entrée.
Sample sides include onion fried potatoes, fried okra, macaroni & tomatoes, and
black-eyed peas. These are brought around constantly and are free with any meal. But
look out, you can get hooked on those fried potatoes. Large portions. No Credit Cards,
but Checks are welcome. Lunch and dinner daily. New store in Ozark, Missouri, too.*

BEGGS FAMILY FARM - FALL HARVEST CELEBRATION

Sikeston *2319 State Highway U. www.beggsfamilyfarm.com/harvest_festival.html. Phone: (573) 471-3879 Activities include a corn maze, moonlight barnyard golf, pig races, a Barnyard Express train, the Barnyard Twister vortex, the Miner Max maze with a real gemstone mining sluice, and a wooden play fort. There's also a rope maze, a corn cannon, wagon rides, bonfires, a milking cow, pick-your-own pumpkins, monster slide, straw jump and plenty of farm animals. Admission. (October)*

MARAMEC SPRING PARK

21880 Maramec Spring Drive (6 miles East of St. James) **St. James** 65559

- ☐   Phone: (573) 265-7387 **www.maramecspringpark.com/maramec/index.html**
- ☐   Hours: Dawn to Dusk. Call or visit website for exact seasonal times.
- ☐   Admission: $5.00 per car.

Two museums, one featuring old tools used in agriculture and a second that explains the history of the Meramec Ironworks. Encompassing almost 2000 acres, the park includes a café, general store, camping, wildlife viewing, picnicking, shelters and trout fishing. Maramec Spring is Missouri's fifth-largest spring. Privately owned. The Missouri Department of Conservation raises thousands of trout in the fish rearing pools located near the head of the Spring. Small fish are hatched at other state hatcheries, transported to Maramec Spring and placed into the rearing pools. The fish are fed 3 times each day. Even if you aren't a fishermen you will enjoy tossing feed to the fish and watching them come to the surface. Fish feeders have been placed along the rearing pools for your convenience.

The **PICK AND SHOVEL CAFE** is located at the entrance to Maramec Spring Park. Breakfast and lunch are served Wednesday through Sunday during the Catch and Keep fishing season.

JESSE JAMES WAX MUSEUM

2432 Route W (I-44 - Exit 230) **Stanton** 63079

- ☐   Phone: (573) 927-5233 **www.jessejameswaxmuseum.com**
- ☐   Hours: Daily 9:00am-6:00pm (June-August). Saturday & Sunday only
     9:00am-5:00pm (April-May) & (September-October). Closed November-March.
- ☐   Admission: $6.00 adult (12+), $2.50 (5-11).

The museum is based on the testimony of Rudy Turilli, who says that Jesse James was not shot by Robert Ford. In fact it was all a ruse, and Jesse lived to be 102. There is a video that you watch when you first enter the exhibit, with live video of Jesse James along with a WAX figure of the 102 year old. Besides the somewhat believable story, touring the museum you'll find amusement viewing the life-like wax figures set in dioramas depicting Jesse's home, the Civil War, robberies and more. It's an old style museum, nothing fancy, but the stories they unfold make it a fun tourist trap.

MERAMEC CAVERNS
Highway W (I-44 west, exit 230) **Stanton** 63079

- ☐ Phone: (573) 468-CAVE (3166) **www.americascave.com**
- ☐ Admission: (Cave Tour) $19.00 adult, $9.50 child (5-11). Additional fees for various other activities.
- ☐ Tours: (Cave Tours - 1 hour) 9:00am-7:00pm+ (Summer). Closes at 4:00 or 5:00pm rest of year. Tours depart every 25 minutes throughout the day.
- ☐ Miscellaneous: Campgrounds.

The oldest tourist attraction on the Mother Road is Meramec Caverns in Stanton. Opened in 1935 by Lester Dill, the "creator" of the bumper sticker, wanderers take a fascinating underground look at the region's history and geology. Fans of bank robber Jesse James can retrace his legendary steps though Missouri and hide out in the same cave as he did over 130 years ago. In the early 1870s, Jesse James and his band returned to Meramec Cavern on numerous occasions because it afforded a complete hideout for men and horses after train and bank robberies. Guided tours by trained rangers along handicapped-accessible lighted passageways offer views of some of the rarest and largest cave formations in the world, including a limestone wine table and a seven-story mansion.

- • <u>CAVEMAN ZIP LINE ADVENTURE</u> - Soar through the tree tops and across the Meramec River on a hour long adventure of a lifetime. Open May-October. Rates: $49.00 Adults, $39.00 Children. Try it, it's worth it.

- • <u>RIVERBOAT RIDES</u> - Enjoy a relaxing, history filled, half hour long excursion on the Meramec River aboard a canopy-topped riverboat. Cavern Queen I and Cavern Queen II can each hold 25 passengers. Boats run April through September, dependant upon weather and river conditions. Additional $5.00-$8.00.

MERAMEC CAVERNS (cont.)

- CANOE FLOATS - Take a six or eleven mile float on the scenic Meramec River. A shuttle bus will take you up river and you can float back to your car, here at the caverns. Reservations are required, please call (573) 468-6463. Canoes and rafts are only available when weather permits. Canoe and multi-person raft rental fees apply.

- PAN FOR GOLD - While parents shop at the Mine Store for beautiful rock gifts or at Granny's Candy Store for home-made fudge, children can pan for fool's gold, fossils, and other gemstones in a 19th century setting. The Meramec Mining Company and Granny's is open during the summer months only. Additional fee for panning. ($7.00-$10.00).

BOLDUC HOUSE MUSEUM COMPLEX

125 South Main Street **Ste. Genevieve** 63670

- ☐ Phone: (573) 883-3105 **www.bolduchouse.com**
- ☐ Hours: Daily except holidays.
- ☐ Admission: $5.00 adult, $2.00 child.

The Bolduc Historic Properties are three historic houses in Sainte Genevieve Missouri: the Bolduc House Museum, the LeMeilleur House, and the Linden House. The Bolduc House is regarded as the first most authentically restored Creole house in the nation. Watch the sign outside the Linden House for the daily schedule of kids' activities including colonial games, a salt making relay race, crafts, and other activities that will connect you to what life in 18th century Ste. Genevieve was like. Touch and explore everything in the Hands-On History Room (located in the Bolduc-LeMeilleur House) at your own pace. There are felt boards, guessing games, matching games, a playable dollhouse, and learn to speak a few French words as you play colonial games like dominoes or continental checkers.

FELIX VALLE STATE HISTORIC SITE

198 Merchant Street **Ste. Genevieve** 63670

- ☐ Phone: (573) 883-7102 **www.mostateparks.com/felixvalle.htm**
- ☐ Hours: Monday-Saturday 10:00am-4:00pm, Sunday Noon-5:00pm (April-October). Thursday-Saturday 10:00am-4:00pm, Sunday Noon-5:00pm (November-March). Tours are available during these times.

For updates & travel games visit: **www.KidsLoveTravel.com**

☐   Admission: The Missouri state park system does not charge entrance fees. However, there are fees associated with camping, lodging, tours, museums and certain special events.

Built in 1818, it was the home of Felix & Odile Pratte Valle; they were from one of Ste. Genevieve's premier colonial families. Many elements of Ste. Genevieve's 18th century streetscape have been preserved in its historic district. Its narrow streets, historic buildings and fenced gardens offer a glimpse of a time when Missouri was part of a vast colonial empire in North America held by France and Spain. The site offers visitors a rare glimpse of Missouri's French colonial past. It has been restored to its original configuration and thus has two doors, one for the mercantile store of the historic trading firm of Menard and Valle. This side has been authentically restocked. The second door was for the family's living quarters.

Just across the street is the Dr. Benjamin Shaw House. The earliest portion of this white frame building was constructed in 1819 by Jean Baptiste Bossier as a storehouse for his mercantile business. Today, the house provides interpretive space for the site.

GREAT RIVER ROAD INTERPRETIVE CENTER
(corner of Market and Main Streets) **Ste. Genevieve** 63670

☐   Phone: (573) 883-7097 **www.ste-genevieve.com/tourism.htm**
☐   Hours: Most days 9:00am-4:00pm.

The Welcome Center is constructed in the tradition of the pioneer French. The Roscoe Misselhorn Gallery is a permanent exhibit and displays a great number of his original sketches of Ste. Genevieve. The main gallery has changing exhibits, many showing the movement of the Mississippi River over the last 500 hundred years. The Center has a walking tour video, gift shop, public rest rooms and brochures on most of the surrounding area. Good stop before you explore the area.

HAWN STATE PARK
12096 Park Drive (Hwy. 144) **Ste. Genevieve** 63670

☐ Phone: (573) 883-3603 **www.mostateparks.com/hawn.htm**
☐ Admission: The Missouri state park system does not charge entrance fees. However, there are fees associated with camping, lodging, tours, museums and certain special events.

One of Missouri's most unspoiled landscapes, this park features Pickle Creek. Pickle Creek, because of its high quality and pristine nature, has been designated as a state natural area. It is also one of the few places in the state where visitors can see such a wide variety of rock types exposed at the surface. It offers a campground, trails and picnic sites under the pine trees. Hawn State Park is the perfect setting for visitors eager to explore the unspoiled natural beauty of the Show-Me-State. Several trails are less than one mile in length and easy to navigate for families.

STE. GENEVIEVE MUSEUM
DuBourg and Merchant Streets (Court House Square)
Ste. Genevieve 63670

☐ Phone: (573) 883-3461
☐ Hours: 9:00am-11:00am & Noon-4:00pm (April-October), Noon-4:00pm (November-March).
☐ Admission: $2.00 adult, $1.00 student

In 1935, as part of the town's bicentennial, the Ste. Genevieve Museum was erected. The museum contains many items of interest relating to the town's history such as artifacts from the salt works at Saline Spring (photo right,) the town's first industry, can be seen. Other items include weapons, prehistoric and historical Native American relics, old documents, and memorabilia of the mid-1800s. The scale model of the Mississippi River Railroad Transfer Boat is neat.

JOUR DE FETE
Ste. Genevieve - *Downtown. www.greatriverroad.com/stegen/sgattract/jourfetehome.htm. Parades, folk dancing, live entertainment, and large craft fair. Actors dressed as early French settlers also reenact frontier life. (mid-August weekend)*

MERAMEC STATE PARK
115 Meramec Park Drive **Sullivan** 63080

☐   Phone: (573) 468-6072 **www.mostateparks.com/meramec.htm**
☐   Admission: The Missouri state park system does not charge entrance fees.
    However, there are fees associated with camping, lodging, tours, museums
    and certain special events.
☐   Tours: 90-minute guided tours thru Fisher Cave with handheld lights are
    available April - mid-October. Most days @ 1:00pm & 3:00pm and in summer
    also at 9:30am & 11:30am. Cave Tour fee $8.00 (20+), $7.00 teen (13-19),
    $6.00 child (6-12).

Naturalist-led tours, offered on a seasonal basis, provide an interesting adventure at Fisher Cave, located within Meramec State Park. From low, narrow streamside passages to huge rooms filled with calcite deposits, Fisher Cave offers a vast array of intricate hellectites, massive columns, and cave wildlife. But what do the kids think is coolest? The well preserved bear claw markings on the walls. The Visitor Center includes a 3500 gallon aquarium and life size diorama. Other features are canoe rentals, lodging, trails and camping.

GRAND GULF STATE PARK
Route W (off Hwy. 19) **Thayer** 65791

☐   Phone: (417) 264-7600 **www.mostateparks.com/grandgulf.htm**
☐   Admission: The Missouri state park system does not charge entrance fees.
    However, there are fees associated with camping, lodging, tours, museums
    and certain special events.

Often called the Little Grand Canyon, Grand gulf was created when the ceiling of a giant cave collapsed. The "Grand Gulf" stretches for nearly a mile with walls almost 130 feet high, making the chasm deeper than it is wide. Boardwalks with overlooks allow visitors to descend partway into the chasm to view one of the largest natural bridges in Missouri. Also, a 118-step descent to the bottom of the gulf can be accessed from the parking lot. From a canyon to a cave to a natural bridge -- this state park has plenty to see and much to do. Picnic tables are scattered among the trees. Note, no guardrails are installed on trails to keep the pristine nature in place so grab hold of little hands if you're going out on hikes.

OZARK NATIONAL SCENIC RIVERWAYS HEADQUARTERS

404 Watercress Drive Van Buren 63965

☐   Phone: (573) 323 4236 **www.nps.gov/ozark**

Missouri's largest national park offers canoeing, hiking, fishing, camping and other activities along 134 miles of the Current and Jacks Fork rivers. Streams in area are classes I & II meaning they provide an easy float and are suitable for novices and families with kids. The headquarters building and website have references to several river and Big Spring float trip companies, some with RV/campgrounds.

OZARK HERITAGE DAYS

Van Buren - *Enjoy a peek into the Ozarks of yesteryear with traditional craftsmen demonstrating the essential skills of life in the Depression era Ozarks. There are woodworkers, fiber craftsmen, fiddle makers, period agricultural techniques, plus live music and storytelling. Held at Big Spring, four miles south of Van Buren, on Route 103. Friday is focused on children, although all are welcome; Saturday is for everyone. FREE. (second weekend in June)*

WEST PLAINS MOTOR SPEEDWAY

10603 Route 63 West Plains 65775

☐   Phone: (870) 994-7447 **www.westplains-speedway.com**

This 3/8 mile red clay, oval track features weekly racing and major national events. Super stock, hobby cars and trucks and cruiser class. $5.00-$50.00. March-October.

WICKLIFFE MOUNDS

94 Green Street (take US 60/62 over the River and stay on US 51/62) Wickliffe, KY 42087

☐   Phone: (270) 335-3681 **http://parks.ky.gov/findparks/histparks/wm/**
☐   Hours: Daily 9:00am-4:30pm (May-September). Closed Monday and Tuesday (March, April, October and November). Closed winter.
☐   Admission: $4.00-$5.00 (ages 6+).

This Research Center and Archeological Site is where they've excavated prehistoric (1100-1350 AD) Mississippian Mound culture villages. Unearthed for current viewing is a burial mound, home sites and a temple mound. The Ceremonial Mound is intact and can be accessed for a beautiful bird's eye view of the park. A Hands-On Activity Touch Table rounds out a museum tour where visitors can use prehistoric tools, and learn about Mississippian artifacts, technology and their environment.

LAKE WAPPAPELLO STATE PARK

Hwy. 172 (Hwy. 172 ends in the park) **Williamsville** 63967

☐   Phone: (573) 297-3232 **www.mostateparks.com/lakewappapello.htm**
☐   Admission: The Missouri state park system does not charge entrance fees.
    However, there are fees associated with camping, lodging, tours, museums
    and certain special events.

Nestled in the southeast region of Missouri, Lake Wappapello State Park offers a variety of recreation opportunities ranging from an exciting day on Lake Wappapello to a quiet stroll through the Ozark forest. Located on Wappapello Lake, the park's scenic coves are known for camping, fishing and picnicking spots. The park also offers cabins, camper cabins, boat ramps, a beach and hiking, backpacking, equestrian and mountain biking trails.

HERITAGE DAY AT TWIN PINES

Winona - *Twin Pines Conservation Education Center. Look back at life the way it was in the 1900 Ozarks Hills as we celebrate the rich forest heritage and the pioneer spirit that made everyday life in the hills possible. See demonstrations of soap making, tie hacking, spinners, paddle makers, blacksmiths, forestry tools, and local forest products. Early logging and mill equipment on display. Fishing and archery for the kids. Shuttle service is available for overflow parking. FREE. www.mdc.mo.gov/areas/ areas/twinpines/. (mid-April Saturday).*

Travel Journal & Notes:

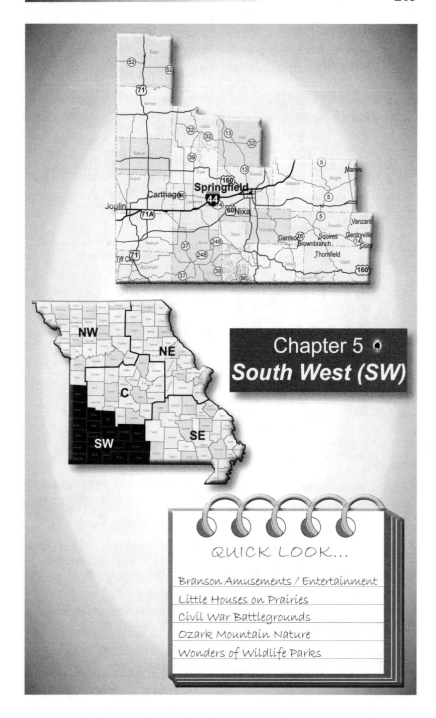

Chapter 5
South West (SW)

QUICK LOOK...

Branson Amusements / Entertainment

Little Houses on Prairies

Civil War Battlegrounds

Ozark Mountain Nature

Wonders of Wildlife Parks

Ash Grove
- Nathan Boone Homestead State Historic Site

Branson
- Branson Amusements
- Branson Campgrounds
- Branson Theaters
- Ozark Mountain Helicopters
- Billy Gail's Café
- Branson Auto Museum
- Branson Landing Cruises
- Branson Scenic Railway
- Branson's Dinosaur Museum
- Dewey Short Visitors Center
- Dick's Oldtime 5 & 10
- Dixie Stampede
- Hollywood Wax Museum
- Imax Entertainment Complex
- Ride The Ducks
- Ripley's Believe It Or Not Museum
- Ruth & Paul Henning Conservation Area
- Shepherd Of The Hills
- Shepherd Of The Hills Fish Hatchery And Conservation Center
- Showboat Branson Belle
- Sight & Sound Theatre
- Silver Dollar City
- Table Rock State Park
- Titanic
- Tribesman Resort
- White Water Water Park
- World's Largest Toy Museum
- Branson Fest
- Port Of Lights

Branson (Ridgedale)
- Big Cedar Lodge Resort

Branson (Walnut Shade)
- Branson Zipline & Canopy Tours

Branson West
- Talking Rocks Cavern

Carthage
- 66 Drive-In Movie Theatre
- Battle Of Carthage State Historic Site
- Civil War Museum
- Precious Moments Park

Cassville
- Mark Twain National Forest - Cassville District
- Roaring River State Park

Diamond
- George Washington Carver National Monument

Joplin
- Candy House Chocolate Factory
- Grand Falls
- Joplin Amusements
- Joplin Museum Complex
- Reptile World Zoo

Joplin (Tipton Ford)
- Undercliff Grill

Lamar
- Harry S Truman Birthplace State Historic Site

Lampe
- Persimmon Hill Berry Farm

Liberal
- Prairie State Park

Mansfield
- Laura Ingalls Wilder Historic Home And Museum

Neosho
- Missouri Renaissance Festival

Nevada
- Bushwhacker Hist'l Museum & Old Jail Historic Site

Noel

- Bluff Dwellers' Cavern & Browning Museum

Ozark

- Doennig Sport Swings & Ozark Paintball
- Ozark Festival Of Lights

Pineville

- Jesse James Days

Point Lookout

- College Of The Ozarks

Rockbridge

- Rockbridge General Store And Restaurant

Springfield

- History Museum For Springfield & Greene County
- Springfield Cardinals Aa Baseball
- Air & Military Museum Of The Ozarks
- Crystal Cave
- Dickerson Park Zoo
- Fantastic Caverns
- Springfield Conservation Nature Center

Springfield (cont.)

- Discovery Center
- Springfield Little Theatre
- Bass Pro Shops Outdoor World
- Incredible Pizza Company
- Springfield Hot Glass Studio
- Wonders Of Wildlife Living Zooquarium
- Missouri Sports Hall Of Fame
- Gray / Campbell Farmstead Lifestyle Exposition
- Festival Of Lights

Springfield (Republic)

- Wilson's Creek National Battlefield

Stockton

- Stockton State Park
- Hammons Products Pantry & Visitors Center

Strafford

- Wild Animal Safari

Walker

- Osage Village State Historic Site

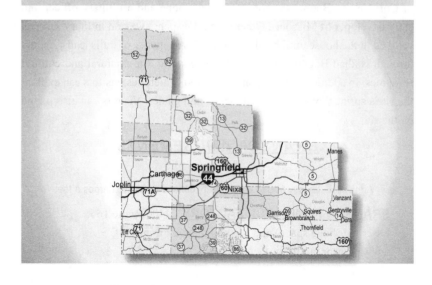

Sites and attractions are listed in order by City, Zip Code, and Name. Symbols indicated represent:

[icon] Festivals   [icon] Restaurants   [icon] Lodging

NATHAN BOONE HOMESTEAD STATE HISTORIC SITE

7850 N. State Hwy. V **Ash Grove** 65604

- Phone: (417) 751-3266 **www.mostateparks.com/boonehome.htm**
- Hours: Wednesday-Saturday 10:00am-4:00pm, Sunday 1:00pm-4:00pm (April -October). Friday & Saturday 10:00am-4:00pm & Sunday 1:00pm-4:00pm. (November-March).
- Admission: The Missouri state park system does not charge entrance fees. However, there are fees associated with camping, lodging, tours, museums and certain special events.
- Tours: Guided tours are available during normal hours and last approximately one hour. $4.00 adult (13+), $2.50 child (6-12).

Early Missourians knew Nathan Boone as a hunter, soldier, surveyor and entrepreneur. They also knew him as his father's son. Boone, youngest child of the famous Daniel Boone, carried his family's legacy deep into the Missouri Ozarks and the American West. This log house, built in 1837, was the home of Col. Nathan Boone, the son of Daniel Boone and a military officer and early developer of Missouri. Other than time spent away on military service, he lived in the house until his death in 1856. A network of trails leads visitors through Nathan Boone Homestead State Historic Site's natural and cultural resources. In addition to the Boone home and cemeteries, visitors can explore the site's springs, woodlands, grasslands and glades. Visitors can also picnic on the site.

BRANSON AMUSEMENTS

Branson

- Admission: usually free to enter facility but each activity charges a fee.

- **BRANSON FAMILY FUN FACTORY** - 2400 Route 165. Laser tag (huge space) and glow in the dark mini-golf. www.bransonfamilyfunfactory.com.

- **THE TRACK FAMILY FUN PARKS** - www.bransontracks.com.
  4 different locations on Route 76
- **PIRATES COVE ADVENTURE GOLF** - www.piratescove.net/
  location/13.
- **BROOKSIDE MINI GOLF** - www.brooksideminiaturegolf.com
- **GREATEST ADVENTURES MINI GOLF** - minigolfinbranson.com.

BRANSON CAMPGROUNDS
Branson

- **CITY OF BRANSON CAMPGROUND** - (on Lake Taneycomo).
  100s of full hookups, fishing docks, boat ramps, and picnic shelters.
- **COMPTON RIDGE CAMPGROUNDS AND LODGE** - Highway
  265. www.comptonridge.com. 25 lodge rooms, over 200 campsites (full
  and tent), planned children's activities each summer.

BRANSON THEATERS
Most are located on Route 76 Branson

☐   Note: most every showplace listed is known for their magical Christmastime
    shows.

Now, after more than 50 years, the cast of entertainers includes singers,
musicians and comedians. Most of the music ranges from Country to Old
Rock tunes - some oldies ballads from the masters, too. Branson, known as
the Las Vegas of the Midwest, offers visitors more than 50 live-performance
theaters. Many shows start around $30.00 for adults and half-price for kids.
Various online and tourism sites offer discounts on admission and you save
bringing a group. To assure seats, make reservations. Most theaters are open
spring thru Christmas but many take off winters. Some of the most popular
are:

- **PRESLEYS' COUNTRY JUBILEE** - www.presleys.com.
- **BALDKNOBBERS HILLBILLY JAMBOREE** -
  www.baldknobbers.com.

BRANSON THEATERS (cont.)

- **INCREDIBLE ACROBATS OF CHINA** - www.acrobatsofchina.com. Very different from the rest, this show has more than 40 acrobats showcasing classic Chinese dance and physical performance art. Circus meets modern dance.

- **RFD TV THE THEATRE** - www.rfdtv.com

- **JIM STAFFORD SHOW** - www.jimstafford.com. Comedy.

- **AMERICANA THEATRE** featuring The Haygoods - www.hotbransonshows.com/haygoods.html

- **BRANSON VARIETY THEATER** - www.bransonvarietytheater.com. Four different themed shows each year.

- **BRETT FAMILY SHOW** - www.brettfamily.com

- **BUCK TRENT MORNING SHOW** - www.bucktrent.com. Country.

- **CIRCLE B CHUCKWAGON & COWBOY MUSIC SHOW** - www.circlebshow.com - Chuckwagon dinner and cowboy show.

- **CLAY COOPER'S COUNTRY MUSIC EXPRESS** - www.claycooper.biz - country.

- **DOUG GABRIEL SHOW** - www.douggabriel.com - morning show.

- **ELVIS & THE SUPERSTARS** - www.elvisbranson.com. Elvis, Hank Williams, Mark Twain and many more.

- **GRAND OLD GOSPEL HOUR** - www.gospelhour.org - gospel, Sunday morning show.

- **HUGHES BROTHERS SHOW** - www.hughes-brothers.com.

- **KIRBY VANBURCH THEATRE** - www.kirbyvanburch.com - magic shows.

- **MANSION THEATRE** - www.themansiontheatre.com. Various shows including National acts.

- **NUMBER 1 HITS OF THE 60s SHOW** - www.1hitsofthe60s.com

- **PIERCE ARROW THEATER** - www.piercearrowtheater.com. Family rock-the-house gospel.

BRANSON THEATERS (cont.)

- **ROY ROGERS-DALE EVANS HAPPY TRAILS THEATER** - www.royrogers.com. Lives of two American icons with descendents performing. Museum, too.

- **SIX** - www.thesixshow.com. Just six human voices with powerhouse vocals.

- **STARLITE THEATRE** - www.starlitetheatre.com

- **YAKOV THEATRE** - www.yakov.com - each season features different performing artist - ex. Dino (piano-Christmas), Neal McCoy (country); Yakov comedy in person and a Moscow Circus.

OZARK MOUNTAIN HELICOPTERS

(Taney County / Point Lookout Airport just 1/2 mile south of 76 on Hwy 65)
Branson 65615

- Phone: (417) 337-7002 or (877) 256-5898 **www.omhllc.com**
- Hours: Call or visit website for current flight availability. Tours vary in length from a 5-7 minute "Taste of Branson" to a 25 minute "Branson Northwest" tour.
- Admission: $40.00-$125.00/person.

The tours take passengers over Branson Landing, Hwy 76, Table Rock Dam, Lake Taneycomo, Inspiration Tower and Silver Dollar City...1000 feet above! The staff have years of experience and are comfortable, yet professional in guiding you through any concerns or anxiety.

BILLY GAIL'S CAFÉ

Branson - *5291 State Highway 265 65616. Phone: (417) 338-8883. While Billy Gail's is said to serve up a mean burger, the restaurant was, in 2009, honored by a regional magazine for having the best breakfast in the entire (417) area code. The pancakes there are literally fall-off-the-plate huge.*

BRANSON AUTO MUSEUM

1335 West Highway 76　**Branson** 65616

- ☐　Phone: (417) 335-2600　**www.bransonmuseum.com**
- ☐　Hours: Opens daily at 9:00am.
- ☐　Admission: $13.95 adult, $11.95 senior, $9.95 child (12-18), $8.95 child (5-11). $34.95 family (2 Adults and up to 4 Children 18 and under).

Branson's newest attraction, the Branson Auto Museum, is located on the world-famous "Strip" in the former "Engler Block" crafts mall. The auto museum features over 100 cool cars inside and 15-20 outside. From celebrity, muscle, and movie cars to a 1925 Chevrolet or a 2010 Camaro. The gift shop features die-cast, apparel, books, magazines (with a reading area), pedal cars and many other unique automotive items.

BRANSON LANDING CRUISES

Branson Landing (Near Branson Landing Blvd and E Main Street)
Branson 65616

- ☐　Phone: (Tickets) (800) 979-3370 or (212) 209-3370
  www.bransonlandingcruises.com
- ☐　Hours: (Sightseeing) departs at 9:45am and/or 1:45pm on select dates. Other tour options available. Call or visit website for current schedule.
- ☐　Admission: (Sightseeing) $15.22 adult (12+), $8.22 child (4-11).
- ☐　Tours: Sightseeing tours last approximately 90 minutes with narration.

The Lake Queen is a modern paddle wheel vessel offering sightseeing, lunch and dinner cruises.

Ozark Sightseeing Cruises - Enjoy daily 1.5 hour sightseeing cruises on Lake Taneycomo on the Lake Queen Paddleboat on select dates. See abundant wildlife, the Historic Lake Taneycomo Bridge, Mt. Branson, and more of the fantastic attractions the Ozark bluffs have to offer. Hear about Baldknobber's, Branson's first roller skating rink, and the Hillbilly Jamboree, or Branson's first music show. Cruise past the Branson Landing waterfront and see the $7.5 million spectacular water attraction of merging water, fire and music! Pass beneath majestic Mt. Branson as you wind your way back north. View the immense diversity of Branson's wildlife, from the American Bald Eagle, Night Heron and Brown Thrasher to foxes, coyote, mink and flying squirrels. Listen to tales of how Branson got its name and why Rockaway Beach is no longer referred to as the Ft. Lauderdale of the Midwest.

BRANSON SCENIC RAILWAY

206 E. Main Street **Branson** 65616

- ☐ Phone: (800) 2-TRAIN-2 (287-2462) or (417) 334-6110
  www.bransontrain.com
- ☐ Hours: Trains run at 9:00am, 11:30am, 2:00pm, 4:30pm (June-July). Similar schedules rest of year (minus the 4:30 train - Closed January & February). Call or visit website for current schedule.
- ☐ Admission: $24.50 adult (13+), $14.00 child (3-12).

Take in the sights of the beautiful Ozark foothills on this 40-mile round trip excursion. The tour takes you through tunnels and across bridges, all while giving passengers a history lesson on the Branson area.

POLAR EXPRESS

Branson - *Branson Scenic Railway. Children...hop aboard The Polar Express, an experience based on the Chris Van Allsburg children's book (and animated motion picture). This journey begins as the train departs from the 1906 original train depot located in Downtown Branson. Once aboard, the porter punches the passengers' tickets, and chefs hand out cups of hot chocolate, as children—dressed in their pajamas—settle down for a nighttime train adventure. The story is read aloud during the train ride, and children can relive the adventure of "The Polar Express" while the train transports them to the North Pole. Admission.*

BRANSON'S DINOSAUR MUSEUM

2020 W Highway 76 **Branson** 65616

- ☐ Phone: (417) 335-TREX (8739) **www.dinowalk.com/mo/**
- ☐ Hours: Daily opens at 9:00am.
- ☐ Admission: $9.95 adult (13+), $8.95 child (4-12). Look for coupons around town and on their website.

More than 50 life-size dinosaurs are displayed, from the very smallest creature (a one-foot micro-raptor) to a towering 42-foot Tyrannosaurus Rex. The models were created by paleo-artists who copied them from actual dino skeletons. As you walk the museum, you'll find small placards sharing details about the animal. As you navigate the path of exhibits, you'll constantly hear screams from the other portion of the museum, the haunted house. These sounds will either add to the "flavor" of the attraction or scare little ones. There are also several movies playing where scientists share recent discoveries about prehistoric animals. They do have computers set up with dinosaur games and they have tables with dino puzzles to put together. The fossil pit is a giant sandbox where kids can dig for fossils. Families with dino-lovin kids will get their money worth here. Otherwise, most families move through this quickly and it's a big price to pay for a short visit. Be sure you find discount tickets.

DEWEY SHORT VISITORS CENTER

(on State Hwy 165 at the south end of Table Rock Dam) **Branson** 65616

- Phone: (417) 334-4101 (Main Office)
  www.swl.usace.army.mil/parks/tablerock/recreation.htm#visitorscenter
- Hours: Daily 9:00am-5:00pm (April-October).
- Admission: FREE.
- Miscellaneous: There is a courtesy dock on the Visitor Center grounds, if you'd like to visit by way of boat.

The center features exhibits detailing the natural history of the area. Exhibits show four seasons of Ozarks looped nature trail and educational tour of the powerhouse to see how the dam generates electricity. There are also three short films you can watch:

- *Taming of the Riviera Blanche* (20 minutes): an introduction to the Table Rock Lake/White River area, detailing the construction and purpose of Table Rock Dam. It also shows what the area was like back in the day.

- *Where Eagles Soar* (14 minutes): the story of how eagles were brought back from endangerment in Missouri.

- *The Expedition of Lewis and Clark, 1804-1806* (32 minutes): tells of their exploration, encounters, objectives and accomplishments during their journey.

Bring a picnic lunch, a swimsuit or a fishing pole for a leisurely afternoon on the shoreline of Table Rock Lake. The Table Rock Lakeshore Trail is adjacent to the Visitors Center, too. This is probably one of the only FREE things you can do in the area.

DICK'S OLDTIME 5 & 10
103 Main Street **Branson** 65616

- Phone: (417) 334-2410
- Hours: Monday-Saturday 8:30am-9:00pm, Sunday 9:00am-9:00pm.
- Admission: FREE.

Features more than 50,000 items you may view or purchase; many hard-to-find items. Displays include a collection of World War II photos, White River Arrow Head collection, baseball hall of fame. Fun stop to browse and buy a unique item or two.

DIXIE STAMPEDE
1525 West Highway 76 **Branson** 65616

- Phone: (417) 337-9400 or (800) 520-5544
  www.dixiestampede.com/branson.php
- Hours: (Showtimes) 5:30pm and 8:00pm.
- Admission: $47.00-$53.00 adult (12+), $26-$32.00 child (4-11). Children 3 years old and younger are free only if they sit in a parent's lap and eat from their plate. If you wish for your child to receive a seat or a meal, a regular children's admission will apply.
- Miscellaneous: Meet the horses in the show before the shows and mornings. Farm animal allergies? Be prepared with antihistamines taken before enter the show arena.

A fun place to eat. The very action-packed dinner and show features dozens of magnificent horses, beautiful costumes, gallant heroes, incredible horsemanship, and a stand-to-your-feet patriotic finale. All this excitement while enjoying a fabulous four-course feast that you have to eat with your hands! The soup and chicken are wonderful and while you're finishing your main course, you may be asked (kids and parents) to participate in several races - don't worry, everyone laughs with you and cheers you on. You'll love the dancing horses and several other unusual animal races.

HOLLYWOOD WAX MUSEUM

3030 W. Hwy. 76 **Branson** 65616

☐   Phone: (417) 337-8277 **www.hollywoodwaxmuseum.com/branson/**
☐   Hours: Daily, 8:00am-Midnight (Summer). Closes earlier between 6:00-
      10:00pm other times of the year. Call or visit website for current hours.
☐   Admission: $13.95 adult (12+), $11.95 senior (55+) $5.95 child (4-11).

Inject your family vacation with a much needed dose of celebrity when you rub elbows with all of your favorite stars, from today and yesteryear. Recent stars like Gwyneth Paltrow, Johnny Depp, Jamie Foxx, and Jennifer Garner stand side by side with classic entertainers like Elvis Presley, Marilyn Monroe, Charlie Chaplin, and John Wayne. You'll rub elbows with the stars—caught in the act of performing the most famous scenes in entertainment history. Skip down the Yellow Brick Road, sail aboard the Titanic, encounter Frankenstein and Freddy, and lots more. Before you leave be sure to take your photo with the gargantuan 40-foot King Kong.

IMAX ENTERTAINMENT COMPLEX

3562 Shepherd of the Hills Expressway **Branson** 65616

☐   Phone: (800) 419-4832 **www.bransonimax.com**
☐   Hours: Open year-round.
☐   Admission: Varies greatly by show selected. Many choices/themes are
      available. Call or visit website for current showtimes and admission fees.

BIG Screens! BIG Shopping! BIG Food! BIG Live Shows! Giant-Screen IMAX© adventures, Hollywood's Biggest Hit Movies, Live Shows, McFarlain's Family Restaurant, IMAX® Food Court, Indoor Shopping Mall, and even Branson, Missouri Vacation Packages. What's Showing at the Branson IMAX? Come see a Branson exclusive and take a powerful journey through the rich history and heritage of the region with the GIANT-screen IMAX® adventure, "Ozarks Legacy & Legend." Or choose from other "New" IMAX® films for a special treat during your vacation! Catch Hollywood's biggest hit movies nightly on the GIANT-Screen IMAX® in Branson.

RIDE THE DUCKS
2320 W Hwy 76 **Branson** 65616

- Phone: (417) 266-7600 (office) or (877) 887-8225 (tickets).
  www.bransonducks.com
- Hours: Ride The Ducks operates seven days a week during daylight hours.
- Admission: $~21.00 adult (12+), $~20.00 senior (62+) and $~12.00 child (ages 4-11). Be sure to check the website for special deals and discount packages.
- Tours: The Classic Table Rock Lake Adventure departs the duck dock on the Strip at 2320 West Highway 76 from early March - mid-December for all six themed adventures. The Lake Taneycomo Adventure departs the Branson Landing from Memorial Day-Labor Day and on select spring and fall weekends.

Splashdown to fun as you see the Ozarks on the famous land and water adventure cruises on amphibious military vehicles that tour land and water. Your trusty mount for this adventure is a duck that travels on land and bucks right into the lake where you can take the reins and drive if you want. Pin on a sheriff's star, dance at a luau, grab your shades, listen to groovy music, try your hand at a trick rope and discover seasonally themed memorabilia in their special exhibit area. As always, your Captain will be full of tall tales and have you quacking Happy Trails as you experience the ride of a lifetime. Hang onto your hat. Duck tours have become our families favorite way to tour the town first to discover all there is to see. Plus, parents, the captain sneaks in lots of history trivia in such an amusing way, kids don't realize they're learning.

RIPLEY'S BELIEVE IT OR NOT MUSEUM
3326 West Hwy 76 **Branson** 65616

- Phone: (417) 337-5300 **www.ripleysbranson.com**
- Hours: Sunday-Thursday, 9:30am-8:00pm. Friday & Saturday 9:30am-9:00pm.
- Admission: $16.95 adult, $8.95 child (4-12). Look for discounts and package deals around town.
- Note: If you are taking in young ones, have one adult go ahead and "scope out" the next hallway or room. Some rooms are creepy and might frighten small or sensitive children.

RIPLEY'S BELIEVE IT OR NOT MUSEUM (cont.)

From the outside, the building looks like an earthquake split it in half. If you want to see the strange, unique, and unusual...this is the place to go. There is some interesting and useful information in there, hidden among all the 2 headed goats and drums made of human skin. There are so many unusual things here to see: brain teasers, artifacts made out of unusual things, small buildings made out of toothpicks and match sticks, a slanted room that makes you fill like you are on ship, a giant ball of string... They even have the Chitty-Chitty Bang-Bang car. We do love the mirror and there are some Branson-themed displays in this one that the others don't have. A little scary and bizarre for younger kids, though.

RUTH & PAUL HENNING CONSERVATION AREA

(located on the west side of Branson on Highway 76) **Branson** 65616

- ☐   Phone: (417) 895-6880 **http://mdc4.mdc.mo.gov/applications/moatlas/ AreaSummaryPage.aspx?txtAreaID=8208**
- ☐   Hours: Open daily, Dawn-Dusk.

This area invites folks to walk in the woods and go to scenic lookout area where you can get a spectacular view of the countryside. On the Boulder Glade Trail - watch for broad-winged hawks on the overlook and lizards on the trail.

SHEPHERD OF THE HILLS

5586 West 76 Country Boulevard (Old Mill Theatre) **Branson** 65616

- ☐   Phone: (800) 653-6288 **www.oldmatt.com**
- ☐   Hours: (May-October)
- ☐   Admission: (Shepherd of the Hills Drama) $37.00 adult (17+), $35.00 senior (55+), $18.00 child (4-16). VIP seating upgrades available at additional cost. Other activities available at additional costs. Combo discounts available.

If you've taking your first trip to Branson and/or you have any interest at all in the history of the area, you should see this play. This moving production of a 1907 novel, "The Shepherd of the Hills," is performed on the very site of the author's home, and your visit includes the show, a tour of the home, a wagon ride, entrance to the Harold Bell Wright Museum and dinner. It's basically a mini-theme park where the story of the early Ozark people is kept alive through:

- HOMESTEAD TOURS: 55-minute tour - you can see places the author stayed while writing the book and ride up 225 foot inspiration tower to get panoramic view of ozarks.

- DRAMA: Each night a spectacular drama based on the book is staged in an authentic outdoor setting, featuring powerful scenes of masked vigilantes on horseback and a burning cabin. The scenes include live animals and a barn dance in which the audience (your family) can join. Before the show, they usually entertain folks with slapstick antics or kids can partake in bullfrog races.

- SONS OF THE PIONEERS CHUCKWAGON DINNER SHOW: A cowboy feast and Western harmonies is served from an authentic 1800s chuck wagon. Dinner bell rings at 4:15pm.

- OLD MATT'S HOMESTEAD: A mini-theme park where the Shepherd in the Hills story is kept alive. Trail rides. Try the new Vigilante Extreme ZipRider. Visitors now have an option of riding down from the top of the observation tower across the 160-acre park at speeds of more than 50 miles per hour. Highest launch point in the world.

SHEPHERD OF THE HILLS FISH HATCHERY AND CONSERVATION CENTER

483 Hatchery Road (on Highway 165 just south of Branson, below the dam at Table Rock Lake) **Branson** 65616

- ☐ Phone: (417) 334-4865 **http://mdc.mo.gov/areas/hatchery/shepherd/**
- ☐ Hours: 9:00am-6:00pm (Memorial Day-Labor Day) Closes at 5:00pm (September-June)
- ☐ Tours: Guided tours, weekday summers at 10:00am, 11:00am & 1:00pm & 2:00pm, and introductory film provide good overview of area. During the remainder of the year, self-guided tours are available. FREE.

This site features guided and self-guided tours showing how the site raises rainbow and brown trout. They raise trout for release in the Missouri lakes. Trails begin at hatchery lead thru from the shoreline of the lake to high rocky bluffs overlooking the white river valley. Inside the center, several aquariums showcase Ozark fish. Did you know fish are raised in raceways? Twelve, outdoor concrete raceways are used for intermediate rearing, and final rearing is completed in twenty outdoor concrete raceways. The area has a boat ramp and several fishing access points along Lake Taneycomo, where trout fishing is allowed year-round.

SHOWBOAT BRANSON BELLE

4800 St Highway 165 **Branson** 65616

- ☐ Phone: (800) 475-9370 **www.showboatbransonbelle.com**
- ☐ Hours: All cruises run approximately two hours and 15 minutes, and begin at noon or 4:00pm and/or 8:00pm. (March-December). Call or visit website for most current operating schedule.
- ☐ Admission: Cruises start at $48.00 adult (12+), $24.00 child (4-11). Optional seating and menu choices available at additional cost. Call or visit website for complete details and most current options.

Take your family on a fantastic lake cruise aboard the magnificent Showboat Branson Belle in Branson, Missouri! Journey past lush Ozark Mountains on the crystal clear waters of Table Rock Lake during your 2-hour lake cruise where you'll experience fabulous Branson dining and the best in Branson shows. Your lake cruise and Branson dinner show features Showstoppers, an exciting production starring a tremendously talented cast showcasing over 30 award-winning numbers. It's fun for the entire family - and kids are always half price!

SIGHT & SOUND THEATRE

1001 Shepherd of the Hills **Branson** 65616

- ☐ Phone: (417) 335-7900 **www.sight-sound.com**
- ☐ Hours: (Showtimes), generally at 3:30pm & 7:30pm. Performances will vary depending on season. As of press time the show was "Noah The Musical". Call or visit website for current schedule.
- ☐ Admission: (Show) $47.00 adult, $23.00 teen, $16.00 child. (Behind the Scenes Tour) $8.00/person.
- ☐ Miscellaneous: the Miracle of Christmas production captures the reason for the season.

Sight and Sound Theaters offer original musical productions that bring biblical stories to life onstage. Shows each year focus on familiar bible characters like Noah, Ruth or Daniel. Through inspirational productions, they seek to encourage others to be dedicated and wise stewards of our God-given talents and resources. Amazing side stage and live isle-way entrances/exits help bring Bible stories fantastically to life! Most major story scenes are mouth-droppers. Don't be afraid of the price, it's worth it. Seasonal shows each Christmas and Eastertime.

SILVER DOLLAR CITY

399 Silver Dollar City Parkway **Branson** 65616

- Phone: (Tickets) (800) 475-9370 **www.bransonsilverdollarcity.com**
- Hours: Vary by season but most days in June and July is 9:30am-7:00pm. Opens earlier and closes later depending on date. (April-December). Call or visit website for most current operating schedule.
- Admission: $53.00 adult (12-61), $51.00 senior (62+), $43.00 child (4-11).

Branson's Number 1 Attraction for 50 years. Meet 100 demonstrating craftsmen, browse 60 unique shops, see 40 live shows daily, thrill to 30 rides and attractions, enjoy a dozen restaurants and six festivals. Smell the fresh-baked bread at Sullivan's Mill, try some Honey Heaven honey, grab an ice cream cone and then ride Fire in the Hole. Tom and Huck's RiverBlast - America's biggest water battle - is the newest feature ride. You look like a bunch of Huck Finn's *"fightin er out on these supped-up bumper boats"*.

Hop on the <u>FRISCO SILVER DOLLAR LINE STEAM TRAIN</u> in the park and enjoy a beautiful 20-minute steam train ride through Ozark country. Watch out for the zany train robbers who briefly interrupt your ride.

Located under Silver Dollar City theme park, <u>MARVEL CAVE</u> is one of the deepest caves in the state with tours included in park admission. To begin, you will travel 300 feet below the surface and enter the Cathedral Room. The breathtakingly beautiful Cathedral Room is the largest cave entrance room in the United States. While the stairs and walkways are strenuous at times, those who venture the 500 feet below the surface can rest on a unique cable train ride out of the cavern.

DID YOU KNOW ? The theme park was literally built around the entrance to Marvel Cave, upon the foundations of a genuine 1800s mining town - Marmaros.

WORLDFEST

Branson - *Silver Dollar City. One of America's largest international festivals, bringing the world's most intriguing cultures to the Ozarks. See incredible performances by Zhejiang Chinese Acrobats starring the Balancing Monks; Fiery Fiddles featuring Janice Martin, The World's Only Flying Fiddler, and Jennifer Roland, Nova Scotia's top fiddle champion; Trinidad's Diego Martin Footprints Folk Performers; plus performers from Ecuador, Russia, Argentina and Mexico. Sample exciting cuisine from around the globe. Admission to Silver Dollar City is required. (early April thru early May)*

KIDSFEST

Branson - *Silver Dollar City. KidsFest's unbelievable shows including the Chris Perondi's Stunt Dog Experience and The Magic of Peter Gossamer. Every member of your family will feel like a kid again with activities such as the Kids Concoctions Interactive Barn, and visits from your all-time favorite characters including SpongeBob and Patrick, Dora and Diego. Plus, experience 30 thrilling rides and attractions, including the RiverBlast, one of America's biggest water battles. Admission to Silver Dollar City is required. (early June thru early August)*

NATIONAL HARVEST FESTIVAL

Branson - *Silver Dollar City, the Home of American Craftsmanship, welcomes hundreds of visiting craftsmen to demonstrate and display their unique talents. The festival includes the Crafts in America Exhibit, displaying 50 of the nation's most stunning works of art; the Caricature Carvers of America Showcase; and a reunion of some of Silver Dollar City's legendary veteran craftsmen. Plus, don't miss America's Biggest Barn Dance in Red Gold Heritage Hall. Admission to Silver Dollar City is required. (mid-September thru October)*

AN OLD TIME CHRISTMAS

Branson - *Silver Dollar City. Celebrate the magic and meaning of the holidays at An Old Time Christmas. More than four million lights, a holiday light parade, a five-story special effects Christmas tree, fun family shows, including A Dickens' Christmas Carol, and festive food await in this dazzling winter wonderland. Admission to Silver Dollar City is required. (early November thru end of December)*

TABLE ROCK STATE PARK
5272 State Hwy. 165 **Branson** 65616

☐ Phone: (417) 334-4704 **www.mostateparks.com/tablerock.htm**
☐ Admission: The Missouri state park system does not charge entrance fees. However, there are fees associated with camping, lodging, tours, museums and certain special events.

Located adjacent to Table Rock Lake and near Branson, Mo., one of the hottest tourism spots in the United States, Table Rock State Park offers easy lake access and is a short drive to area attractions and entertainment. This park is ideal for water sports as it features a marina, parasailing equipment, a boat ramp, picnic sites, campgrounds, hiking and mountain biking trails and a paved walking and bicycle trail. Other facilities at Table Rock State Park include picnic sites, a sand volleyball court and playground equipment. The Lake is know for great fishing. Here's some other amenities you may be interested in, especially if you're spending the day:

- **STATE PARK MARINA** - www.boatbranson.com. Rent water vehicles, including jet skis, pontoon boats, ski boats, canoes, paddleboats, and fishing boats. They also have para-sailing rides offered.

- **SPIRIT OF AMERICA** - www.sailbranson.com. 90 minute excursions on 49 passenger catamaran tours.

- **THE BOATHOUSE BBQ AND BURGERS CAFE** - Open Memorial Day through Labor Day at the marina. The cafe offers park guests premium-quality fun foods such as burgers, barbecue and hand-dipped ice cream treats. You can walk in or boat in...and pig out.

TITANIC
3235 West 76 Country Boulevard **Branson** 65616

☐ Phone: (417) 334-9500 **www.titanicbranson.com**
☐ Hours: Daily 10:00am-7:00pm. Open later in summer and peak seasons. Call or visit website for current boarding schedule.
☐ Admission: $18.82 adult (13+), $9.99 child (5-12). $52.87 Family Pass (2 Adults, minimum of 2 children, maximum of 4 children ages 5 -18, that still reside within the residence).

TITANIC (cont.)

☐ Miscellaneous: Parents and preteens interested in the storyline should purchase the audio tour, it offers more information and back story and you can hear firsthand accounts from survivors. Educators: a varied and curriculum specific Teachers Guide page is available here: www.titanicbranson.com/titanic_guide_home.php. Some really great ideas on how to approach the dynamics of wealth and the working class plus interesting studies about the science of the boat and the waters it sailed in.

Towering 100 feet above street level, this ship-shaped venue holds more than 400 artifacts and historic treasures. It allows each visitor to encounter the personal, heroic and tragic stories of Titanic's passengers. Each guest is assigned a passenger or crew member to follow on the timeline. Often, you see items from that person during the tour. The museum does a wonderful job to re-create many parts of the ship including the magnificent grand staircase and the dining room. See where each class slept for the night or try to stay afoot as the museum floor slopes down like the sinking ship. You also have the opportunity to see what 28 degrees feels like (temperature of frozen water surrounding the ship). Younger kids may be a little scared when they get to the part of the ship sinking (noises). There are staff peppered throughout in period costume who are kind and very helpful. This themed exhibit is very well done and well worth admission if you are sure to engage your kids to follow the storyline of their assigned character. Did your passenger survive?

TRIBESMAN RESORT
416 Cave Lane **Branson** 65616

☐ Phone: (417) 338-2616 or (800) 447-3327 **www.tribesman.com**

The Tribesman is located on a peninsula called Indian Point. Which is located by Branson on Table Rock Lake. The Tribesman Resort has seven unique sections. This resort, whether staying at the fully-equipped condos, apartments or cabins is family oriented and may remind you of an upscale summer camp. Activities include: indoor and outdoor pools, fireplaces, boat rentals, golf cart rentals, fishing dock, shuffleboard, paddle boats, scavenger hunts, and themed parties like Captain Kids Day. It isn't a luxury resort and it's a bit dated (like most other resorts in Branson) but it is very clean and well kept with everything needed for a family to have a comfortable stay at a fair price. Oh, and you'll love the close proximity of a Super Walmart (10 miles - for meal supplies) and Silver Dollar City (3 miles away). Rates range $60.00 (quiet season) to about $150 average during peak season.

WHITE WATER WATER PARK
3505 West 76 Country Blvd **Branson** 65616

☐ Phone: (800) 475-9370 (tickets) **http://whitewater.silverdollarcity.com**
☐ Hours: Daily 10:00am-6:00pm+ (Memorial Day Weekend - Labor Day Weekend). Open 1+ hours longer in summer. Call or visit website for current schedule.
☐ Admission: $36.00 adult (12-61), $25.00 senior (62+), $30.00 child (4-11). Cabana rental extra.

Dive into summer fun at White Water, your family's tropical adventure featuring plenty of sun and more than 2 million gallons of fun. White Water is Branson's only outdoor water park and offers water-blasters, super-soakers, speed water slides, and a wave pool. Plus, Kalani Towers - the 6-lane Freefall and Racing thrill slide! Choose between two 75-foot freefall drop lanes or four mat racing lanes over 310-feet long. They have a few tube slides, a kid area for ages 6-12(Raintree Island w/ dumping bucket and chutes and ladders), and an area that is mostly sprinklers for the younger kids, plus a wave pool. Folks rave about the rush of the water slides and the food - good, fresh choices at modest prices. The Kalani Towers slides probably give the most thrills. Lots of rides, and the park is relatively small, so you can walk from one end of the park to the other. White Water is clean and well staffed, plenty of lifeguards everywhere.

WORLD'S LARGEST TOY MUSEUM
3609 W 76 Country Blvd **Branson** 65616

☐ Phone: (417)-332-1499 **www.worldslargesttoymuseum.com**
☐ Hours: Monday-Saturday 9:00am-8:00pm.
☐ Admission: $9.95 adult, $7.95 child. Children 6 and under are FREE.

It's like Christmas morning every day here as parents and grandparents rediscover the joy of their favorite toys and reminisce about childhood heroes. You'll find toys as old as the 1800s and as new as Star Wars, tiny objects and big boy toys (like a full-size Rolls Royce). Girls may gravitate to the dollhouses and boys to the toy cars and trucks. Barbies, action figures, antique toy train sets and cap pistols, too.

On the premises: <u>HAROLD BELL WRIGHT MUSEUM</u> - Original hand-written manuscript of the book "The Shepherd of the Hills." Discover how tourism began in the Ozarks. Closed Sundays.

BRANSON FEST

Branson - *www.explorebranson.com. 5 day sampler of everything Branson offers. Indoor and outdoor events, a parade, celebrity autograph sessions, food booths. (late March or early April)*

PORT OF LIGHTS

Branson - *Off Highway 13 on a peninsula that juts into the Lake. Thousands of glittering Christmas displays light up the night on a Table Rock Lake peninsula, offering a 3 mile stretch of holiday displays. These include a giant Jack-In-The-Box, Cinderella with her coach and castle, hillbilly fishermen, and a massive American flag. Two drive-through displays are Snowflake Tunner and Hollywreath Tunnel, while the Candy Cane forest will lead visitors past doll houses, glittering buggies, and trucks. Each year the display grows larger. www.tablerocklake.org/port_of_lights. Admission. (early November through December during the evenings).*

BIG CEDAR LODGE RESORT

612 Devil's Pool Road (10 miles south of Branson on Table Rock Lake)
Branson (Ridgedale) 65739

☐   Phone: (800) 225-6343 **www.bigcedar.com**

Have kids and want to get away for a few days to a private cabin on the lake? This resort meets your fix. They also have hotel rooms. It is a very large resort set on the side of a steep hill overlooking Table Rock Lake. The theme is a wooded cedar lodge and fishing resort...probably because it is owned by the same people who own and operate Bass Pro Shops. Do not be afraid of the size of the resort as they have free shuttles on hand that will take you anywhere you want to go (within the resort). Most families walk anyway. Most activities were included in the room rates, canoes, paddleboats, mini golf, shuffleboard, volleyball, 4 swimming pools, several hot tubs, even the paddle boats down at the Marina. Boat and watersport rentals are a little pricey so you might want to consider bringing your own. Horseback riding is available for a fee. It is fun in the warm months because of the pools, hot tubs and lazy river. But it is also fun in the cold months to enjoy the indoor pool and have a fire with movies in the cabin at night. They have plenty of walking trails, too. A small grocery store is about 10 miles away to purchase food to prepare in your cabin. If staying in the lodge rooms, all of their restaurants have fair pricing and good food...especially the breakfast buffet. During the day, it's a 20 minute ride into the strip of Branson. The kids favorite part - a visit from the cookie lady each evening. Best online price we found: $200/night.

BRANSON ZIPLINE AND CANOPY TOURS

Hwy 65, seven miles north of downtown **Branson (Walnut Shade)** 65771

- ☐   Phone: (417) 561-2500 **www.BransonZipline.com**
- ☐   Admission: Ozarks Xplorer (2.5 hour tour)-$89.00-$99.99. Flying Prospector(1.5 hour tour)-$66.00-$69.99. Blue Streak Fast Line (one zip)-$38.99-$39.99.
- ☐   Tours: Schedule changes with the seasons and weekdays vs. weekends. Usually at least two of each type of tour per day.

Using a system that originated in the jungles of Costa Rica, the Branson Zipline and Canopy Tour allows guests to soar in the Ozark Mountains. After learning the simple in's and out's of operating a zip line, you and your party will be escorted to the top of our Wolfe Creek Preserve by way of tram and prepare for the adventure of a lifetime. As visitors "zip" from observation platform to platform, through and over the trees, certified guides accompany participants pointing out unique topographical and historical features of the Ozarks.

Branson visitors will be able to experience the Ozarks Xplorer Canopy Tour® a two and a half hour, interactive tour which features a variety of zip lines, walkways and platforms; and the Blue Streak Fast Line®, a thrilling one-stop ride from the top of the property to the base.

The kids take to it well and even middle-aged moms (like me) found it easily manageable and so memorable. Soft adventure, good for anyone who likes mild amusement rides and doesn't have a fear of heights.

TALKING ROCKS CAVERN
423 Fairy Cave Lane **Branson West** 65737

- ☐ Phone: (417) 272-3366 or (800) 600-CAVE (2283)
  www.talkingrockscavern.com
- ☐ Hours: Daily, 9:30am-6:00pm. Tours depart frequently.
- ☐ Admission: $16.95 (13+), $8.95 (4-12). Online coupon.
- ☐ Miscellaneous: gemstone panning for extra fee.

Talking Rocks Cavern near Branson offers guided 50-minute tours of thousands of living crystal cave formations of many different kinds, colors and textures. Perhaps you'll see a glimpse of one of the cave's occupants, the Ozark blind salamander. The main chamber of the cavern is more than 100 feet tall and 600 feet long, and stalactites and stalagmites along the way are a testament to years of water trickling down to shape the brilliant formations. Above ground, you can walk on the nature trail or climb up to the top of the 40-foot Treetop Tower. A crawl through their SpeleoBox maze is always a favorite. Students enter one side and crawl along 150 feet of winding, twisting passage to pop out the other side. This activity is used by "cavers" to practice safe caving techniques in this fun, simulated cave passage. These extra activities are included in admission ticket pricing.

66 DRIVE-IN MOVIE THEATRE
17231 Old 66 Blvd **Carthage** 64836

- ☐ Phone: (417) 359-5959 **http://66drivein.com/**
- ☐ Hours: Open April - mid-September. Friday-Sunday nights mostly.
- ☐ Admission: $6.00 adult, $3.00 child (car seat to age 12). If kids still use a car seat they are FREE. (admission includes viewing 2 movies).
- ☐ Miscellaneous: No outside food is allowed. See FAQ's on website.

66 Drive-In movie theatre, the last of the original six drive-ins named after this famous road. The screen is 96 feet wide and 44 feet tall, making it one of the largest remaining outdoor screens in America. Get your flicks on Route 66.

BATTLE OF CARTHAGE STATE HISTORIC SITE
Chestnut Street **Carthage** 64836

☐ Phone: (417) 682-2279 **www.mostateparks.com/carthage.htm**
☐ Admission: The Missouri state park system does not charge entrance fees. However, there are fees associated with camping, lodging, tours, museums and certain special events.

The battle was the first major land battle of the Civil War. The 7.4-acre tract is the site of the 12-hour battle's final confrontation, which began nine miles north of town on the morning of July 5, 1861. Missouri Gov. Claiborne Fox Jackson commanded the 6,000 Southerners who forced Col. Franz Sigel and his 1,000 Union men to retreat down the stagecoach road to Sarcoxie. An interpretive shelter with displays explains the history of the battle, and the site remains just as it was when the victorious Southern troops camped there the evening after the battle.

DID YOU KNOW ? The nearby town of Marionville is known for one attraction: hundreds of albino (white) squirrels.

CIVIL WAR MUSEUM
205 Grant Street **Carthage** 64836

☐ Phone: (417) 237-7060 **www.carthage-mo.gov**
☐ Hours: Tuesday-Saturday 8:30am-5:00pm, Sunday 1:00-5:00pm.

The Civil War Museum in downtown Carthage presents artifacts and information about the Battle of Carthage and the Civil War in southwest Missouri. The focal point is a mural painted by Andy Thomas that features battle action on the courthouse square, as well as mini-displays on Belle Starr, African-American and American Indian contributions to the war. Girls will especially like hearing tales of how townswomen handled the war and how they could be sneaky, too.

PRECIOUS MOMENTS INSPIRATION PARK

4321 S Chapel Road (off I-44, near US 71) **Carthage** 64836

☐ Phone: (800) 445-2220

www.preciousmoments.com/content.cfm/park_chapel

☐ Admission: The Fountain of Angels show, the music show and any traveling exhibits charge a fee. The main chapel and welcome center do not.

☐ Tours: Daily, FREE Chapel Tours hourly from 9:00am-4:00pm (March-December). Tuesday-Saturday 10:00am-4:00pm, Sunday 11:00am-3:00pm (January & February).

☐ Miscellaneous: A neat video of how they draw, sculpt, mold and paint each new Precious Moments figure is online here: www.preciousmoments.com/content.cfm/how_pm_made. Also, a fun seasonal event happens here in November & December called *Carthage At Christmastime*.

It all began more than thirty years ago, when Precious Moments® creator Sam Butcher began drawing the endearing teardrop-eye children he called "Precious Moments" as gifts for family and friends. Today, his Precious Moments artwork is among the most recognized art in the world, sharing messages of loving, caring and sharing with collectors from around the globe. The Gardens, a Christian chapel (50 biblical murals in stained glass and paintings depicting stories from the Bible), art museum, restored Victorian house, and inspirational show are all found at this one park. The Fountain of Angels laser light and water show is accompanied by outstanding inspirational music and vocals. There's a neat island with a playhouse that provokes wishful thinking in all kids. Plus an "upside-down" decorated Christmas tree in the gift shop. Getting hungry? The property has Royal Delights - a small restaurant and Souper Sam's Homestyle Buffet for big appetites. While somewhat sappy for youngsters, the parents and grandparents will soften as they look inward and then outward at artistic happiness. Once you know the story behind the figurines and the chapel you understand why so many people love Precious Moments.

MARK TWAIN NATIONAL FOREST - CASSVILLE DISTRICT

Highway 248 East **Cassville** 65625

☐ Phone: (417) 847-2144

www.fs.fed.us/r9/forests/marktwain/ranger_districts/ava/

Visitors to Ava/Cassville/Willow Springs District will find different landscapes, contrasting the typical oak-hickory forests of the Midwest. Open areas of native tall prairie grasses characterized by dry, shallow soils and limestone outcroppings are reminiscent of the historic pioneer trails to the Old West not far away. The unique blending of eastern forest and western desert habitats makes a home for such varied wildlife as the bald eagle and the roadrunner, armadillos and wild turkey, white-tailed deer and black bears. The sunlit balds and deep hollows, narrow ridgetops and steep slopes, secluded pastures and clear streams characteristic of the Ozarks are the trademark of Cassville Area. This is the landscape so eloquently described in Harold Bell Wright's famous book, The Shepherd of the Hills. As you drive through the district, take your time and get out and stop to wander a little on the marked pathways.

ROARING RIVER STATE PARK

12716 Farm Road 2239 (7 miles south of Cassville on Hwy. 112)
Cassville 65625

- Phone: (417) 847-2539 **www.mostateparks.com/roaringriver.htm**
- Admission: The Missouri state park system does not charge entrance fees. However, there are fees associated with camping, lodging, tours, museums and certain special events.

Nestled in the rugged and scenic terrain of the Ozarks is Roaring River, which is stocked daily during trout season. In addition to fishing, the park features a pool, hiking trails, camping, lodging, dining, a store and a nature center. Explore the natural wonders of the park on one of seven trails totaling over 10 miles. Deer Leap Trail is the shortest trail (0.2 miles) that leads to an overlook and boardwalk above the fish hatchery and the spring that is the head of Roaring River. Ozark Chinquapin Nature Center exhibits interpretive displays and park naturalists present programs on the park's natural history. Overnight guests have a variety of options. Campers will find 187 campsites ranging from basic to electric hookup. The elegant Emory Melton Inn and Conference Center features 26 guest rooms, a restaurant, gift shop and meeting rooms. Twenty-six secluded, rustic cabins with kitchens are perfect for families. Reservations for the inn and cabins are required.

GEORGE WASHINGTON CARVER NATIONAL MONUMENT

5646 Carver Road (From Exit 18A on I-44, take Highway 59 south to Diamond. Go west 2 miles on Highway V, then south ½ mile on Carver Road) **Diamond** 64840

- ☐ Phone: (417) 325-4151 **www.nps.gov/gwca/index.htm**
- ☐ Hours: Daily, 9:00am-5:00pm.
- ☐ Admission: FREE.
- ☐ Educators: http://www.nps.gov/gwca/forteachers/curriculummaterials.htm has a page full of themed curriculum as it relates to Carver. We love the wonderful puzzles and quizzes at the end of each lesson that tie what kids learn into current life application.

The national park covers land that belonged to Moses and Susan Carver, the family who owned George's mother at the time of his birth and who raised him after the Civil War. GW enjoyed freedom early in life. It was at this site, once a working family farm, where Carver's love for science and the outdoors was born. Although he sought to further his education, he often was denied access to schools because of his color. But he persevered and earned a master's degree in agriculture in 1896 – the same year Booker T. Washington asked him to head the Agriculture Department at the Tuskegee Institute. The GW Carver site tells the inspirational story of the slave child who grew up to become one of the greatest scientists of his day. The monument features the mile-long Carver Trail, the Carver Family Cemetery and the 1881 Carver House. Additionally, park staffers conduct hands-on experiments in plant science at an on-site lab. Kids realize anyone can overcome odds, hone in on their special talents and work to have their dreams come true.

CARVER DAY

Diamond - G. Washington Carver Nat'l Monument - Celebrate the life of George Washington Carver with an fun event that includes storytelling, exhibitors, musical performers, guided tours, interpretive talks, children's programs and more. (July)

PRAIRIE DAY

Diamond - *G. Washington Carver Nat'l Monument - Features activities that celebrate early pioneer life, including living history demos, musical performances, wagon rides and hayrides.(September).*

CANDY HOUSE CHOCOLATE FACTORY
510 Kentucky Avenue **Joplin** 64801

- ☐   Phone: (417) 623-7171 **www.candyhouse.net**
- ☐   Store Hours: Monday-Saturday 9:30am-5:30am, Sunday 12:30-5:30pm. Seasonal hours may vary.
- ☐   Tours: Tours are free, and available to be scheduled Monday through Friday 9:30am to 2:00pm. (Sorry, no tours between December 1-24 or the week before Valentine's Day and Easter.)

Ever wondered just how chocolates and candies are made? Bring your family on a tour of the Candy House. Visitors will see how peanut brittle and English toffee are made, how candies are enrobed in chocolate (39 feet of chocolate waterfalls) and see chocolates being dipped by hand. Did you know most toffees, brittles and caramels are made from the same ingredients? The best part of the tour comes at the end when you get to taste some of these delightful treats.

GRAND FALLS
Riverside Drive From 1-44 West take Joplin exit 6 (Hwy 86 south)
Joplin 64801

- ☐   Phone: (417) 624-4150

Grand Falls on Shoal Creek are only a few minutes from Wildcat Park and have been one of Missouri and the Ozarks' most scenic destinations for several decades. As the largest, continuously flowing natural waterfall in Missouri, Grand Falls plunges over 25 feet down a ledge of solid chert before flowing southward. You can walk on outcrops of this chert to get to the best viewing spots. Missouri's Grand Falls is like a miniature Niagara Falls. On a breezy day, you'll feel the mist hit your face.

JOPLIN AMUSEMENTS
Joplin 64801

- **ROUTE 66 CAROUSEL PARK** - www.route66carouselpark.com. Family entertainment for all ages, including 36-hole mini-golf, go-karts, arcade, batting cages, bumper boats and amusement rides.

- **GLOWGOLF** - www.opryglowgolf.com. GlowGolf is a glow-in-the-dark miniature golf course. You can play up to three rounds at a time which equals 54 holes! Located inside Northpark Mall.

- **HOUSE OF BOUNCE** - www.joplinhob.com. 2 locations of family friendly fun on inflatables (one located inside Northpark Mall).

JOPLIN MUSEUM COMPLEX
504 S. Schifferdecker Avenue (Schifferdecker Park) Joplin 64801

- ☐ Phone: (417) 623-1180 **www.joplinmuseum.org**
- ☐ Hours: Tuesday 10:00am-7:00pm, Wednesday-Saturday 10:00am-5:00pm, Sunday 2:00pm-5:00pm.
- ☐ Admission: $2.00 adult, $5.00 family.

Tri-State Mineral Museum -portrays mining in the Tri-State district where Joplin once led world production of zinc and lead. The Everett J. Ritchie Tri-State Mineral Museum details mining processes and methods used from the 1870s to the 1960s, and houses one of the world's best collections of lead and zinc ores. Tools of the mining trade, various mining models, maps and photographs from Joplin's mining days are also on display. And best of all, the Mineral Museum sits in a reproduced mine shaft so it feels like you are actually under ground experiencing firsthand the workings of a real zinc mine.

Other rooms in the complex detail Joplin's foundings and history plus areas are spattered with Route 66 memorabilia, Bonnie & Clyde's adventures in Joplin, and the National Cookie Cutter Historical Museum. Afterwards, kids might like to head over to the **COUNTRY CABOOSE** museum and gift shop inside a real caboose. www.countrycaboose.com.

DID YOU KNOW ? Zinc is the 23rd most abundant element in the earth's crust. The zinc and lead produced in Joplin was 3rd in the world for materials produced from 1850-1950 with more than 500 million tons of ore taken from the ground.

REPTILE WORLD ZOO
1733 Kodiac Road Joplin 64804

☐   Phone: (417) 206-4443 **www.reptileworldzoo.com**
☐   Hours: Monday-Saturday 10:00am-4:00pm.
☐   Admission: $8.00 adult (13+), $4.50 child (12 and under).
☐   Miscellaneous: The Safari Café is a great place for a snack offering very reasonable prices ($1.00-$5.00) and great variety. FREEBIES: the website has online, printable coloring pages of reptiles: http://reptileworldzoo.com/coloring.htm.

This small zoo showcases an amazing collection of exotic reptiles and creepy, crawly things including cobras, anacondas, alligators, crocodiles, dragons, iguanas, tortoises and tarantulas. The biggest draw is the snakes - lots of snakes - the largest is about 16 feet long and 300 pounds. The guides take time to talk about the animals, taking some out of their cages so visitors that want to touch or hold the snakes get plenty of opportunity. You can even pose for a picture with a 75 pound albino python. The Safari Café is open next door.

UNDERCLIFF GRILL

Joplin (Tipton Ford) - *6385 Old Highway 71 64804. http://undercliff.net. Phone: (417) 623-8382 Hours: Wedsday-Friday 11:00am-9:00am, Saturday 9:00am-9:00pm, Sunday 9:00am-3:00pm. Breakfast is served Saturday & Sunday from 9:00am-11:00am. The Undercliff is a restaurant built into the side of a cliff that gives you the feeling of eating in a cave. The coolest thing about the space is that it's literally a shack built into the side of a cliff. The back wall of the dark dining room looks like a cave. The interior decor is a mix of old Hollywood and vintage sports stuff. OK, kooky places like this always have something to order that's a little different. Here, it's the fries with cheese sauce. The sauce has a special flavor and it may become you favorite dipping sauce. If the weather is fine, and you're in the mood for less cave, they have patio dining. The Kids Menu is served with drink, fries and a surprise (around $5.00). Adults will want to order make your own burgers starting at $5.99.*

HARRY S TRUMAN BIRTHPLACE STATE HISTORIC SITE

1009 Truman (Off U.S. Hwy. 71, 2 miles on Hwy. 160, one block north on Truman) **Lamar** 64759

- ☐ Phone: (417) 682-2279 **www.mostateparks.com/trumansite.htm**
- ☐ Hours: At press time, site hours were currently under review. Wednesday-Saturday 10:00am-4:00pm. Tours are offered during these hours.
- ☐ Admission: The Missouri state park system does not charge entrance fees. However, there are fees associated with camping, lodging, tours, museums and certain special events.

President Harry S. Truman – the only Missourian ever elected president - was born here on May 8, 1884. Truman's family stayed in the six-room home until he was almost 1. Furnishings from the period fill the house. Visitors today can view its four downstairs rooms and two upstairs rooms, as well as the smokehouse, well and outhouse located in the back. The modest furnishings inside the house and the surrounding landscaping accurately represent a typical home of its style during the time the Truman's resided in Lamar. It has neither electricity nor indoor plumbing. Guided tours are FREE. The Austrian pine planted the day he was born by his father, a livestock dealer, still stands in the front yard.

PERSIMMON HILL BERRY FARM

367 Persimmon Hill Lane **Lampe** 65681

- ☐ Phone: (417) 779-5443 **www.persimmonhill.com**
- ☐ Hours: (Farm) Daily 7:00am-7:00pm (noon on Sundays) (June and July). Closes at 5:00pm (August-September). Call or vist website for additional store hours in other seasons.

This self-sustaining farm prides itself on its high quality products and ecological practices, including manufacturing its own bio fuels from recycled cooking oils. What tasty treats might you find? Among the farm's specialties are "thunder" muffins; shiitake mushroom sauce; blueberry barbeque sauce; spicy raspberry sauce and sweet blackberry glaze; elderberry juice; and the nutty blue goose - a combo of blueberry, gooseberry and black walnut jam. Everything is done in small batches to prevent overcooking and preserve natural flavors and color. The drive to Persimmon Hill Farm will take you through some of the Ozarks' most beautiful countryside.

PRAIRIE STATE PARK
128 NW 150th Lane **Liberal** 64769

☐ Phone: (417) 843-6711 **www.mostateparks.com/prairie.htm**
☐ Hours: (Visitor Center) Wednesday-Saturday 10:00am-4:00pm (April-October). Thursday-Saturday 10:00am-4:00pm (November-March).
☐ Admission: The Missouri state park system does not charge entrance fees. However, there are fees associated with camping, lodging, tours, museums and certain special events.

This nearly 4000 acre park is the state's largest public example of native prairie. It protects a variety of prairie grasses, flowers and animals, including bison and elk, and features a visitor center with displays, a prairie diorama, hands-on exhibits, and frequently a naturalist who can answer questions or give the kids an idea for a project. Upon entering the Visitors Center, the large, central diorama depicts the prairie in spring, summer and autumn with the colors and diversity of the prairie. The "Furs and Fence Row" room flows across time and the effects of humans on the prairie. Hands-on items in the "Learning Center" allow everyone the chance to explore the special features of a tallgrass prairie. A 50-person capacity "audio/visual room/auditorium" offers video and more exhibits. If you would like to have a quick snack or taste what people may have eaten more than 200 years ago, try the bison jerky and wash it down with a cool bottle of water. There are also hiking trails and primitive campsites. And, if you're wanting to walk the trails after 4pm Mid-March thru Mid-May, forget it. The trails are closed to protect the greater prairie chicken during its mating season.

LAURA INGALLS WILDER HISTORIC HOME AND MUSEUM
3068 Highway A (45 miles east of Springfield on highway 60)
Mansfield 65704

☐ Phone: (417) 924-3626 **www.lauraingallswilderhome.com**
☐ Hours: Monday-Saturday 9:00am-5:00pm, Sunday 12:30pm-5:00pm (March - mid-November).
☐ Admission: $8.00 adult (18+), $6.00 senior (65+), $4.00 child (6-17).
☐ Note: Before you go, your family will get so much more out of the visit if you read at least one 'Little House" book or watch a few shows of the same title to "set the scene." FREEBIES: Pioneer coloring pages, word finds and quizzes are found here: www.lauraingallswilderhome.com/kids.htm

LAURA INGALLS WILDER HISTORIC HOME & MUSEUM (cont.)

Rocky Ridge Farm, in the Ozark Hills, is where Laura Ingalls Wilder wrote the Little House books. The museum exhibits include artifacts from the pioneer lifestyle described in "Little House" books. Laura's daughter, Rose is also featured. Recreations of rooms from both homes, her desks, her manuscripts, and souvenirs from her world travels are also displayed. Many of the rooms were left nearly exactly as if Laura had just left the room. The little homes are so sweet and Almanzo built much of the first home and Laura, Rose, and Almanzo's graves are nearby. Why are the countertops so low? Also, look for Pa's actual fiddle. This is a must for children and adults interested in the early American pioneers and history or big "Little House on the Prairie" fans.

LAURA'S MEMORIES PLAY

Mansfield - *Laura Ingalls Wilder Historic Home & Museum. Experience the past with Laura Ingalls Wilder as she reminisces about her childhood, pioneer days, her incredible family, and her beloved Almanzo. Laura's life unfolds through a live theater production that culminates on that momentous day in 1951 when Mansfield dedicated its library in her honor. Laura's Memories captures Mrs. Wilder's journeys through Iowa, Minnesota, the Dakota Territory, Kansas, and finally Mansfield, Missouri where Laura and Almanzo spent their remaining years. The pageant is a family oriented production. Proceeds go to high school scholarships for participating students. Performed by the Ozark Mountain Players, under the starry canopy of the Ozark sky. Concessions are available. Admission. (first two weekends in August and first three weekends in September).*

MISSOURI RENAISSANCE FESTIVAL

Neosho - *Morse Park, 1100 E. Spring St. Neosho's Morse Park is transformed to the sixteenth century English garrison town of Drogheda-on-the-Boyne, Ireland. Shop the wares of artisans; listen to the strains of Celtic music; thrill to the thunder of hooves as Mounted Fury, an all-female troupe of Dames enchant patrons with their knightly feats of skill. Enjoy the summer revels of the Wylde Irish and the Civilized Ways of the English lords. Admission. www.morenfest.com. (last weekend in July)*

DID YOU KNOW? The World's Largest Flower Box is located in Neosho on N. College Street. A 66-foot gondola car has been transformed into what may well be the world's largest flower box, filled with a wide variety of trees, shrubs, and flowers.

BUSHWHACKER HISTORICAL MUSEUM & OLD JAIL HISTORIC SITE

212 W. Walnut Street (main bldg. Is the basement of the Nevada library)
Nevada 64772

- ☐ Phone: (417) 667-9602 **www.bushwhacker.org**
- ☐ Hours: Tuesday-Saturday 10:00am-4:00pm (May-October).
- ☐ Miscellaneous: The Old Jail Historic Site is located at 231 N. Main Street.

Known as the "Bushwhacker Capital" during the war, learn about "bushwhackers," Confederate guerrillas who played an important role in Missouri's Civil War. Nevada was burned to the ground by Federal troops on May 26, 1863. The city's Bushwhacker Museum and Bushwhacker Jail offer permanent exhibits about the region's Civil War history. Visitors see the cell room in the 1860 stone jail and the sheriff's home. The women prisoners were kept in an upstairs cell room away from the men prisoners. Find out what life was like for the POWs. The final exhibit at the main location- and probably the largest is the Hornback House Exhibit. Dr. Hornback was a physician that worked in Vernon County in 1896. The Hornback family donated the family home to the museum. The exhibits range from the doctor's office to the dining room.

A short video describes the time period and they are trying to add interactive stations each year. The first such exhibit: incorporating the actual telegraph key from Nevada's old railroad depot. Visitors are able to sit and tap out a message and see what it was like to use this early form of communication. There is a Morse Code guide sheet to help visitors, and they are able to transmit copies of famous telegrams, such as the SOS from the Titanic. A new exhibit on joinery, or the way carpenters put things together, also is ready. Examples of the different kinds of woodwork are available for people actually to take apart and see how they are put together. "Flips" are also used on some exhibits to engage the Museum's visitors. A flip is a placard in front of an object that asks what that particular thing is or is used for. A visitor tries to figure it out and then "flips" the placard to reveal the answer underneath.

BLUFF DWELLERS' CAVERN & BROWNING MUSEUM

954 Highway 59 South (2 miles South of Noel) **Noel** 64854

- ☐ Phone: (417) 475-3666 **www.bluffdwellerscavern.com**
- ☐ Hours: Daily, 8:00am-6:00pm (March-October). Winter schedule may vary.
- ☐ Admission: $12.00 adult, $6.00 child (4-11).
- ☐ Miscellaneous: The temperature is 56 degrees all year long so please dress appropriately. Pan for gemstones and fossils for extra fee.

This is a guided cave tour and a museum site. The same family has operated the cave since its discovery in 1925. The cave entry is almost straight uphill so plan on wear comfy shoes as there are a lot of stairs to navigate from the parking lot to the cave entrance and tour. In the still pools you'll find cave coral, sponges, lilly pads, popcorn and "one of the most striking rimstone dams in the state."

And, for the avid adventuresome families: FLOAT & STAY RESORTS in Noel plus another handful of others:

- **RIVER RANCH RESORT** - www.riverranchresort.com. Campsites and 40 cabins on a full mile of riverfront. You can rent a canoe, raft, or kayak and resort guides will launch you 4 to 8 miles upstream and you can float back to your cabin or campsite.

- **SYCAMORE LANDING** - www.noelrafting.com. Float and camp packages.

DOENNIG SPORT SWINGS & OZARK PAINTBALL

671 Jackson Spring Road **Ozark** 65721

- ☐ Phone: (417) 443-4444 **www.swingsandpaintball.com**
- ☐ Hours: Public Session: Friday and Saturday nights only or by appointment. Prices vary. Generally $5.00-$10.00 per person.

Sports Swings offers jousting, bungee basketball, a mechanical bull, rock climbing, fun cycles, whirly bird and giant inflatables. They even have a goofy Hillmobilly Hayride - wait until you see the "wagon." Paintball with underground tunnels, bridges and trenches. Everything extreme but anyone, any age, physically active can enjoy these sports - even the challenging sport swings. Please wear modest clothing and tennis shoes…no flip-flops.

OZARK FESTIVAL OF LIGHTS

Ozark - *Finley River Park. Over 200 displays to enjoy in the drive-thru exhibit. Hours are 5:00pm-10:00pm. There are new exhibits each year. Penguins playing on an ice berg, two reindeer skating, and a train with waving engineer. It's free to drive through but donations are accepted to help pay the expenses and improve the displays for next year. (evenings in December)*

JESSE JAMES DAYS

Pineville - *Five day event commemorating the fact that actors Tyrone Power, Henry Fonda, Randolph Scott, and Nancy Kelly came to town with a crew from Hollywood to shoot the film "Jesse James" in 1938. Carnival, contests for kids, bingo, food and nightly music. Memorabilia from the film is on display at the McDonald Country Library in Pineville and one afternoon a fake bank robbery at the McDonald County State bank (shootouts, too). (weekend in August)*

COLLEGE OF THE OZARKS
1 Industrial Place **Point Lookout** 65726

☐   Phone: (417) 334-6411 **www.cofo.edu**

This 4-year liberal arts college requires all students to work on campus to defray the cost of tuition. There are 80 work areas on campus, ranging from a theater and radio station to a dairy farm and a bakery. Most areas are open to public, including Edward's Mill, where you can purchase whole-wheat flour, cornbread mix, and grits; a weaving studio featuring hand-woven items from pot holders to clothing; and greenhouses where houseplants and flowers are sold.

•   **RALPH FOSTER MUSEUM** - 750,000 items pertaining to Ozark history and folklore. See the car from The Beverly Hillbillies television show, a miniature circus, life-sized stuffed animals, a hands-on discovery room for children ages four to eight where kids can crawl thru a cave, try on clothing, examine a wide assortment of crazy objects. www.rfostermuseum.com or (417) 334-6411 ext 3407. Admission: $6.00 adult, $5.00 senior, FREE child (high school age and under). Hours: Monday-Saturday, 9:00am-4:30pm.

__COLLEGE OF THE OZARKS__ (cont.)

- __FRIENDSHIP HOUSE__ - Prepared and served by students, the food here ranges from hamburgers, sandwiches, french fries and dinners to a complete buffet on Sunday. Inexpensive.

ROCKBRIDGE GENERAL STORE AND RESTAURANT

Rockbridge - 65741. The resort sits on 1,500 acres of the scenic Ozarks, sporting to nature trails for hiking and one mile of sparkling, spring-fed creek stocked with rainbow trout. Guests will find a bait and tackle shop, gift shop and a beautiful sitting lounge with a fireplace. There's a pay phone in the lobby, but Rockbridge is an oasis away from the phone and the blare of the television. Rainbow Trout Restaurant is of the finest, specializing in a variety of menu choices: fresh caught trout from the stream, old-fashioned hash browns, handcut chops and steaks, skillet-fried chicken or tender chicken-fried steak and gravy.

HISTORY MUSEUM FOR SPRINGFIELD & GREENE COUNTY

830 Boonville Avenue **Springfield** 65802

- ☐ Phone: (417) 864-1976 **www.springfieldhistorymuseum.org**
- ☐ Hours: Tuesday-Friday 10:30am-4:30pm. Open second Saturday 10:30am-4:30pm.
- ☐ Admission: There is not an admission fee, but a modest suggested donation ranging from $1.00 to $3.00 is used to offset museum expenses.

Located in Springfield's City Hall, this history museum traces local history from prehistoric times through the 1950s. In addition, The History Museum has three hands-on areas for younger guests. These include a Native American grinding stone, a Civil War tent, and a variety of household items similar to those used in pioneer households. These items are historically accurate reproductions, so visitors are encouraged to handle them in order to better understand the lives of our ancestors.

DID YOU KNOW ? The Jefferson Avenue Footbridge (Commercial St. at Jefferson Ave.) is the country's longest. You can watch trains from the sturdy decking. Double-decker trains glide by on 13 sets of tracks below.

DID YOU KNOW ? Officially recognized as the birthplace of Route 66, it was in Springfield on April 30, 1926, that officials first proposed the name of the new Chicago-to-Los Angeles highway. www.missouri66.org.

SPRINGFIELD CARDINALS AA BASEBALL

955 E. Trafficway (Hammons Field) **Springfield** 65802

- [ ] Phone: (417) 863-0395 or (417) 863-2143 (Tickets)
  www.springfieldcardinals.com
- [ ] Admission: $6.00-$24.00 depending on seat location.

Visit Hammons Field for Springfield Cardinals Baseball, the AA affiliate of the St. Louis Cardinals. Meet Louie the mascot, come on Fireworks Fridays or Ice Cream Sundays (kids can run the bases, too). April-September.

AIR & MILITARY MUSEUM OF THE OZARKS

2305 East Kearney **Springfield** 65803

- [ ] Phone: (417) 864-7997 **www.ammomuseum.com**

This hands-on environment features a Cobra helicopter, a T-33 jet aircraft, Army Jeeps, trucks and other restored military equipment. Guests can even take a simulated flight in a real Cobra helicopter or have a personalized dog tag made.

CRYSTAL CAVE

7225 N. Crystal Cave Lane (5 Miles North of I-44 on Hwy. H, Exit 80B)
Springfield 65803

- [ ] Phone: (417) 833-9599 **www.CrystalCaveMissouri.com**
- [ ] Hours: 9:00am-1:00pm. Call for additional tour information.
- [ ] Admission: $9.00 adult, $5.00 child.
- [ ] Tours: Guided tours last approximately 80 minutes. The cave has a constant temperature of 59 degrees so be sure to dress for this temperature.

Enjoy the beauty of Crystal Cave as you walk through natural paths. Handrails and stone steps guide you along to see wells and symbols that indicate American Indian habitation. Crystal Cave is charmingly underdeveloped allowing a more natural feel. Guided tours are often led by the Richardson family, owners of the private cave.

DICKERSON PARK ZOO

1401 West Norton Road (Interstate 44 and Missouri Highway 13 - exit 77)
Springfield 65803

☐ Phone: (417) 864-1800 **www.dickersonparkzoo.org**
☐ Hours: Daily 9:00am-5:00pm (April-September), Daily 10:00am-4:00pm
(October-March).
☐ Admission: $8.00 adult (13+), $5.00 senior (60+) & child (3-12).

Exhibit themes include habitats from Africa, Tropical Asia, South America, Australia and Missouri habitats. Missouri Habitats area shows animals and habitats native to the Ozarks, including black bears, bobcats, and river otters. The Diversity of Life center houses reptiles, insects and amphibians. A three-car train circles the zoo. The zoo is nationally known for its Asian elephant breeding program.

FANTASTIC CAVERNS

4872 North Farm Road 125   **Springfield** 65803

☐ Phone: (417) 833-2010 **www.fantasticcaverns.com**
☐ Hours: 8:00am-6:00pm. (open about 2 hours later in summer, closes about 2
hours earlier in winter.) Call or visit website for current season hours.
☐ Admission: $21.50 adult (13+), $13.50 child (6-12).
☐ Tours: Depart every 20-30 minutes throughout the day and each tour takes
about an hour. The temperature inside the cave is 60 degrees.
☐ Educators: a wonderful, easy to follow study guide and quiz about caves is
found under Education>Classroom Study Guide online.

Fantastic Caverns is America's only drive-through cave with tours conducted from a vehicle-draw tram in order to protect the delicate formations. Look for cave pearls and delicate drapes. Fragile species of wildlife include cave crayfish and grotto salamanders. Be especially on the lookout for blind Ozarks cavefish - a reclusive little creature no longer than a finger. View sites and formations carved into Missouri limestone one drop of water at a time. Your tram driver gives you a 55-minute talk that combines history, ecology, conservation and geology.

Since today's tour is entirely by tram, with no walking required, families with small children, senior citizens and the physically challenged can all sit back and enjoy the ride. Temperatures inside the cave always hover around 60 degrees making it a wonderful adventure regardless of the season.

For updates & travel games visit: **www.KidsLoveTravel.com**

SPRINGFIELD CONSERVATION NATURE CENTER
4600 South Chrisman Avenue **Springfield** 65804

- ☐ Phone: (417) 888-4237 **http://mdc.mo.gov/areas/cnc/springfd/**
- ☐ Hours: Daily 8:00am-5:00pm.

The park has six hiking trails of varying lengths, a visitor center with exhibits, but camping and fishing are not allowed. Nearly three miles of trails, as short as a fifth of a mile, as long as two miles. A boardwalk goes over the marshy shallows of the lake. Some trails are paved - all are easily accessed. No bikes or pets allowed. There's an indoor bird watching space inside the center. Experience the sounds of the nighttime forest and discover how rainwater becomes spring water, all in the center's multi-sensory exhibit room. Towards evening, you might even catch the eyes of a deer, raccoon, a duck or even bobcats.

DISCOVERY CENTER
438 East Saint Louis Street **Springfield** 65806

- ☐ Phone: (417) 862-9910 **www.discoverycenter.org**
- ☐ Hours: Tuesday-Thursday 9:00am-5:00pm, Friday 9:00am-8:00pm, Saturday 10:00am-5:00pm, Sunday 1:00pm-5:00pm.
- ☐ Admission: $9.00 adult, $8.00 senior (60+), $7.00 child (3-15). There may be some additional fees for special exhibits.

This is an interactive hands-on science center for all ages. Imagine, create, have fun and learn with hundreds of exhibits that explore physics, chemistry, energy, health and culture. You can stroll through a giant eyeball, dig for a dinosaur, mix oozing bubbling chemicals in the Exploratory Lab, or be a star on the Evening News. Sense-Sational Hall houses unique exhibits like Big Mouth, Eye Spy, and Brain Central that allow visitors to investigate the workings of the human body through giant-sized anatomic models. Play pretend or be creative in Discovery Town. Next, ride the HighWire Bike or create a dam in waterworks. Every space is designed to draw the kids in on their level to start experimenting. Well done.

SPRINGFIELD LITTLE THEATRE

311 E. Walnut Avenue **Springfield** 65806

☐ Phone: (417) 869-1334 **www.springfieldlittletheatre.org**

The Springfield Little Theatre at the historic Landers Theatre is Missouri's oldest and largest civic theater. Most shows are very family-friendly with titles like: High School Musical, Peter and the Wolf, Willy Wonka and Disney productions. Tickets run $15.00-$25.00. Wednesday-Sunday evenings and weekend matinees.

BASS PRO SHOPS OUTDOOR WORLD

1935 S. Campbell **Springfield** 65807

☐ Phone: (417) 887-7334 **www.basspro.com**
☐ Hours: Monday-Saturday 7:00am-10:00pm, Sunday 9:00am-7:00pm.

There's a theme park atmosphere in the store including: four story waterfall, indoor bow and arrow range, fish feeding shows in a 140,000 gallon aquarium - one of five large aquariums - with divers and a video. Their newest acquisition ...alligators. Restaurant on premises.

DID YOU KNOW ? This is usually one of Missouri Tourism's most visited attractions.

INCREDIBLE PIZZA COMPANY

Springfield - *2850 S Campbell Avenue 65807. www.incrediblepizza.com/springfield. Phone: (417) 887-3030 Hours: Sunday-Thursday 11:00am-8:00pm. Friday & Saturday 11:00am-9:00pm (game room stays open 1 hour later). This attraction starts with a pizza, pasta, dessert buffet; bottomless drinks. Go-karts, bumper cars, mini golf, dozens of interactive games.*

SPRINGFIELD HOT GLASS STUDIO

314 S. Campbell Street, downtown **Springfield** 65807

☐ Phone: (417) 868-8181 **www.springfieldhotglass.com**

This studio is a working glass-making center, featuring glassblowing and torch-working demos and a gallery of original glass art for sale (look, don't touch). Don't miss continuous glass blowing demonstrations Tuesday, Thursday, Saturday and every First Friday.

WONDERS OF WILDLIFE LIVING ZOOQUARIUM

500 W. Sunshine Street **Springfield** 65807

☐ Phone: (417) 890-9453 or (877) 245-9453 **www.wondersofwildlife.org**

At press time The Wonder of Wildlife facilities and site were closed for major expansion and renovation. The site is on schedule to re-open in late 2010. The new museum will feature exhibits modeled after the great nocturnal exhibit at The Henry Doorly Zoo and the Rain Forest Exhibit at The Dallas World Aquarium. The new museum will also include some new surprises not found in any of the major aquariums. Many of these are aimed at entertaining and educating young visitors. Some of the displays and features include a flooded rain forest exhibit, shark and ray touch tanks, sturgeon touch pool, a large living coral tank, a bird aviary and a nocturnal swamp just to name a few. The Museum will increase in size from 126,100 to more than 200,000 square feet with many new exhibits. WOW will house a 220,000-gallon shark tank, 140,000-gallon freshwater pond, live otter pool, cave, "walk in the Ozarks," and more. WOW is also planning a new Conservation Education Center for the WOW educational programs and WOLF school to provide a fun and educational space for young people in the Springfield Public School System. Please call or visit website for latest details.

MISSOURI SPORTS HALL OF FAME

3861 E. Stan Musial Drive (1 mile east of U.S. Hwy. 65 on U.S. Hwy. 60)
Springfield 65809

☐ Phone: (417) 889-3100 or (800) 498-5678 **www.mosportshalloffame.com**
☐ Hours: Monday-Saturday 10:00am-4:00pm, Sunday Noon-4:00pm.
☐ Admission: $5.00 adult, $4.00 senior, $3.00 child (6-15). Immediate Family $14.00.

The Missouri Sports Hall of Fame is a family-friendly environment that includes a museum with more than 4,000 pieces of sports memorabilia, hands-on exhibits and displays. All those famous uniforms and signed game balls and quotes...make a young athletes head spin!

GRAY / CAMPBELL FARMSTEAD LIFESTYLE EXPOSITION

Springfield - *Nathanael Greene Park. www.graycampbellfarmstead.org. The Lifestyle Exposition Activities will include: Blacksmith Demonstrations, Apple Butter Making, Apple Cider Making, Open Hearth Cooking, Lye Soap Making, Clogging, Wagon Rides, Music, Leather-crafting, Fiber Arts, Story Telling and Food from a concession stand. Admission is free - Donations Accepted. (third weekend in September).*

FESTIVAL OF LIGHTS

Springfield - *www.itsalldowntown.com. Twinkling lights atop a 30-foot tree in Jordan Valley Park and fireworks at nearby Hammons Field will light up the evening sky during the kick-off ceremony for the Festival of Lights. The Festival of Lights is a six-week celebration featuring a number of no- or low-cost activities for people to enjoy during the holiday season along with a variety of music and theater performances in the spirit of the season. (starting right before Thanksgiving thru December)*

WILSON'S CREEK NATIONAL BATTLEFIELD

6424 West Farm Road 182 **Springfield (Republic)** 65738

- ☐ Phone: (417) 732-2662, ext. 227 **www.nps.gov/wicr**
- ☐ Hours: (Visitor Center) Daily 8:00am-5:00pm, (Museum) Daily 9:00am-Noon & 1:00-4:00pm, Note: The museum is closed December-March. Park (Tour Road) Daily, 8:00am-5:00pm.
- ☐ Admission: The entrance fee to the park is $5.00 per adult to a maximum of $10.00 per vehicle. The receipt is honored for seven days. An adult is defined as anyone 16 years old and older.
- ☐ Tours: A 4.9 mile paved tour road provides a self-guided auto tour. There are eight interpretive stops at significant battle-related locations. There are five walking trails off the tour road, varying in length from 1/4 to 3/4 of a mile. A seven mile trail system for horseback riding and hiking is accessible from the tour road.
- ☐ Educators: an excellent Common Soldier/Common Man unit study is found off the main website: www.nps.gov/wicr/forteachers/curriculum.

Near Springfield is Wilson's Creek National Battlefield, perhaps the most important Civil War battle fought west of the Mississippi River. Fought Aug. 10, 1861, this battle was the first Confederate victory in the early stages of the war in Missouri, and the battle in which Gen. Nathaniel Lyon became the first Union general to be killed in the Civil War.

This National Park Service battlefield contains a state-of-the-art visitor center as well as a self-guided auto tour of the battlefield itself. Inside the center and the Civil War Museum are camp life dioramas, a fiberoptic map of the battle and a film about the battle.

The Ray House, dating from the 1850s, served as a temporary field hospital for Southern soldiers following the battle. General Nathaniel Lyon's body was brought to the house and placed in a bed for examination. The bed is on exhibit in one of the rooms. The Ray House is open on weekends (subject to staff and volunteer availability), Memorial Day through Labor Day.

STOCKTON STATE PARK
19100 S. Hwy. 215 **Stockton** 65635

☐ Phone: (417) 276-4259 **www.mostateparks.com/stockton.htm**
☐ Hours: Sunrise-Sunset (year-round).
☐ Admission: The Missouri state park system does not charge entrance fees. However, there are fees associated with camping, lodging, tours, museums and certain special events.

Located along the rolling Springfield plateau, this park overlooks the Stockton Reservoir. A steady breeze makes it a destination for sailing. Stockton State Park's marina rents a variety of boats ranging from personal watercrafts to sail boats. The park has two launching ramps, making lake access easy. A swimming beach accommodates visitors who would rather play in the water than on it. The park has a marina, a beach, lodging, picnic sites and campsites. The grill is a seasonal restaurant at the marina offering burgers, catfish, chicken, etc. After a fun-filled day of activity, visitors can relax and camp under the stars at one of the park's basic or electric campsites, or rent a camper cabin, cabin with kitchenette or duplex cabin with kitchenette.

HAMMONS PRODUCTS PANTRY & VISITORS CENTER
414 North Street **Stockton** 65785

- [ ] Phone: (417) 276-5800 **www.hammonspantry.com** or **www.black-walnuts.com**
- [ ] Note: To understand how Hammons processes nuts watch their online video on HOW WE PROCESS/Video Link.

Welcome to Hammons Products Company, the world's largest processor and supplier of American Black Walnuts! Wild, hand-harvested Black Walnuts stand alone in the nut world as a flavorful, nutritional ingredient to some of your favorite baked goods, dishes, and ice cream. Here you'll find everything there is to know about the American Black Walnut. You'll learn how they hand-harvest every year across 15-states, how to use black walnuts in delicious recipes, and how Hammons Products Co. has been a family-owned company for over 60 years. Black walnut harvesting occurs in the fall, when the wild nut crop is hulled, bagged and sold to a network of buying stations, or "hullers," for Hammons Products Company. The Visitors Center is a retail store with some information about the process and, of course, black walnut products to purchase.

WILD ANIMAL SAFARI
124 Jungle Drive **Strafford** 65757

- [ ] Phone: (417) 859-5300 **www.goanimalparadise.com**
- [ ] Hours: 10:00am-5:00pm. Open until 6:00pm or 7:30pm spring and summers. Be sure to call or visit website for current closing schedule. The park is open everyday possible but snow, ice, or severe cold conditions do cause them to close as they cause unsafe driving conditions in the park.
- [ ] Admission: Covers the Drive-Thru and Walk-About. $15.95 adult, $11.95 senior (65+) and child (4-12). Small additional charge for animal feed.
- [ ] Tours: Tour bus runs spring & fall weekends and Daily in summer.
- [ ] Miscellaneous: Safari Grill and gift shop on premises. Note: it's recommended (and we agree) to go on a safari bus/van tour vs. riding your own vehicle. It will be covered with slobber. Also, keep the young kids and squeamish teens sitting in the middle so they don't have to have direct contact with the animals if they don't want.

Have your cameras ready as you embark on this two-part animal adventure. Experience up-close encounters with all sorts of animals. You can drive your own vehicle (or take the complimentary bus tour- seasonal) thru the Drive-Thru safari and get to experience hand feeding the animals. On the safari the exotic animals will literally come up to your car and eat right out of the palm of your hand. Scattered through the park they have approx. 650 animals, (and counting!) including: Rhinoceros, Tigers, Lions, Black Panthers, Spotted Leopards, Kangaroos, Wallabies, Hyenas, Zebras, Camel, Gaurs, Ostriches, Emus, Lemurs, Monkeys, Deer, Elk, Buffalo, Bison, and more. They even have 2 adult and 2 baby "Ligers" for you too see! This is one of those "you have to be there" experiences. For the full experience, it is wise to purchase the feed (giant pellets) so you can get close to animals (they love you more when you give them food). Choose to feed timid deer or aggressive ostrich. Our favorites: the elk, bison (wait til you see their tongues!) and the zebra (like feeding horses).

Hop out of the car and take a stroll through their Winding Path and the Walk-About. Here you will find some of the smaller animals, or the more friendly. You can take a moment and gaze at the Lemurs as they jump around and leap from rope to rope. See the beautiful Peacock spread his feathers and show off. Then, walk through the winding path where you will be able to feed more animals and even pet them as they come up to you. Hand feed a Four-Horned Sheep, an Alpaca, Zedonk, or even a Wallaby!

OSAGE VILLAGE STATE HISTORIC SITE
(6 miles north on Route C, west 3 miles on a gravel road, Vernon County)
Walker 64790

- ☐ Phone: (417) 682-2279 (c/o Harry S Truman Birthplace State Historic Site) **www.mostateparks.com/osagevillage.htm**
- ☐ Hours: Open Daily (year-round).
- ☐ Admission: The Missouri state park system does not charge entrance fees. However, there are fees associated with camping, lodging, tours, museums and certain special events.

This site was once a Big Osage Indian village occupied from 1700-1775. At its height, the village contained thousands of people and about 200 lodges. Tons of artifacts have been excavated from this land, including many items used in trading. In the late 18th and early 19th centuries, the Osage Indians accounted for more than half of the total trade in furs along the Missouri River. After the United States government took control of the Louisiana Purchase territory in 1804, the Osage Indians were gradually forced to retreat to Oklahoma. Today, Osage Village State Historic Site features a walking trail and outdoor exhibits that help visitors visualize the village and the everyday bustle of this once powerful Indian tribe.

Travel Journal & Notes:

Activity Index

AMUSEMENTS

ANIMALS & FARMS

SCIENCE

SCIENCE (cont.)

SPORTS

Travel Journal & Notes:

Travel Journal & Notes:

Travel Journal & Notes:

For updates & travel games visit: **www.KidsLoveTravel.com**